1,001 Dating Ideas

By: Sarah Melland

Table of Contents

Disclaimer: Not all of these are you going to want to do. Some you might not like, some you might disagree with. But, hey, I couldn't get to 1,001 without breaking some rules.

Introduction

Let's just say it, dating today is a dumpster fire wearing lip gloss. Every scroll feels like déjà vu: gym selfie, fishing photo, "6 feet (actually 5'9")", "just ask" in the bio, and that one mirror pic with toothpaste splatter in the corner. We're all out here trying to find connection, but most people can't even find good lighting.

I care about your dating life because I've been in the trenches. I've seen enough half-effort messages and beige small talk to last a lifetime. Somewhere between the ghosters, the love-bombers, and the emotionally unavailable men who "aren't ready for a relationship but want one someday," we forgot that dating is supposed to be fun.

This book is your antidote. It's not about finding "The One," it's about remembering what it feels like to be alive again. To laugh until your cheeks hurt. To do something ridiculous with someone you actually like, or maybe just tolerate with wine. Whether it's a first date where you want to make an impression, or the thousandth night where you're trying to keep the spark from dying in a sea of takeout and streaming options, these ideas will help you remember that joy is not optional, it's essential.

Because when you strip away the algorithms and bad bios, we all want the same thing: connection, curiosity, and a reason to look up from our phones. So, let's bring a little magic back to the madness. You don't need a soulmate to have a great time, you just need a plan and the right kind of chaos.

I made this for the lovers, the cynics, the hopefuls, and everyone who's ever texted "wyd" and immediately regretted it, and even the men who didn't. Dating doesn't have to suck, but it does need a little imagination.

So, pour a drink, turn off your notifications, and pick your next adventure. You've got 1,001 of them waiting, and probably a lot more, I stopped counting, but I know it's at least 1,001. Lol, you'll love it. I promise. I'll even let you be a little surprised☺

Food and Beverage

☐ **Make a homemade pinata together.** This one might stretch over a couple of date nights. Basically, you can plan and start your pinata on one date, let it dry, and then on another date, you can decorate it and smash it. It pairs well with the above adult kids party idea. Fill it with whatever fun stuff you want. Maybe even each sneak in some surprises for each other.

How to Make a Pinata

Protect your work area. Making your pinata has the potential to get a little messy, so make sure you give yourself plenty of room to work. Cover your work area with layers of newspaper or a disposable plastic tablecloth. This will keep your tabletop clean, and make cleanup afterward a breeze. Keep yourself clean too by wearing an old shirt or apron as well as latex gloves.

Make the paper mache paste. In a bowl, mix 2 cups of flour, 2 cups of water, and a tablespoon of salt. Stir the mixture until it starts to thicken like a batter. Don't worry about breaking down all the lumps; you want the batter to be relatively smooth but it will likely still have chunks of flour in it.

Prepare your paper mache strips. Tear some newspaper into strips that are about 1 to 2 inches wide and 6 to 8 inch (15.2 to 20.3 cm) long. This will make the newspaper lay nice and flat on the balloon. You will need to prepare many of these strips of paper so that you have enough to cover your balloon in several layers.

Choose a shape for your pinata. Make your pinata whatever you like! The easiest shape to make is an oblong sphere based on a balloon form, but you can create anything you want.

- To create a more elaborate shape, tape or glue cardstock, and cardboard onto your balloon form.
- Traditional pinatas are made with a ceramic pot as the form, but these can be messy and dangerous. Stick with a pliable form made from paper products.

Inflate your balloon. This will form the body of your pinata, so make sure you make it nice and big. Round balloons are preferable because they will create a larger space for all of the candy. You may also use a box if you prefer a square shape for your pinata. Add any additional shapes to make legs, arms, tails, snouts, hats, etc, using cardboard, newspaper or construction paper. Tape these shapes on with masking tape or clear tape.

Apply the paper mache paste to your paper strips. Dip the strips into your paste and remove any excess paste by running the strips through your pinched fingers or dragging them along the edge of the bowl.

Apply the paper mache to the balloon. Lay the strips down all over the balloon in a crisscross pattern until the entire balloon is covered. Leave the knot of the balloon uncovered to make removal of the balloon easier. Complete this step 3 to 4 times, allowing each layer to dry before adding another.

Let the pinata dry. Once you have finished adding layers of paper mache, let the pinata sit until it is completely dry and has hardened. How long this will be will depend on many factors, including how thick the paper mache is, and the humidity and temperature of the air. In general, plan on several days.

Paint the piñata. Use a single color to smooth out the paper and to create an even surface. It does not need to be especially well-painted, just enough to cover the paper. Choose a color that matches the decorations you'll be adding on or to match the animal or character that you're turning your piñata into, as it'll probably show through.

Glue crepe paper to the pinata. This will give your pinata a more traditional look. It is also a festive and inexpensive touch. Cut or tear strips of crepe paper and glue it onto the pinata. Leave the paper in strips, or bunch it up into small tassel-like balls and glue on.

Add finishing touches. Once you've gotten the base of crepe paper on, add other neat details to your pinata. Colorful cupcake liners and brightly colored tissue squares can be added as fringe. If you made an animal, add googly eyes for a fun look.

Cut a hole for the candy. If the balloon has not yet popped, go ahead and pop it and remove it. Since you did not cover the knot of the balloon with your paper mache, you should have a small hole already.

Make the hole bigger if needed. If the candy doesn't fit, cut away at the edge of the hole until it is large enough to pass the candy through.

Punch two small holes around the main hole. Tie a string or ribbon to the holes to create a loop. This will come in handy later when it comes time to hang the pinata.

Put the goodies in the piñata. Start adding in candy, streamers, stickers, confetti, small toys or anything else you like.

- Avoid adding any candy that isn't wrapped.
- Toys that may break easily are also a poor choice.

Cover the hole. Glue down some crepe paper on top of the hole, or use masking tape. The goal is to prevent the filling of the pinata from falling out before you've actually hit it.

Hang the pinata. Tie another piece of string, ribbon, or rope to the loop you've already made and use this to attach the pinata to whatever you'd like to hang it from.

☐ **New food night.** Try out some new food items you have no idea if you will like or not. Grab a bunch of fruit from the grocery store you have never eaten. Get snacks/food/drinks from an international food store that you have no idea what they taste like. Have a taste testing night. You could also film each of your reactions, and if you feel the need to post on social media, do so.

☐ **Russian Roulette with a dish from a different country.** Here is a list of all the most popular dishes from each country. Run your finger up and down this list and have your partner yell stop. This is the dish you will make for the night. NO MATTER WHAT! If you both love to cook, this could also be 186 recipes to go down the list and make all of them as of a sort of food bucket list.

☐ **Afghanistan** – *Kabuli Pulao*
☐ **Albania** – *Albanian Spinach Pastry*
☐ **Algeria** – *Algerian Bourak*
☐ **Andorra** –*Trinxat*
☐ **Angola** – *Chicken Moamba*
☐ **Antigua & Barbuda** – *Ducana*
☐ **Argentina** – *Chimichurri*
☐ **Armenia** – *Armenian Garmir Pilaf*
☐ **Australia** – *Australian Chocolate Lamingtons*
☐ **Austria** – *Austrian Potato Salad*
☐ **Azerbaijan** – *Traditional Lamb Stew*
☐ **Bahamas** – *Conch Salad*
☐ **Bahrain** – *Chicken majoboos*
☐ **Bangladesh** – *Bangladeshi Chicken Roast*
☐ **Barbados** – *Bajan Coconut Turnovers*
☐ **Belarus** – *Draniki*
☐ **Belgium** – *Belgian Waffles*
☐ **Belize** – *Belizean Panades*
☐ **Benin** – *Spicy Peanut Sauce*

☐ **Bhutan** – *Jaju*
☐ **Bolivia** – *Salteña*s
☐ **Bosnia and Herzegovina** – *Traditional Bosnian Meatballs*
☐ **Botswana** – *Beef Oxtail*
☐ **Brazil** – *Pão De Queijo*
☐ **Brunei** – *Nasi Katok*
☐ **Bulgaria** – *Banitsa*
☐ **Burkina Faso** – *Du Riz Graz Au Poulet*
☐ **Burundi** – *Matoke*
☐ **Cabo Verde** – *Cachupa*
☐ **Cambodia** – Cambodian Lemongrass Beef Skewers
☐ **Cameroon** – *Ndole*
☐ **Canada** – *Canadian Poutine*
☐ **Central African Republic** – Kanda ti Nyma (Beef Meatballs in Peanut Butter Stew)
☐ **Chad** – *Chadian Pasta*
☐ **Chile** – *Chilean Pebre*
☐ **China** – *Chinese Lo Mein*
☐ **Colombia** – *Arepas de Queso*
☐ **Comoros** – *Broiled Lobster in a Vanilla Sauce*

- [ ] **Congo, Democratic Republic of the** – *Pondu*
- [ ] **Congo, Republic of the** – Liboké de Viande (Meat in Banana-Leaf)
- [ ] **Costa Rica** – *Gallo Pinto*
- [ ] **Cote d'Ivoire** – *Ivory Coast Style Kedjenou Chicken Stew with Boiled White Rice*
- [ ] **Croatia** – *Mlinci*
- [ ] **Cuba** – *Cubano Sandwich*
- [ ] **Cyprus** – *Sheftalia Cypriot BBQ*
- [ ] **Czechia** – *Hovězí guláš (Beef Goulash)*
- [ ] **Denmark** – *Overnight Danish Rolls*
- [ ] **Djibouti** – *Fah Fah Soup*
- [ ] **Dominica** – *Souse*
- [ ] **Dominican Republic** – *Mangú con Los Tres Golpes*
- [ ] **Ecuador** – *Llapingachos*
- [ ] **Egypt** – *Koshari*
- [ ] **El Salvador** – *Pupusas*
- [ ] **Equatorial Guinea** – *Banana Bake*
- [ ] **Eritrea** – *Kulwha*
- [ ] **Estonia** – *Kringel*
- [ ] **Eswatini (formerly Swaziland)** – *Karoo Roast Ostrich Steak with Pumpkin Mash and Slaai*
- [ ] **Ethiopia** – *Ethiopian Injera*
- [ ] **Fiji** – Fijian Palusami
- [ ] **Finland** – *Mustikkapiirakka (Traditional Finish Blueberry Pie)*
- [ ] **France** – *Ratatouille*
- [ ] **Gabon** – *L'épinard au poisons et crevettes*
- [ ] **Gambia** – *Grilled Dibi Gambian Style*
- [ ] **Georgia** – *Khachapuri*
- [ ] **Germany** – *Stollen*
- [ ] **Ghana** – *Waakye*
- [ ] **Greece** – *Greek Moussaka*
- [ ] **Grenada** – *Oil down*
- [ ] **Guatemala** – *Pepian*
- [ ] **Guinea** – *Peanut Sauce*
- [ ] **Guinea-Bissau** – *Cafriela de Frango*
- [ ] **Guyana** – *Guyanese Pepperpot*
- [ ] **Haiti** – *Griot and Pikliz*
- [ ] **Honduras** – *Baleadas*
- [ ] **Hungary** – *Töltött káposzta*
- [ ] **Iceland** – *Icelandic Fish Stew*
- [ ] **India** – *Indian Chicken Curry*
- [ ] **Indonesia** – *Nasi Goreng*
- [ ] **Iran** – *Persian Beef Koobideh Kebab*
- [ ] **Iraq** – *Dolma*
- [ ] **Ireland** – *Irish Shepherd's Pie*
- [ ] **Israel** – *Israeli Shakshuka*
- [ ] **Italy** – *Spaghetti Carbonara*
- [ ] **Jamaica** – *Jamaican Jerk Chicken*
- [ ] **Japan** – *Onigiri*
- [ ] **Jordan** – *Mansaf*
- [ ] **Kazakhstan** – *Baursaki*
- [ ] **Kenya** – *Mutura*
- [ ] **Kiribati** – *Kiribati Glazed Mahi Mahi*
- [ ] **Kuwait** – *Gabout*
- [ ] **Kyrgyzstan** – *Chicken Shashlik Kebab*
- [ ] **Laos** – *Papaya Salad*
- [ ] **Latvia** – *Dark Caraway Bread*
- [ ] **Lebanon** – *Kibbeh*
- [ ] **Lesotho** – *Lipabi*
- [ ] **Liberia** – *Liberian Dry Rice*
- [ ] **Libya** – *Libyan-style Aseeda*
- [ ] **Liechtenstein** – *Käsknöpfle*
- [ ] **Lithuania** – *Cepelinai*
- [ ] **Luxembourg** – *Gromperekichelcher*
- [ ] **Madagascar** – *Romazava*
- [ ] **Malawi** – *Nsima*
- [ ] **Malaysia** – *Nasi Lemak*
- [ ] **Maldives** – *Plantain Curry*

- Mali – *Nandji*
- Malta – *Maltese Baked Rice*
- Marshall Islands – *Marshallese Coconut Fish*
- Mauritania – *Mauritanian Green Tea*
- Mauritius – *Chicken Biryani*
- Mexico – *Elotes*
- Micronesia – *Coconut Chicken Curry*
- Moldova – *Cheese Dumplings*
- Monaco –*Barbajuans*
- Mongolia – *Goat Jembii*
- Montenegro –*Crunchy Montenegrin Steak*
- Morocco –*Zaalouk*
- Mozambique –*Xima*
- Myanmar (formerly Burma) – *Mohinga*
- Namibia – *Potjiekos*
- Nauru – *Coconut Crusted Fish*
- Nepal – *Dal Bhat*
- Netherlands – *Hutspot and Stampot*
- New Zealand– *Mince and Cheese Pies*
- Nicaragua – *Salpicón*
- Niger – *Spicy Green Kuka Sauce*
- Nigeria – *Fufu*
- North Korea – *North Korean style Spicy Stuffed Steamed Eggplant*
- North Macedonia (formerly Macedonia) – *Pitulici*
- Norway – *Bacalao*
- Oman – *Shuwa*
- Pakistan – *Karahi Chicken*
- Palau – *Fried Mekebud*
- Palestine – *Musakhan*
- Panama – *Panamanian Sancocho*
- Papua New Guinea – *Mumu*
- Paraguay – *Paraguayan Sopa*

- Peru – *Lomo Saltado*
- Philippines – *Pancit Bihon*
- Poland – *Haluski*
- Portugal – *Cod Fritters*
- Qatar – *Lentil Machboos*
- Romania – *Romanian Cabbage Rolls*
- Russia – *Russian Rice Pilaf with Braised Beef (Plov)*
- Rwanda – *Potatoes with Peanut Sauce*
- Saint Kitts and Nevis – *Banana Fritters*
- Saint Lucia – *St Lucian Dahl*
- Saint Vincent and the Grenadines – *Ducana*
- Samoa – *Faiai Eleni*
- San Marino – *Corned Tuna Sisig*
- Sao Tome and Principe – *Fish Stew*
- Saudi Arabia – *Sambusa*
- Senegal – *Thiéboudiène*
- Serbia – *Serbian cevapi*
- Seychelles – *Coconut Crab Curry*
- Sierra Leone – *Peanut Butter Soup*
- Singapore – *Fried Hokkien Noodles*
- Slovakia – *Halušky*
- Slovenia – *Štrukli*
- Solomon Islands – *Papaya Chicken*
- Somalia – *Somali Bariis*
- South Africa – *Chakalaka Chicken*
- South Korea – *Korean Breakfast Banchan*
- South Sudan – *Shaiyah*
- Spain – *Spanish Tapas*
- Sri Lanka – *Pineapple Curry*
- Sudan – *Chicken & Vegetable Stew*
- Suriname – *Saoto Soup*

- [ ] **Sweden** – *Chokladbollar (Swedish Chocolate Balls)*
- [ ] **Switzerland** – *Potato Rösti*
- [ ] **Syria** – *Chicken Shawarma*
- [ ] **Tajikistan** – *Qurutob*
- [ ] **Tanzania** – *Tanzanian Style Chicken & Bananas*
- [ ] **Thailand** – *Thai Fried Rice with Shrimp (Khao Pad Goong)*
- [ ] **Timor-Leste** – *Hakmerik*
- [ ] **Togo** – *Fetri Dessi*
- [ ] **Tonga** – *Faikakai*
- [ ] **Trinidad and Tobago** – *Trinidadian Roti*
- [ ] **Tunisia** – *Brik*
- [ ] **Turkey** – *Gozleme*
- [ ] **Turkmenistan** – *Turkmen Dumplings*
- [ ] **Tuvalu** – *Tuna Curry*
- [ ] **Uganda** – *Katogo*
- [ ] **Ukraine** – *Ukrainian Perogies*
- [ ] **United Arab Emirates (UAE)** – *Balaleet*
- [ ] **United Kingdom (UK)** – *Fish & Chips*
- [ ] **United States of America (USA)** – *New York Style Hot Dog*
- [ ] **Uruguay** – *Chivito*
- [ ] **Uzbekistan** – *Uzbek Plov*
- [ ] **Vanuatu** – *Tanna Soup*
- [ ] **Vatican City (Holy See)** – Fettuccine alla Papalina
- [ ] **Venezuela** – *Arepas*
- [ ] **Vietnam** – *Vietnamese Coconut Rice Cake*
- [ ] **Yemen** – *Bint al Sahn*
- [ ] **Zambia** – *Cassava & Groundnuts*
- [ ] **Zimbabwe** – *Traditional Peanut Butter Rice*

- [ ] **Fancy fast food feast.** Dress in your finest and use your best plates, glasses, and silverware and candles and have a fancy fast food meal. It can be at home or in the fast-food restaurant. Go super fancy and sophisticated with your burger and fries. You could even pair it with a nice box wine.

- [ ] **Create a new type of dessert together.** Desserts are great for experimentation because if you slap enough sweet stuff together, it will probably still taste good. So, let your creativity run wild, make a mess of your kitchen, and get decadent with some sweets.

- [ ] **Recreate a "Nailed It" Cake.** Watch an episode of "Nailed It" on Netflix and try to recreate one of their desserts. Or you can go to an exquisite bakery and take a pic of beautiful cake and try to put your spin on it.

- [ ] **Make a difficult dessert you always see in restaurants together.** Have a sweet tooth and always wanted to know how to make some of the most delectable deserts that restaurants serve? Well, here is your chance. Pick from the list and have at it. Some recipes also if on this list are staples that need a fresh take like chocolate chip cookies or a hot fudge sundae, put some of your own specialty ingredients in.

11

- ☐ Key Lime Pie
- ☐ Flan
- ☐ Apple Pie
- ☐ Red Velvet Cake
- ☐ Cream Brulee
- ☐ Mochi
- ☐ Nanaimo Bar
- ☐ Pakhlava
- ☐ Tres Leches
- ☐ Panna Cotta
- ☐ Cannoli
- ☐ Éclair
- ☐ Hot Fudge Sundaes
- ☐ Parfait
- ☐ Baklava
- ☐ Chocolate Chip Cookies (Make them with a twist)
- ☐ Fudge
- ☐ Chocolate Mousse
- ☐ Churros
- ☐ S'mores
- ☐ Tiramisu
- ☐ Doughnut
- ☐ Milkshake (with a twist)
- ☐ Gelato al Pistacchio
- ☐ Macarons
- ☐ Brownies (with a twist)
- ☐ Carrot Cake
- ☐ German Chocolate Cake
- ☐ Raspberry Crumble Bars
- ☐ Brigadeiro
- ☐ Stroopwafel
- ☐ Kremes
- ☐ Beijinho
- ☐ Sfogliatella
- ☐ Ile Flottante
- ☐ Kaiserschmarrn
- ☐ Sernik
- ☐ Affogato
- ☐ Kheer
- ☐ Pastiera
- ☐ Crema Catalana
- ☐ Pancakes
- ☐ Bread Pudding
- ☐ Medovik
- ☐ Tong Sui
- ☐ Bavarian Cream
- ☐ Riz au Lait

- ☐ Okoshi
- ☐ Molten Chocolate Cake
- ☐ Amaretti
- ☐ Babka
- ☐ Pound Cake
- ☐ Strawberry Short Cake (homemade whip cream or it doesn't count)
- ☐ Beignets
- ☐ Cassata
- ☐ Cream Pie
- ☐ Apfelstrudel
- ☐ Knedliky
- ☐ Souffle au Chocolat
- ☐ Madeleines
- ☐ Tarts (any kind)
- ☐ Granita
- ☐ Better Than Sex Cake
- ☐ Pineapple Whip Cream Cake
- ☐ New York-Style Cheesecake
- ☐ Monaka
- ☐ Fenglisu
- ☐ Lokum
- ☐ Banana Bread
- ☐ Lebkuchen
- ☐ Varenye
- ☐ Ice Cream Sandwich
- ☐ Schwarzwalder Kirschtort* (saving for myself to remember because this looks flipping amazing)
- ☐ Profiteroles
- ☐ Banana Split
- ☐ Cremeschnitte
- ☐ Sachertorte
- ☐ Dango
- ☐ Pecan Pie
- ☐ Snickerdoodle
- ☐ Kakigori (shaved ice with toppings)
- ☐ Dulce de Leche
- ☐ Meringue
- ☐ Gaufre (A true Belgian waffle)
- ☐ Kasutera
- ☐ Pumpkin Pie
- ☐ Blini
- ☐ Manju

- ☐ Ma'amoul
- ☐ Alfajor
- ☐ Pavlova
- ☐ Nougat
- ☐ Dondurma
- ☐ Wagashi
- ☐ Cupcakes

☐ **Make cupcakes and decorate them with weird candy.** This goes along with all the fun of the one above. Make a totally different cupcake than anyone has ever tried. Use your imagination. Maybe figure out how to put alcohol in your cupcake. Or make a bacon maple cupcake. Always be creative, if you're not just make regular cupcakes and try not to get in a food fight or fight over who gets to eat the leftover batter.

☐ **Enjoy a night making creative pancakes.** Again, another one with mixing and matching ingredients. Just another easy way to get to know your partner and their taste level.

CREATIVE PANCAKE IDEAS

Classic with a Twist
- Chocolate Chip Pancakes
- Blueberry Lemon Zest Pancakes
- Banana Walnut Pancakes
- Strawberry Shortcake Pancakes (with whipped cream)
- Cinnamon Roll Pancakes (swirled with cinnamon-sugar butter)

Indulgent Dessert-Inspired
- Oreo Cookie Pancakes
- S'mores Pancakes (chocolate, marshmallow, graham cracker)
- Red Velvet Pancakes (cream cheese drizzle)
- Carrot Cake Pancakes (with cream cheese glaze)
- Tiramisu Pancakes (coffee syrup, mascarpone cream, cocoa dusting)

Savory & Unexpected
- Bacon & Cheddar Pancakes
- Chive & Sour Cream Potato Pancakes (latke-inspired)
- Cornbread Pancakes with Jalapeños
- Smoked Salmon & Dill Pancakes
- Pizza Pancakes (cheese, pepperoni, marinara drizzle)

International Flavors
- Japanese Soufflé Pancakes (extra fluffy)
- Dutch Baby Pancake (oven-baked, topped with fruit or sugar)
- Crepe-Style Pancakes (French-inspired, thin and filled)
- Churro Pancakes (sugar-cinnamon coated with caramel drizzle)
- Matcha Green Tea Pancakes

Fruit & Fresh Options
- Peach Cobbler Pancakes
- Pineapple Upside-Down Pancakes
- Apple Cinnamon Pancakes
- Coconut & Mango Pancakes
- Watermelon & Mint Pancakes (with yogurt drizzle)

Healthy & Wholesome
- Protein Pancakes (oats, banana, protein powder)
- Vegan Pancakes (almond milk, flax egg)
- Gluten-Free Almond Flour Pancakes
- Whole Wheat & Honey Pancakes
- Greek Yogurt Pancakes (extra fluffy with more protein)

The beauty of this is couples can pick a few and make a "Pancake Flight Night." Each person invents/customizes a stack, then they taste-test each other's creations.

☐ **Take a factory, brewery or bakery tour.** Sounds like a field trip, but it's usually pretty entertaining. If nothing else, it's a date idea that neither of you has tried! Plus, if you go for a bakery or brewery tour, you get some tasty samples.

☐ **Craft brew tasting/Wine tasting/Coffee tasting.** Perfect if you both like beer. You can do this at a bar that serves craft beers or if you want to save some money you can buy individual bottles at a liquor store. Always good to support local, and you get some wine in the process! It's an excellent way to find a new wine you like, plus wine has a way of relaxing nerves. This also could consist of going to a local brewery or vineyard as well.

☐ **Share a glass of red.** This could be another fun game. Go to the grocery store and pick the most expensive bottle of wine, or the one you guys think has the most interesting label. Like oh this label looks neat, I will try it.

☐ **Have a wine pairing night.** Research your favorite wine and see what goes along with it and how it makes your pallet sing. You can make stuff up when you tell your partner why these pairings go together or really know your shit. However, you want to make this fun and intriguing, have at it. Be a real wine connoisseur after this.

<u>WINE PAIRING NIGHT: THE WILD LIST</u>

1. **Popcorn + Champagne or Cava.** Salty, buttery crunch with sparkling bubbles? It's basically turning Netflix into the Cannes Film Festival.

2. **Potato Chips + Sauvignon Blanc.** Crisp on crisp. The citrusy zing from the wine snaps against the salt. Suddenly that bag of Lay's feels gourmet.

3. **Fried Chicken + Sparkling Rosé.** Fat loves bubbles, and rosé is flirty enough to pull off Southern comfort with Paris chic.

4. **Sushi + Riesling.** Slight sweetness tamps down wasabi fire. Sip, bite, kiss. Repeat.

5. **Tacos al Pastor + Pinot Noir.** Street food, smoky pineapple, and a playful red. Who knew taco Tuesday could taste like a vacation?

6. **Burgers + Syrah/Shiraz.** Juicy, charred meat loves bold, peppery reds. If you make sliders, it's practically a wine flight.

7. **Mac & Cheese + Oaked Chardonnay.** Creamy richness meets buttery oak. The comfort food glow-up you didn't know you needed.

8. **Spicy Thai Curry + Gewürztraminer.** Floral, aromatic, and just sweet enough to make fire taste like a tango instead of a dare.

9. **Chocolate-Covered Bacon + Malbec.** Dark fruit, smoky meat, and sweet chaos. This one gets a "trust me" stamp.

10. **PB&J Sandwich + Lambrusco (chilled red).** Nostalgia with bubbles. It's childhood, but with adult supervision (and better taste).

11. **French Fries + Rosé.** Dip in aioli, sip rosé, pretend you're at a seaside café in Nice. Fries never looked so fashionable.

12. **Brownies + Port.** Dense chocolate + velvety Port = end credits roll.

13. **Pizza Margherita + Chianti.** Classic red sauce + rustic Italian red. Even delivery pizza feels like Florence.

14. **Buffalo Wings + Riesling.** Sugar calms spice. A glass of Riesling is basically blue cheese in liquid form.

15. **French Toast + Moscato.** Breakfast for dinner. Fluffy, syrupy, sparkling sweet.

16. **Pasta Carbonara + Pinot Grigio.** Cream + crisp, bacon + brightness. You'll look like you actually studied pairing charts.

17. **BBQ Ribs + Zinfandel.** Sticky, smoky, messy ribs with a bold American red. Grab napkins and dig in.

18. **Pho + Grüner Veltliner.** Herbal soup with an herbal white. A pairing that whispers "I travel."

19. **Pop-Tarts (Strawberry) + Rosé.** Trashy meets classy. And it *works.*

20. **Nachos + Garnacha.** Cheesy, spicy, crunchy chaos meets flexible Spanish fun. Party pairing.

21. **Hot Dogs + Riesling.** Mustard, relish, even jalapeños — Riesling says, "I got this."
22. **Oysters + Muscadet.** The classic most people don't know. The ocean never tasted sexier.
23. **Ramen (Tonkotsu) + Alsace Pinot Gris.** Savory pork broth + crisp minerality. College noodles have never been so bougie.
24. **Cheesecake + Late-Harvest Riesling.** Sweet on sweet, creamy on fruity. A sugar bomb you'll want seconds of.
25. **S'mores + Shiraz.** Smoke + chocolate + a fire in your glass. Basically, camping without mosquitoes.
26. **Elote (Mexican Street Corn) + Albariño.** Spicy, creamy corn with a zesty white. Pure summer.
27. **Grilled Cheese + Beaujolais.** Comfort food + playful red = nostalgia date. Add tomato soup for bonus cozy points.
28. **Spaghetti & Meatballs + Barbera.** High acid + tomatoes + meat. A classic that feels like Sunday dinner at Nonna's.
29. **Grilled Pineapple + Torrontés.** Floral, fruity, caramelized, and tropical. Dessert that drinks like vacation.
30. **Corn Dogs + Merlot.** Fairground fun meets smooth red. Sweet batter + mellow fruit = guilty pleasure pairing.
31. **Ramen Noodles (Chicken Flavor) + Rosé.** Budget-friendly brilliance. Salty broth meets crisp pink.
32. **Grilled Peaches + Prosecco.** Bubbly peaches on peaches. Serve warm, sip cold.
33. **Caesar Salad + Pinot Grigio.** Anchovy tang, creamy dressing, sharp white. Your salad just graduated.
34. **Fried Pickles + Champagne.** Sharp, salty, fried — it's chaos, but Champagne always saves the day.
35. **Sliders + Grenache.** Mini burgers + playful Spanish red. Bite-sized fun.
36. **Donuts + Sparkling Moscato.** Glazed sugar meets sweet bubbles. Breakfast-for-dessert magic.
37. **Sushi (Spicy Tuna Roll) + Rosé Champagne.** Bubbles kill heat, rosé hugs the tuna. Date night flex.
38. **Deviled Eggs + Albariño.** Tangy yolks + bright white. Picnic food just found its soulmate.
39. **Philly Cheesesteak + Cabernet Sauvignon.** Beefy, cheesy, caramelized onions. Bold red says "yes."
40. **Fried Calamari + Vermentino.** Crisp seafood + crisp coastal white. Mediterranean energy.
41. **Apple Pie + Riesling Spätlese.** Sweet spice + sweet apple + sweet love.
42. **Chocolate-Covered Strawberries + Sparkling Rosé.** Obvious. But obvious is sometimes perfect.
43. **Sushi (Eel Roll) + Gewürztraminer.** Eel sauce + floral, aromatic white = surprise harmony.

44. **Fried Rice + Chardonnay (unoaked).** Simple, versatile, and secretly refined.
45. **Chili Cheese Fries + Zinfandel.** Spicy, gooey mess. Zin says, "bring it."
46. **Caesar Wrap + Sauvignon Blanc.** Herb, cream, crunch — green on green.
47. **Lobster Roll + Chablis.** Butter + mineral white. East Coast summer date.
48. **Fish & Chips + Champagne.** Greasy fried fish + high bubbles = genius.
49. **BBQ Pizza + Shiraz.** Spicy, sweet, smoky. Shiraz handles it like a pro.
50. **Burrata + Rosé of Grenache.** Creamy heaven with pink brightness.
51. **Chicken Tenders + Pinot Noir.** Kid food + grown-up red. Playful clash.
52. **Falafel Wrap + Beaujolais Nouveau.** Earthy chickpeas + light fruity red. Pure fun.
53. **Gyros + Assyrtiko (Greek white).** Lamb + tzatziki + wine from the homeland.
54. **Cheeseburger Pizza + Syrah.** The chaos pairing you didn't know you needed.
55. **Gnocchi with Pesto + Soave.** Herbal pasta + herbal Italian white.
56. **Cereal (Fruity Pebbles) + Moscato d'Asti.** Ridiculous, but it slaps. Trust the bubbles.
57. **Pancakes + Late-Harvest Chenin Blanc.** Breakfast sugar bomb meets dessert wine.
58. **Quesadillas + Tempranillo.** Cheesy, smoky tortilla meets Spanish flair.
59. **Chicken Alfredo + Chardonnay.** Cream + butter + buttery white.
60. **Shrimp Cocktail + Sauvignon Blanc.** Tangy sauce + crisp zing. Cocktail hour win.
61. **Garlic Bread + Lambrusco.** Carbs + bubbles. Always yes.
62. **Pad Thai + Riesling.** Peanuts, tamarind, spice + sweet acidity.
63. **Tater Tots + Prosecco.** Nostalgia meets sparkle.
64. **Roast Chicken + Beaujolais.** Simple dinner + fruity red.
65. **Crab Rangoon + Pinot Gris.** Creamy, crunchy, crabby. Pinot Gris saves the day.
66. **Poutine + Syrah.** Cheese curds + gravy + bold red. Canada says cheers.
67. **Baked Brie + Chardonnay.** Warm cheese + buttery wine. Indulgence squared.
68. **Smoked Brisket + Malbec.** Dark fruit + smoky beef. Cowboy romance.

69. **Chips & Salsa + Albariño.** Zesty, salty, fresh = party snack upgrade.
70. **Grilled Sausage + Riesling Kabinett.** Spicy sausage meets sweet-acid balance.
71. **Churros + Pedro Ximénez Sherry.** Cinnamon sugar + liquid caramel. Unreal.
72. **Fried Green Tomatoes + Chenin Blanc.** Southern tart + crisp white.
73. **Sloppy Joes + Zinfandel.** Messy + bold = date-night laughter.
74. **Peanut Butter Cookies + Tawny Port.** Nutty dessert + nutty dessert wine.
75. **Sweet Potato Fries + Rosé.** Earthy, sweet, salty, pink.
76. **Bagels & Lox + Champagne.** Smoked salmon + sparkling. NYC brunch vibes.
77. **Spicy Nachos + Verdejo.** Green wine with green heat.
78. **Biscuits & Gravy + Viognier.** Creamy, peppery gravy with lush aromatic white.
79. **Cornbread + Rosé.** Slightly sweet bread + summer pink.
80. **Mozzarella Sticks + Barbera.** Gooey cheese + bright red.
81. **Sushi (California Roll) + Prosecco.** Basic roll, fancy bubbles.
82. **Spicy Ramen + Gewürztraminer.** Heat tamed by floral sweetness.
83. **Pizza Bagels + Lambrusco.** Childhood snack, adult flair.
84. **Hot Chocolate Lava Cake + Banyuls.** Molten chocolate + fortified wine. Seduction pairing.
85. **Leftover Cold Pizza + Chardonnay.** Because sometimes romance is realest the morning after.
86. **Ceviche (limey white fish) + Vinho Verde.** Zippy, spritzy, and coastal—like eating sunshine with a sea breeze.
87. **Peking Duck + Pinot Noir (Burgundy or Oregon).** Crispy fat + cherry-bright acid = silk robe energy.
88. **Blue Cheese (Roquefort/Stilton) + Sauternes.** Salty funk meets honeyed velvet. The enemies-to-lovers of wine pairings.
89. **Moroccan Lamb Tagine (apricot/almond) + Grenache.** Warm spice and dried fruit lock step with juicy, sun-soaked red.
90. **Bibimbap (with gochujang) + Chilled Gamay.** Fresh veg, fried egg, chili heat—Gamay keeps it playful and crushable.
91. **Banh Mi (pork) + Rosé of Pinot Noir.** Herbs, pâté, pickles and pink—street food meets chic.
92. **Padrón Peppers + Txakolina.** Slightly salty, sometimes spicy; the Basque fizz snaps everything into focus.
93. **Shakshuka + Grenache Blanc.** Tomato, cumin, and eggs with a rounded white that won't get steamrolled.
94. **Moussaka + Xinomavro.** Layers of eggplant and lamb with a structured Greek red that brings graphite and grip.
95. **Cedar-Plank Salmon + Pinot Noir (Oregon).** Smoky salmon and red fruit—forest and river holding hands.

96. **Prosciutto & Melon + Verdicchio**. Salty-sweet classic lifted by a crisp, almond-tinged Italian white.
97. **Jerk Chicken + Dry Chenin Blanc (Loire)**. Scotch bonnet heat meets green apple snap and a cool, waxy finish.
98. **Ethiopian Doro Wat + Cabernet Franc**. Berbere spice + herbal, savory red—ink and incense vibes.
99. **Char Siu (Chinese BBQ pork) + Zinfandel**. Sticky-sweet glaze, peppery fruit, big grin. It just slaps.
100. **Fried Plantains + Madeira (Bual)**. Caramelized edges with nutty, toffee'd warmth. Dessert that purrs.
101. **Ratatouille + Côtes du Rhône (GSM blend)**. Herby Provençal veg cuddles up to peppery, sun-baked red. Garden party in a glass.

Get Another Great Wine Pairing Game:

https://www.etsy.com/listing/4406479677/wine-pairing-challenge-game-printable

☐ **Attend any free tasting**. Pretty much any free tasting event you can find, just go to it. Maybe even crash an event that has food. The sky is the limit.

☐ **Brew some beer together.** You'll need a kit or a bunch of equipment for this one, and it can get a little expensive. Also, unfortunately, you both won't get to try the beer you brewed together that day. But then again, that could be the next date night. All that being said, though, doing something together is very rewarding.

HOW TO BREW BEER AT HOME
Ingredients (for ~5 gallons / 19 liters)
- 6.6 lbs (3 kg) liquid malt extract (or 6 lbs dry malt extract)
- 1–2 oz (28–56 g) hops (bittering, flavor, or aroma depending on recipe)
- 1 packet of ale yeast (like Safale US-05 or Nottingham)
- 5 oz (140 g) priming sugar (for bottling carbonation)
- Optional: specialty grains for extra flavor (e.g., crystal malt, roasted barley)

Equipment
- Large brew pot (at least 5 gallons)
- Fermenter with airlock (plastic bucket or glass carboy)
- Thermometer
- Hydrometer (to measure sugar/alcohol content)
- Stirring spoon (sanitized)
- Sanitizer (Star San or Iodophor)
- Siphon tubing
- Bottles & caps (or a keg system if fancy)

Step-by-Step Brewing Process

1. Sanitize Everything. Beer is 90% cleaning and 10% fun. Anything that touches your beer after the boil needs to be sanitized — fermenter, airlock, siphon, etc.

2. Steep Specialty Grains (Optional, adds flavor)
- Heat ~2.5 gallons of water to 150–160°F (65–70°C).
- Place crushed specialty grains in a mesh bag and steep for 20–30 minutes.
- Remove grains before the water boils.

3. The Boil
- Bring water to a boil, then remove from heat and stir in malt extract.
- Return to heat and boil for 60 minutes.
- Add hops according to recipe:
  - **Bittering hops** (at 60 min) give backbone bitterness.
  - **Flavor hops** (at 30 min) add taste.
  - **Aroma hops** (last 5 min or flameout) add smell.

4. Cooling the Wort
- After the boil, you now have "wort" (unfermented beer).
- Cool it quickly to ~70°F (21°C) using an ice bath or wort chiller.

5. Fermentation
- Transfer wort into sanitized fermenter.
- Add cold water to bring total volume to 5 gallons.
- Aerate by shaking or stirring.
- Pitch (sprinkle) the yeast.
- Seal with airlock.
- Let it ferment in a dark, cool place (65–72°F / 18–22°C) for 1–2 weeks.

6. Bottling & Carbonation
- After fermentation, boil 5 oz priming sugar in 2 cups water.
- Add to bottling bucket.
- Siphon beer into bucket (avoiding sediment).
- Bottle and cap.
- Store bottles at room temp for 2 weeks to carbonate.

7. Enjoy!
- Chill bottles.
- Pour carefully into a glass (leave sediment in the bottle).

- Drink the fruits of your labor!
Once you're comfortable, you can start experimenting with recipes: stouts, IPAs, wheat beers, fruit beers, etc.

☐ **Drink and write dirty limericks.** What sounds better than cuddling up in sweats, drinking and writing dirty lines to each other? All you need is some booze, a pen and paper or cell phone, and the rhyming scheme of limericks. Here are some examples to get you started:

There once was a man from Devizes
Whose balls were of differing sizes
One was so small you couldn't see it at all
The other so big it won prizes.

There once was a man from leeds
who ate a packet of seeds
within the hour
his dick was a flour
and his balls were all covered in weeds.

There once was a Senator from Mass
Who wanted a strange piece of ass
He lucked up and found it
But screwed up and drowned it
And now his future is past.

There once was a man from Nantucket
with a d**k so long he could suck it
he said with a grin as he licked off his chin
"if my ear was a c**t I would f**k it."

There once was a man from China
who wasn't a very good climba'
he slipped on a rock and cut of his c**k
and now he's got a va**na.

Get the Full Dirty Limerick Game:

https://www.etsy.com/listing/4404297587/dirty-limerick-night-the-drunk-poetry

☐ **Go foraging for edible plants and berries and make a meal with them.** You'd be surprised how many plants we consider weeds are edible. You and your date definitely need to be very open minded for this one, but it can be a fun way to cook dinner together and learn about what plants and weeds are edible.

☐ **Play Pancakes vs. Waffles.** In this imaginative game that exposes core identity values, you have to pick one forever. Start with waffles vs. pancakes. If you choose pancakes, waffles are gone forever. Next, challenge your partner with pancakes vs. french fries…and suddenly you'll be arguing about whether you want to keep oral sex or government (that one is a gimme in my book lol) in this mental jungle of a future you're designing together. Someone at Middlebury College takes credit for creating the game and explains it with an example script. We think the origins are more nebulous and played widely at freshman orientations and company bonding events.

> Below is an accelerated demonstration of how the game would work and a short note on why these choices were made.
>
> Player 1: Pancakes or Waffles?
>
> Player 2: Waffles! [I just like waffles more. Goodbye pancakes!] Waffles or Strawberries?
>
> Player 1: Waffles! [This was tricky… This means we never have strawberries, strawberry jam etc.] Waffles or Sleeping-in?
>
> Player 2: Sleeping-in! [Sleeping-in is just one of those joys in life.] Sleeping-in or Comfortable beds?
>
> Player 1: Comfortable beds! [Why sleep in if the bed isn't comfortable? This one was pretty straightforward. It's still unfortunate that we can't sleep-in…] Comfortable beds or Shoes?
>
> Player 2: Shoes! [Shoes just seem more fundamentally important. For example, people in cooler climates need shoes to keep their feet warm. The health consequences of bare feet in sub-zero temperatures seriously outweigh the luxury of a comfortable bed.] Shoes or the Internet?
>
> Player 1: Shoes! [Again, a hard choice, but I felt that shoes are more of a fundamental necessity than the internet.] Shoes or Roads?
>
> Player 2: Roads! [Well, we've lost shoes, but at least humans can move from one place to another easily via a roads network. I am pretty confident that roads are more important to how humans function as a society than shoes are.] Roads or Primary education?

22

Player 1: Primary education! [Eliminating primary education would, in my opinion, not only influence human productivity but also during this phase in life, a child is instilled with certain social skills which I weigh as being more important than roads. At the same time, we have to keep in mind what we losing now that we are sacrificing roads.] Primary education and Trade?

Player 2: Primary education! [In another circumstance, I would have chosen Trade, but as roads don't exist already, that means trade, in the world we've developed, would be fairly fragmented and difficult to traverse. Because we don't have roads, the institution of trade cannot be as influential as it is in our world today. Therefore, I think Primary education plays a more important role in the society we've created.]

… And this is how the game progresses.

As you can see, the game gets more complicated and the questions get harder to answer. With each successive round, the reasoning behind making these choices gets more nuanced and sophisticated.

For the full Pancakes vs. Waffles game:

https://www.etsy.com/listing/4404203265/pancakes-vs-waffles-the-relationship

☐ **Play dinner-delivery roulette.** This potential partner already knows plenty about you, and you'd invite them over if you could. Instead, exchange addresses for a surprise takeout night that also helps support a local business. Set a time for delivery, and schedule your favorite local dish to land on their doorstep. Watching them unbox and enjoy your favorite food, and you, theirs, is perfect whether you're a plate-sharer or not.

☐ **Eat samples at a food market.** Feeling hungry but don't want to splurge on a restaurant date? Head over to a local food market or food festival with your date and snack on some delicious samples. Low-key, Costco works, too.

☐ **Do some pub trivia.** This one is a fun option if you want some drinks, but don't want to just sit at the bar together. Now you can sit at the bar and try to answer trivia questions! It gives you a lot to talk about, and you can find out what they are interested in. Whether you win or lose, it's still a fun way to spend a couple of hours.

☐ **Adult kids party.** Have a kids birthday party for yourselves. With a cake (the sillier, the better), a present for each of you, a pinata, pin the tail on the donkey, etc. Basically, whatever party games and decorations you want to rock. Because why should kids have all the fun?

☐ **Make some different types of homemade salsa.** After you make the salsa, what else is there to do but to have some margaritas, and taste test your salsa with chips. Maybe make it into a taco or nacho night. Loads of different types of salsa to try to make to suit all different types of tastes.

TYPES OF HOMEMADE SALSAS

Classic Fresh Salsas
- Salsa Fresca / Pico de Gallo (chopped tomatoes, onion, jalapeño, cilantro, lime)
- Salsa Roja (tomato-based, blended smooth)
- Salsa Verde (made with tomatillos, tangy and green)
- Salsa Taquera (thin, red taco-shop salsa with dried chiles)

Roasted & Cooked Salsas
- Fire-Roasted Tomato Salsa (smoky flavor from charred tomatoes & peppers)
- Charred Tomatillo Salsa (earthy, tangy, roasted green salsa)
- Salsa Ranchera (cooked tomato & chili salsa, often for huevos rancheros)
- Salsa Borracha (beer-infused chili salsa, great with meats)

Chile-Focused Salsas
- Salsa de Chile de Árbol (bright red, spicy, made with dried chile de árbol)
- Salsa de Chipotle (smoky with chipotle peppers in adobo)
- Guajillo Salsa (smooth, deep red, slightly sweet)
- Pasilla Salsa (dark, rich, mild heat)
- Habanero Salsa (very spicy, citrusy flavor)
- Salsa Macha (oil-based salsa with dried chiles, garlic, nuts, and seeds)

Fruit Salsas
- Mango Salsa (sweet-spicy with jalapeño or habanero)
- Pineapple Salsa (bright, citrusy, great with grilled meats)
- Peach Salsa (fresh and slightly floral)

- Strawberry Salsa (sweet-tart with jalapeño and cilantro)
- Watermelon Salsa (refreshing summer salsa with cucumber and lime)

Unique & Regional Salsas
- Salsa Negra (dark, smoky salsa made with dried chilies and garlic)
- Salsa de Cacahuate (peanut-based salsa, nutty and spicy)
- Salsa de Aguacate (creamy avocado salsa, thinner than guacamole)
- Salsa Criolla (Peruvian style with onion, vinegar, and peppers)
- Salsa de Molcajete (chunky, stone-ground in a mortar and pestle)

Creamy & Fusion Salsas
- Avocado Tomatillo Salsa (silky and green)
- Yogurt-Cilantro Salsa (cooling with spice)
- Sour Cream & Chile Salsa (mild, tangy blend)
- Salsa de Queso Fresco (cheese-based dip-like salsa)

☐ **Try to make convoluted cocktails.** This always a lot of fun. You can either try to make some crazy cocktails/shots that have recipes, or you can try to make an original cocktail. This one can be expensive if you go all out, but if you find the right recipe, it doesn't have to be too crazy expensive. If you make up your own cocktail, you, obviously, have to give it a name. I made up the drink Tequila Rose and Mountain Dew, don't knock it until you try it. I call it a Rose Garden…just made that up on the spot, probably a terrible name but it just felt right.

<u>**Craft Cocktail Recipes for Date Night (Sample)**</u>
1. **Smoked Maple Old Fashioned**. Bourbon, maple syrup, Angostura bitters, orange peel, smoked glass. Warm, woodsy, seductive.
2. **Lavender Gin Fizz**. Gin, lavender syrup, lemon juice, club soda, egg white. Floral, frothy, Instagram-ready.
3. **Espresso Martini**. Vodka, Kahlúa, espresso shot, coffee beans garnish. The ultimate sexy pick-me-up.
4. **Pineapple Jalapeño Margarita**. Tequila, pineapple juice, lime juice, triple sec, muddled jalapeño. Sweet fire.
5. **Cucumber Basil Gimlet**. Gin, lime juice, basil, cucumber slices. Fresh, green, garden-in-a-glass.
6. **Blood Orange Negroni**. Gin, Campari, sweet vermouth, blood orange juice. Bitter-sweet, jewel-toned.
7. **Rosemary Grapefruit Paloma**. Tequila, grapefruit juice, rosemary syrup, soda. Earthy and citrusy.

8. **Coconut Rum Painkiller**. Dark rum, pineapple juice, orange juice, coconut cream, grated nutmeg. A tiki trip without leaving home.
9. **Smoked Mezcal Mule**. Mezcal, ginger beer, lime juice, agave. Smoky cousin of the Moscow Mule.
10. **Matcha White Russian**. Vodka, Kahlúa, cream, matcha powder. Dessert cocktail with a zen twist.
11. **Blackberry Sage Smash**. Bourbon, blackberries, sage leaves, simple syrup, lemon juice. Rustic, mysterious, delicious.
12. **Pear & Prosecco Spritz**. Pear nectar, prosecco, elderflower liqueur. Elegant bubbles with orchard sweetness.
13. **Pomegranate Gin Sour**. Gin, pomegranate juice, lemon juice, egg white, bitters. Jewel-pink froth.
14. **Banana Rum Flip**. Aged rum, banana liqueur, egg, cream, nutmeg. Tropical custard in a coupe glass.
15. **Chocolate Chili Martini**. Vodka, crème de cacao, chili-infused syrup, cayenne dust rim. Sweet with a burn.
16. **Fig & Thyme Manhattan**. Rye whiskey, sweet vermouth, fig syrup, thyme garnish. Complex, sultry, autumn in a glass.
17. **Salted Caramel Martini**. Vanilla vodka, Baileys, caramel syrup, sea salt rim. Dessert masquerading as a drink.
18. **Blueberry Mojito**. Rum, blueberries, mint, lime, soda, sugar. Classic mojito with a violet-blue glow.
19. **Cranberry Rosemary Spritz**. Vodka, cranberry juice, rosemary simple syrup, soda. Winter wonderland vibes.
20. **Spicy Mango Caipirinha**. Cachaça, muddled lime, mango puree, chili flakes. Sweet, sour, hot — Brazil on fire.
21. **Cotton Candy Champagne**. Drop a puff of cotton candy in a flute, pour sparkling wine over it. Childlike wonder meets adult luxury.
22. **Watermelon Basil Cooler**. Vodka, watermelon juice, basil syrup, lime. Summer romance in a glass.
23. **Pumpkin Pie Martini**. Vanilla vodka, pumpkin purée, Baileys, cinnamon sugar rim. Autumn date night treat.
24. **Hibiscus Tequila Sour**. Tequila, hibiscus syrup, lime juice, egg white, bitters. Bright pink and bold.
25. **Charcoal Lemonade Cocktail**. Vodka, activated charcoal, lemon juice, simple syrup, soda. Dark, mysterious, and conversation-starting.

☐ **Cook a new recipe together.** Find a recipe for something neither of you has ever made and make it. It's easy to chat while cooking and you get a dinner out of it as well. You can even make shopping for ingredients part of the date. A bottle of wine or beers helps the cooking process stay fun.

☐ **Meet for breakfast.** The great thing about a breakfast date is that it opens up the rest of the day for you. If you two hit it off over bacon and eggs, you can keep the date going. No sparks? Your evening's still open for something else to come along. Pick a restaurant with a type of cuisine that neither of you has tried. This one is a bit of a gamble because you won't know if you both will like the food or not. If you are both adventurous, it can be a lot of fun experiencing a new cuisine together. And you've both got a natural topic of conversation to fall back on, the new food! It can lead to a very memorable date. An example would be a Brazilian Steakhouse.

☐ **Go pick some fruit at a pick your own fruit farm.** Most towns or cities will have a farm where you can pay to pick your own fruit. You can take it back home and eat it fresh or make it into a dessert. Either way, it'll give you a chance to get out of the house and chat while doing something together. Obviously, the Apple Orchard in the fall is a must!

☐ **Make your own sundaes.** I know this is in the make your own desserts, but this one is absolutely customized. There are tons of DIY homemade ice cream methods. You can ask each other why they would ever pick such a thing to put on their ice cream. If you don't want to buy all the ingredients, find a frozen yogurt place near you, like a Yogurtland or whatever.

☐ **Have a multi-venue meal.** Okay, so this is technically dinner. But it's more of an adventure than a typical sit-down meal. Have your appetizer, main course, and dessert at different spots, because who doesn't want to have nachos followed by sushi followed by flan?

☐ **Make pizzas at home.** This is a fun one. Don't just make a traditional pizza. Have fun with it like a macaroni and cheese pizza. Pizza with the weirdest ingredients maybe even a white sauce with corn. I went to a Brazilian pizza place once, Google pizzas like that.

CREATIVE PIZZA IDEAS

1. **Mac & Cheese Pizza.** Cheese sauce, elbow macaroni, mozzarella, cheddar, breadcrumbs.
2. **Brazilian Corn & Catupiry Pizza.** Catupiry cheese, sweet corn, mozzarella, oregano.

3. **Stroganoff Pizza**. Beef stroganoff, mushrooms, cream sauce, mozzarella.
4. **Banana & Cinnamon Dessert Pizza**. Sliced bananas, cinnamon sugar, mozzarella, sweetened condensed milk.
5. **Hot Dog Pizza (Cachorro-Quente)**. Sliced hot dogs, mozzarella, ketchup drizzle, corn, potato sticks.
6. **Chicken Catupiry Pizza**. Shredded chicken, Catupiry cheese, mozzarella, oregano.
7. **Egg & Bacon Brazilian Pizza**. Fried eggs, crispy bacon, mozzarella, green onions.
8. **Shrimp with Garlic Cream Pizza**. Shrimp, garlic cream sauce, mozzarella, parsley.
9. **Brigadeiro Dessert Pizza**. Chocolate brigadeiro spread, strawberries, chocolate sprinkles.
10. **Tuna & Onion Pizza**. Canned tuna, red onions, mozzarella, oregano.
11. **Palm Heart Pizza (Palmito)**. Hearts of palm, mozzarella, olives, tomato slices, oregano.
12. **Calabresa & Onion Pizza**. Brazilian linguiça sausage (calabresa), caramelized onions, mozzarella.
13. **Portuguesa Pizza**. Ham, onions, black olives, boiled eggs, bell peppers, mozzarella.
14. **Chocolate & Strawberry Pizza**. Melted chocolate, sliced strawberries, white chocolate drizzle.
15. **Chicken & Corn Pizza**. Shredded chicken, sweet corn, mozzarella, green onions.
16. **Cheeseburger Pizza**. Ground beef, cheddar, pickles, onions, ketchup-mustard drizzle.
17. **Spinach & Ricotta Pizza**. Sautéed spinach, ricotta, mozzarella, garlic.
18. **Cream Cheese & Guava Pizza (Romeo & Juliet)**. Guava paste, cream cheese, mozzarella.
19. **Shrimp & Catupiry Pizza**. Shrimp, Catupiry cheese, mozzarella, parsley.
20. **Caramelized Banana & Dulce de Leche Pizza**. Banana slices, dulce de leche drizzle, cinnamon sugar.
21. **BBQ Chicken Pizza**. Shredded chicken, BBQ sauce, mozzarella, red onions, cilantro.
22. **Broccoli & Alfredo Sauce Pizza**. Broccoli florets, Alfredo sauce, mozzarella, Parmesan.
23. **Prosciutto & Arugula Pizza**. Prosciutto, arugula, mozzarella, Parmesan shavings.
24. **Chocolate Hazelnut Pizza**. Nutella, strawberries, chopped hazelnuts, powdered sugar.
25. **Four-Cheese Brazilian Style Pizza**. Mozzarella, Catupiry, gorgonzola, provolone.

☐ **Have a drink at a rooftop bar.** If you don't have this in your area, maybe take a road trip and find a place that does. Or just find a great place to sip a cocktail with a great ambiance and scenery.

☐ **Make your own homemade sushi.** I feel like rolling sushi kits aren't that expensive. This is like anything get whatever your heart desires and make it fun. Maybe watch some YouTube videos for ideas.

CREATIVE SUSHI ROLL IDEAS

1. **California Roll.** Imitation crab, avocado, cucumber, sesame seeds.
2. **Spicy Tuna Roll.** Raw tuna, sriracha mayo, cucumber, scallions.
3. **Dragon Roll.** Eel, cucumber, avocado, eel sauce, sesame seeds.
4. **Rainbow Roll.** California roll topped with tuna, salmon, yellowtail, avocado.
5. **Philadelphia Roll.** Smoked salmon, cream cheese, cucumber.
6. **Crunchy Tempura Shrimp Roll.** Tempura shrimp, avocado, cucumber, spicy mayo, crunchy tempura flakes.
7. **Volcano Roll.** Spicy crab, avocado, cucumber, baked spicy scallops on top, spicy mayo.
8. **Caterpillar Roll.** Eel, cucumber, avocado slices layered on top, eel sauce.
9. **Spider Roll.** Soft-shell crab tempura, cucumber, avocado, sprouts, spicy mayo.
10. **Vegetable Garden Roll.** Cucumber, avocado, carrots, asparagus, pickled radish.
11. **Mango Tango Roll.** Shrimp tempura, cucumber, topped with mango slices and sweet chili sauce.
12. **Boston Roll.** Cooked shrimp, avocado, lettuce, Japanese mayo.
13. **Alaskan Roll.** Salmon, avocado, cucumber.
14. **Lobster Roll.** Tempura lobster, cucumber, avocado, spicy aioli drizzle.
15. **Spicy Scallop Roll.** Scallops, sriracha mayo, cucumber, masago.
16. **Crispy Chicken Katsu Roll.** Fried chicken katsu, avocado, cucumber, spicy mayo.
17. **Tropical Roll.** Crab, avocado, cucumber, topped with pineapple chunks and coconut flakes.
18. **Snow Crab Roll.** Snow crab, avocado, cucumber, Japanese mayo.
19. **Tempura Sweet Potato Roll.** Tempura sweet potato, avocado, eel sauce drizzle.

20. **Sake Lover's Roll.** Raw salmon, avocado, cucumber, topped with salmon sashimi slices.
21. **Futomaki (Jumbo Roll).** Egg omelet, cucumber, spinach, pickled radish, crab, shiitake mushrooms.
22. **Tuna Tataki Roll.** Seared tuna, avocado, cucumber, ponzu sauce drizzle.
23. **BBQ Eel & Cream Cheese Roll.** Eel, cream cheese, cucumber, eel sauce.
24. **Spicy Jalapeño Roll.** Spicy tuna, avocado, cucumber, topped with jalapeño slices.
25. **Dessert Sushi Roll.** Sweet rice, banana, strawberries, Nutella, rolled in soy paper with powdered sugar.

☐ **Make homemade pasta.** Why not? Anything else you can think of to make homemade, do it. What is your favorite pasta? Tortellini, linguini or Spaghetti?

☐ **Pick a mishmash of ingredients and cook something crazy.** This is a fun one. You can grab an ingredient at the grocery store and then your partner grabs another, and you keep going until you have a the most random meal you could make. There is also another way this game could work and that is cooking whatever you have in the fridge and pantry. It really shows how good of a cook you really are. (You can also cheat on this and put the ingredients into Google, and see what recipes come up, or have ChatGPT make you a whole new recipe.)

☐ **Do a Master Chef competition.** Get a meat, some random ingredients to choose from. Now do a cookoff and only have thirty minutes to prepare. The loser has to rub the other person's feet.

☐ **Have a cooking competition with whatever food you have in your or their house.** If both of you are comfortable with visiting the other's house on a date or if you live together, this can be an enjoyable way to spend the evening. It forces you both to be creative and can lead to some hilarious results.

☐ **Gross food test.** You know you want to. Anything you can think of like pig ears, crickets, brain, etc. You name it! Let's try it!

TOP 50 SHOCK FOODS

1. **Century Egg (China).** Preserved duck or chicken egg turned black and jelly-like.
2. **Balut (Philippines).** Fertilized duck embryo boiled and eaten straight from the shell.

3. **Surströmming (Sweden).** Fermented Baltic herring known for its infamously rotten smell.
4. **Casu Marzu (Italy).** Sardinian sheep's milk cheese filled with live maggots.
5. **Hákarl (Iceland).** Fermented Greenland shark, ammonia-rich and pungent.
6. **Fugu (Japan).** Pufferfish that can be deadly if improperly prepared.
7. **Rocky Mountain Oysters (USA).** Fried bull testicles, served like bar food.
8. **Escamoles (Mexico).** Ant larvae, nicknamed "insect caviar."
9. **Sannakji (Korea).** Live octopus chopped and still wriggling on the plate.
10. **Tuna Eyeball (Japan).** Huge fish eye boiled or steamed, jelly-like texture.
11. **Fried Tarantulas (Cambodia).** Crispy whole spiders, legs and all.
12. **Bat Soup (Palau/Guam).** Fruit bat boiled in broth, sometimes with wings intact.
13. **Pig's Blood Cake (Taiwan).** Sticky rice mixed with pig's blood, served on a stick.
14. **Snake Wine (Vietnam).** Rice wine bottled with a preserved venomous snake inside.
15. **Stink Bugs (Africa/Asia).** Crunchy insects eaten fried or raw.
16. **Chicken Feet (China/Worldwide).** Boiled or fried, gelatinous texture with tiny bones.
17. **Sheep's Head (Norway – Smalahove).** A whole sheep's head, boiled and served.
18. **Kopi Luwak Coffee (Indonesia).** Coffee beans eaten and excreted by civet cats, then roasted.
19. **Muktuk (Alaska/Greenland).** Whale skin and blubber eaten raw or frozen.
20. **Lutefisk (Norway).** Whitefish soaked in lye, gelatinous when cooked.
21. **Horse Meat Sashimi (Japan – Basashi).** Thinly sliced raw horse meat.
22. **Camel Hump (Middle East).** Fatty hump meat, roasted or stewed.
23. **Guinea Pig (Peru – Cuy).** Whole roasted guinea pig, head and feet included.
24. **Tong Zi Dan (China).** "Virgin boy eggs" boiled in the urine of young boys (yes, really).
25. **Blood Sausage (Various).** Sausage made from pig or cow's blood.

26. **Duck Blood Soup (Poland/China).** Thick soup made with coagulated duck's blood.
27. **Fermented Stingray (Korea).** Strong-smelling fish with ammonia-rich flesh.
28. **Lamprey Pie (England).** Medieval delicacy made of blood-sucking fish.
29. **Snake Bile Wine (China).** Rice wine infused with snake bile.
30. **Shirako (Japan).** Cod fish sperm sacs, creamy texture.
31. **Jellied Moose Nose (Canada).** Moose snout boiled and set into jelly.
32. **Beondegi (Korea).** Steamed or boiled silkworm pupae.
33. **Brain Masala (Pakistan/India).** Spiced goat or lamb brains.
34. **Tripe Soup (Romania – Ciorbă de burtă).** Cow stomach soup with garlic and vinegar.
35. **Haggis (Scotland).** Sheep's stomach stuffed with offal, oats, and spices.
36. **Fermented Fish Sauce (Southeast Asia).** Intensely pungent fermented anchovy sauce.
37. **Goat Eyeballs (Mongolia).** Often served in soup for hangovers.
38. **Alligator Jerky (USA).** Chewy dried alligator meat.
39. **Grasshoppers (Mexico – Chapulines).** Toasted grasshoppers with lime and chili.
40. **Duck Tongues (China).** Tiny tongues, often stir-fried or deep fried.
41. **Sea Cucumber (Asia).** Slimy sea creature served braised or raw.
42. **Cow's Udder (Spain).** Roasted or grilled cow mammary glands.
43. **Pig's Ear Salad (China/Spain).** Chewy cartilage slices in salads or tapas.
44. **Boiled Sheep Intestines (Middle East – Usban).** Stuffed with rice, spices, and minced meat.
45. **Sea Urchin (Japan – Uni).** Bright orange, creamy gonads of sea urchins.
46. **Fermented Horse Milk (Mongolia – Airag).** Alcoholic drink made from fermented mare's milk.
47. **Crocodile Skewers (Africa/Asia).** Grilled croc tail meat on skewers.
48. **Wasp Crackers (Japan).** Rice crackers with baked wasps inside.
49. **Live Ant Salad (Denmark – Noma style).** Salad garnished with live ants for sour, citrusy pop.
50. **Ox Penis Soup (China).** Stewed bull penis served as "strength food."

☐ **Tapas Restaurant**. These are my favorite, just cause, I love to sample. Go to a genuine tapas restaurant. Don't look, just point and order four or five things off the menu to try together.

☐ **A foreign country-themed date night.** Make that country's food, listen to music from there, drink booze from there, watch a movie or TV show from there. It's a fun way to experience a different country's traditions. This one works best if you pick a country you don't know much about.

France
Movie: *Amélie* (2001)
Food: Coq au vin or crepes
Drink: Bordeaux
Music: Édith Piaf

Italy
Movie: *La Dolce Vita* (1960)
Food: Homemade pasta or pizza Margherita
Drink: Chianti
Music: Andrea Bocelli

Spain
Movie: *Vicky Cristina Barcelona* (2008)
Food: Tapas or paella
Drink: Sangria
Music: Flamenco guitar

Japan
Movie: *Your Name* (2016)
Food: Sushi or ramen
Drink: Sake
Music: City pop

India
Movie: *The Lunchbox*
Food: Butter chicken and naan
Drink: Chai
Music: India love songs

Mexico
Movie: *Like Water for Chocolate* (1992)
Food: Tacos al pastor
Drink: Tequila or horchata
Music: Mariachi

Greece
Movie: *Before Midnight*
Food: Souvlaki or Greek salad
Drink: Ouzo
Music: Bouzouki

Brazil
Movie: *City of God* (2002)
Food: Feijoada
Drink: Caipirinha
Music: Bossa nova

Argentina
Movie: *The Secret in Their Eyes* (2009)
Food: Chimichurri Steak
Drink: Malbec
Music: Tango

South Korea
Movie: *Decision to Leave*
Food: Korean BBQ or bibimbap
Drink: Soju
Music: Korean ballads

Germany
Movie: *Run Lola Run*
Food: Bratwurst or pretzels
Drink: Beer
Music: Kraftwerk

Australia
Movie: *The Dressmaker*
Food: BBQ prawns or meat pie
Drink: Shiraz
Music: Angus & Julia Stone

Ireland
Movie: *Once* (2007)
Food: Shepherd's pie
Drink: Guinness
Music: The Cranberries

England
Movie: *About Time* (2013)
Food: Fish and chips or scones
Drink: Tea
Music: The Beatles

Scotland
Movie: *Local Hero* (1983)
Food: Shortbread or haggis
Drink: Whisky
Music: Celtic folk

Iceland
Movie: *Rams* (2015)
Food: Lamb stew
Drink: Brennivín
Music: Sigur Rós

Sweden
Movie: *A Man Called Ove* (2015)
Food: Swedish meatballs
Drink: Aquavit
Music: ABBA

Denmark
Movie: *Another Round* (2020)
Food: Smørrebrød
Drink: Beer
Music: Danish jazz

Norway
Movie: *The Worst Person in the World* (2021)
Food: Salmon
Drink: Aquavit
Music: Aurora

Finland
Movie: *The Man Without a Past* (2002)
Food: Karelian pies
Drink: Vodka
Music: Finnish folk

Portugal
Movie: *Night Train to Lisbon* (2013)
Food: Caldo verde
Drink: Port wine
Music: Fado

Turkey
Movie: *The Water Diviner* (2014)
Food: Doner kebab or baklava
Drink: Turkish coffee
Music: Sufi-inspired chill

Morocco
Movie: *Casablanca* (1942)
Food: Chicken tagine or couscous
Drink: Mint tea
Music: Gnawa rhythms

Egypt
Movie: *Cairo Time* (2009)
Food: Koshari or falafel
Drink: Hibiscus tea
Music: Arabic lounge

Israel
Movie: *The Band's Visit*
Food: Hummus and shawarma
Drink: Arak
Music: Middle Eastern jazz

Lebanon
Movie: *Capernaum* (2018)
Food: Shawarma and tabbouleh
Drink: Arak
Music: Fairuz

South Africa
Movie: *Tsotsi* (2005)
Food: Bobotie or braai
Drink: Pinotage
Music: Amapiano

Nigeria
Movie: *The Wedding Party*
Food: Jollof rice
Drink: Palm wine
Music: Afrobeats

Kenya
Movie: *Rafiki* (2018)
Food: Ugali with sukuma wiki
Drink: Tusker beer
Music: Benga

Ghana
Movie: *Beast of No Nation*
Food: Fufu groundnut soup
Drink: Palm wine
Music: Highlife

Ethiopia
Movie: *Difret* (2014)
Food: Injera with doro wat
Drink: Tej (honey wine)
Music: Ethio-jazz

Iran
Movie: *A Separation* (2011)
Food: Fesenjan
Drink: Pomegranate juice
Music: Persian classical

Afghanistan
Movie: *The Kite Runner*
Food: Mantu dumplings
Drink: Green tea
Music: Afghan folk

Pakistan
Movie: *Bol* (2011)
Food: Biryani
Drink: Chai
Music: Coke Studio

Nepal
Movie: *Himalaya* (1999)
Food: Dal bhat
Drink: Milk tea
Music: Tibetan chants

China
Movie: *In the Mood for Love* (2000)
Food: Dumplings
Drink: Plum wine
Music: Guzheng instrumentals

Taiwan
Movie: *Eat Drink Man Woman* (1994)
Food: Dim sum
Drink: Bubble tea
Music: Mandopop

Hong Kong
Movie: *Chungking Express*
Food: Noodles or congee
Drink: Tsingtao beer
Music: Cantopop

Thailand
Movie: *The Beach* (2000)
Food: Pad Thai
Drink: Thai iced tea
Music: Thai lounge

Vietnam
Movie: *The Scent of Green Papaya* (1993)
Food: Pho
Drink: Saigon beer
Music: Vietnamese

Indonesia
Movie: *Eat Pray Love*
Food: Nasi goreng
Drink: Bintang beer
Music: Gamelan

Malaysia
Movie: *The Garden of Evening Mists* (2019)
Food: Laksa
Drink: Kopi
Music: Malaysian jazz

Philippines
Movie: *That Thing Called Tadhana* (2014)
Food: Chicken adobo
Drink: San Miguel beer
Music: OPM ballads

Singapore
Movie: *Crazy Rich Asians*
Food: Chili crab
Drink: Tiger beer
Music: Swing jazz

Cambodia
Movie: *First They Killed My Father* (2017)
Food: Amok
Drink: Iced coffee
Music: Khmer pop

Laos
Movie: *Good Morning Luang Prabang* (2008)
Food: Laap
Drink: Beerlao
Music: Traditional Laotian

Myanmar
Movie: *The Lady* (2011)
Food: Mohinga
Drink: Green tea
Music: Burmese folk

Mongolia
Movie: *The Story of the Weeping Camel* (2003)
Food: Dumplings
Drink: Fermented milk
Music: Throat singing

Russia
Movie: *Burnt by the Sun*
Food: Pelmeni
Drink: Vodka
Music: Tchaikovsky

Ukraine
Movie: *The Guide* (2014)
Food: Varenyky
Drink: Horilka
Music: Ukrainian folk rock

United States
Movie: *La La Land* (2016)
Food: Burgers
Drink: Bourbon
Music: Jazz or indie rock

Canada
Movie: *One Week* (2008)
Food: Poutine
Drink: Canadian whisky
Music: The Tragically Hip

Cuba
Movie: *Buena Vista Social Club* (1999)
Food: Ropa vieja
Drink: Mojito
Music: Cuban jazz

Jamaica
Movie: *The Harder They Come* (1972)
Food: Jerk chicken
Drink: Rum punch
Music: Bob Marley

Dominican Republic
Movie: *Sugar* (2008)
Food: Mangu and fried plantains
Drink: Presidente beer
Music: Bachata

Puerto Rico
Movie: *West Side Story*
Food: Mofongo
Drink: Piña colada
Music: Salsa

Haiti
Movie: *Murder in Pacot*
Food: Griot (fried pork)
Drink: Prestige beer
Music: Kompa

Bahamas
Movie: *Thunderball* (1965)
Food: Conch fritters
Drink: Bahama Mama
Music: Junkanoo

Barbados
Movie: *Hit for Six* (2007)
Food: Flying fish and cou-cou
Drink: Rum punch
Music: Calypso

Trinidad & Tobago
Movie: *Bazodee* (2016)
Food: Doubles
Drink: Carib beer
Music: Soca

Costa Rica
Movie: *After Words* (2015)
Food: Gallo pinto
Drink: Guaro sour
Music: Latin chill

Panama
Movie: *Hands of Stone*
Food: Sancocho
Drink: Seco Herrerano
Music: Reggaeton

Guatemala
Movie: *Ixcanul* (2015)
Food: Pepian stew
Drink: Atol de elote
Music: Marimba

Honduras
Movie: *La Condesa* (2020)
Food: Baleadas
Drink: Salva Vida beer
Music: Punta rock

El Salvador
Movie: *The Hand That Paints the Sky* (2018)
Food: Pupusas
Drink: Horchata salvadoreña
Music: Cumbia salvadoreña

Nicaragua
Movie: *La Yuma* (2009)
Food: Nacatamales
Drink: Flor de Caña rum
Music: Marimba

Belize
Movie: *2012: Curse of the Xtabai* (2012)
Food: Stewed chicken
Drink: Belikin beer
Music: Garifuna drumming

Colombia
Movie: *Embrace of the Serpent* (2015)
Food: Bandeja paisa
Drink: Aguardiente
Music: Cumbia

Venezuela
Movie: *From Afar* (2015)
Food: Arepas
Drink: Polar beer
Music: Salsa and joropo

Ecuador
Movie: *Proof of Life* (2000)
Food: Ceviche
Drink: Pilsener beer
Music: Andean pan flute

Peru
Movie: *The Milk of Sorrow*
Food: Lomo saltado
Drink: Pisco sour
Music: Afro-Peruvian fusion

Bolivia
Movie: *Yvy Maraey* (2013)
Food: Salteñas
Drink: Singani cocktail
Music: Andean folk

Chile
Movie: *A Fantastic Woman* (2017)
Food: Empanadas
Drink: Carménère wine
Music: Nueva Canción

Paraguay
Movie: *7 Boxes* (2012)
Food: Sopa paraguaya
Drink: Tereré
Music: Guarania

Uruguay
Movie: *Whisky* (2004)
Food: Chivito sandwich
Drink: Tannat wine
Music: Candombe

Guyana
Movie: *The Terror and the Time* (1978)
Food: Pepperpot stew
Drink: Banks beer
Music: Chutney

Suriname
Movie: *Wan Pipel* (1976)
Food: Roti
Drink: Parbo beer
Music: Kaseko

French Guiana
Movie: *Savages* (2012)
Food: Creole curry
Drink: Ti' Punch
Music: Zouk

Greenland
Movie: *Inuk* (2010)
Food: Fish stew
Drink: Aquavit
Music: Inuit throat singing

New Zealand
Movie: *The Piano* (1993)
Food: Lamb roast
Drink: Sauvignon Blanc
Music: Māori traditional

Fiji
Movie: *Blue Lagoon* (1980)
Food: Kokoda (fish ceviche)
Drink: Kava
Music: Island reggae

Samoa
Movie: *Three Wise Cousins*
Food: Palusami
Drink: Coconut water
Music: Polynesian folk

Tonga
Movie: *The Legend of Baron To'a* (2020)
Food: Lu pulu
Drink: Otai
Music: Pacific fusion

Papua New Guinea
Movie: *Tukana: Husat i Asua?* (1984)
Food: Mumu (earth oven feast)
Drink: Coffee
Music: Tribal drumming

Solomon Islands
Movie: *Tanna* (2015)
Food: Taro and coconut fish
Drink: Local beer
Music: Island folk

Vanuatu
Movie: *Tanna* (2015)
Food: Laplap
Drink: Kava
Music: Island chants

Madagascar
Movie: *Madagascar Skin*
Food: Romazava
Drink: Litchel
Music: Salegy

Mauritius
Movie: *Lonbraz Kann*
Food: Dholl puri
Drink: Phoenix beer
Music: Sega

Seychelles
Movie: *A Love Like This*
Food: Grilled red snapper
Drink: Takamaka rum
Music: Moutya

Reunion Island
Movie: *Le Plein de Super*
Food: Cari chicken
Drink: Rhum arrangé
Music: Maloya

Tunisia
Movie: *The Silences of the Palace* (1994)
Food: Brik and couscous
Drink: Mint tea
Music: Arabic jazz

Algeria
Movie: *The Battle of Algiers* (1966)
Food: Chakchouka
Drink: Coffee
Music: Raï

Libya
Movie: *Lion of the Desert* (1981)
Food: Couscous bil-bosla
Drink: Arabic coffee
Music: Tuareg folk

Sudan
Movie: *You Will Die at Twenty* (2019)
Food: Ful medames
Drink: Hibiscus juice
Music: Sudanese jazz

Tanzania
Movie: *Darwin's Nightmare*
Food: Nyama choma
Drink: Safari lager
Music: Swahili fusion

Zimbabwe
Movie: *Cook Off* (2017)
Food: Sadza with beef stew
Drink: Castle lager
Music: Zimdancehall

Namibia
Movie: *The White Line*
Food: Biltong and pap
Drink: Windhoek lager
Music: Desert folk

Botswana
Movie: *The Gods Must Be Crazy* (1980)
Food: Seswaa
Drink: St. Louis beer
Music: Kora

Tanzania (Zanzibar)
Movie: *Zanzibar Soccer Queens* (2007)
Food: Zanzibar biryani
Drink: Sugarcane juice
Music: Taarab

☐ **Fondue Night.** It's basically legalized playing with your food. Melt down cheese for bread and veggies or go sweet with chocolate for strawberries and marshmallows. Half the fun is in fishing out the chunk you dropped and maybe sneaking in a stolen bite from your partner's skewer.

☐ **Charcuterie Board Challenge.** Forget Instagram perfection, this is about outdoing each other in creativity. One of you goes bougie with cured meats and truffle honey, the other piles Goldfish crackers next to pepperoni sticks. At the end, you've built edible artwork and probably found a new snack obsession.

☐ **Homemade Bread Night.** There's something ridiculously satisfying about pulling a warm loaf out of the oven. Make it a focaccia art challenge with herbs and veggies, or just stick to a rustic sourdough. Once it cools, turn it into gourmet sandwiches or rip it apart caveman-style while you butter and devour.

BREAD TYPES
1. **Baguette (France).** Long, crusty, chewy white bread perfect for tearing apart or dipping.
2. **Ciabatta (Italy).** Rustic Italian bread with a crisp crust and open, airy holes.

3. **Focaccia (Italy).** Flat, olive-oil-rich bread topped with herbs, tomatoes, or even art.
4. **Sourdough (Worldwide).** Tangy, chewy bread made with a wild yeast starter.
5. **Brioche (France).** Soft, buttery, slightly sweet bread — dreamy for French toast.
6. **Challah (Jewish).** Braided egg bread, light and golden, often eaten on holidays.
7. **Pita (Middle East).** Round pocket bread, perfect for stuffing with falafel, shawarma, or dips.
8. **Naan (India).** Soft, pillowy flatbread often brushed with butter or garlic.
9. **Paratha (India).** Flaky, layered flatbread fried with ghee or oil.
10. **Roti (South Asia/Caribbean).** Simple unleavened flatbread, versatile and wholesome.
11. **Injera (Ethiopia/Eritrea).** Spongy, tangy flatbread made with teff flour, used as an edible plate.
12. **Lavash (Armenia/Georgia).** Thin, pliable flatbread, sometimes baked on hot stones.
13. **Matzo (Jewish).** Crisp, unleavened flatbread, traditionally eaten during Passover.
14. **Arepa (Venezuela/Colombia).** Cornmeal bread patties, grilled or fried, stuffed with fillings.
15. **Cornbread (USA).** Sweet or savory quick bread made from cornmeal.
16. **Banana Bread (Worldwide).** Moist, sweet quick bread made with ripe bananas.
17. **Zopf (Switzerland).** Braided Swiss bread, similar to challah but richer with milk and butter.
18. **Rye Bread (Northern Europe).** Dense, hearty bread with a deep, earthy flavor.
19. **Pumpernickel (Germany).** Dark, slightly sweet rye bread, great with cheese or smoked fish.
20. **Barmbrack (Ireland).** Yeast bread with dried fruit, often served with tea.
21. **Damper (Australia).** Bush bread, traditionally cooked over campfires.
22. **Pan de Muerto (Mexico).** Sweet, round bread decorated with bone-like shapes, eaten for Day of the Dead.
23. **Pandoro (Italy).** Tall, star-shaped sweet bread, dusted with powdered sugar at Christmas.
24. **Panettone (Italy).** Sweet, fluffy bread studded with dried fruit, iconic for the holidays.
25. **Khachapuri (Georgia).** Cheesy bread boat filled with egg and butter — ridiculously indulgent.

☐ **Fermentation Night.** Kimchi, kombucha, sauerkraut, pickles, fermentation is slow magic. It won't be ready right away, but watching jars bubble and transform is part of the fun. Plus, in a couple weeks, you'll get to taste the fruits (and funky smells) of your labor.

BEST FERMENTED FOODS

1. **Kimchi (Korea).** Spicy, sour napa cabbage and radish with chili, garlic, and ginger.
2. **Sauerkraut (Germany/Eastern Europe).** Fermented shredded cabbage, tangy and crunchy.
3. **Kombucha (China/Worldwide).** Sweetened tea fermented with SCOBY, fizzy and tart.
4. **Miso (Japan).** Fermented soybean paste used in soups, marinades, and sauces.
5. **Tempeh (Indonesia).** Fermented soybeans pressed into a firm, nutty cake.
6. **Natto (Japan).** Sticky, stringy fermented soybeans with an umami punch.
7. **Pickles (Worldwide).** Cucumbers brined in saltwater until sour and crisp.
8. **Kvass (Russia/Ukraine).** Lightly fermented rye bread drink with a tangy, malty flavor.
9. **Fermented Hot Sauce (Worldwide).** Chilies, garlic, and salt left to ferment for bold, fiery heat.
10. **Yogurt (Middle East/Worldwide).** Fermented milk thickened with bacteria cultures.
11. **Kefir (Caucasus Mountains).** Fermented milk drink with tangy, probiotic fizz.
12. **Cheese (Worldwide).** Milk fermented and aged into infinite textures and flavors.
13. **Buttermilk (Traditional).** Soured milk leftover from churning butter, tangy and refreshing.
14. **Idli/Dosa Batter (India).** Fermented rice and lentil batter for fluffy idlis and crisp dosas.
15. **Injera (Ethiopia/Eritrea).** Spongy sour flatbread made from fermented teff flour.
16. **Sourdough Bread (Worldwide).** Wild-yeast fermented bread with a tangy bite.
17. **Fish Sauce (Southeast Asia).** Fermented anchovies into salty, funky liquid gold.
18. **Soy Sauce (China/Japan).** Fermented soybeans and wheat aged into umami depth.
19. **Fermented Black Beans (China).** Salty, funky beans used in stir-fries and sauces.
20. **Chhaang (Tibet/Nepal).** Mildly alcoholic Himalayan millet/barley drink.
21. **Palm Wine (Africa/Asia).** Fermented sap from palm trees, lightly sweet and boozy.
22. **Pulque (Mexico).** Fermented agave sap, milky and slightly sour.

23. **Gundruk (Nepal).** Fermented leafy greens, tangy and savory.
24. **Fermented Tofu (China).** Soft tofu cubes preserved in brine, funky and creamy.
25. **Fermented Garlic Honey (Modern Trend).** Garlic cloves aged in honey until sweet, sharp, and medicinal.

☐ **Blindfold Taste Test.** Grab random items from the pantry or grocery store and take turns feeding them to each other blindfolded. Could be strawberries, could be mustard, could be wasabi. The reactions are priceless, just try not to laugh so hard you choke on the surprise bite.

☐ **Food Sculptures.** Channel your inner kindergartener and turn dinner into an art project. Build a broccoli forest, a mashed potato volcano, or arrange olives into googly eyes. Take photos, laugh at how ridiculous you both are, then destroy your masterpieces with your forks.

Other Ideas that really need no explanation:

☐ Cook a park -or garden- bbq together
☐ Take turns cooking each other breakfast in bed
☐ Have some cocktails at a local landmark
☐ Share a lunch hour date
☐ Go whiskey tasting, or get whiskey delivered to your home with a subscription service!
☐ Dress up to the nines and sip cocktails and from home with candlelight
☐ Go for brunch
☐ Make each other's favorite meals
☐ Go to the grand opening of a restaurant
☐ Go on a picnic
☐ Make a ginger bread house

Classes/Learning

☐ **Take a class for something new.** There are tons of places that have classes. You can often find them at the local library, a community college, a community center, or even at a craft store or hardware stores. There are numerous classes you can take together, here are some ideas:

101 CLASSES FOR COUPLES

Food & Drink
☐ Cooking Basics
☐ Pastry Baking
☐ Bread Making
☐ Sushi Rolling
☐ Wine Tasting & Pairing
☐ Craft Beer Brewing
☐ Cocktail Mixology
☐ Cheese Making
☐ Chocolate & Confections
☐ Barista Coffee Art
☐ Ice Cream Making

Arts & Creativity
☐ Painting (oil, acrylic, watercolor)
☐ Pottery & Ceramics
☐ Sculpture
☐ Drawing & Sketching
☐ Photography Basics
☐ Digital Photography Editing
☐ Printmaking
☐ Mural Painting
☐ Calligraphy
☐ Stained Glass Making
☐ Jewelry Design
☐ Knitting & Crochet
☐ Quilting
☐ Sewing & Fashion Design
☐ Embroidery
☐ Candle Making
☐ Soap Making
☐ Origami
☐ Wood Carving
☐ Leather Crafting
☐ Basket Weaving
☐ Flower Arranging (Ikebana)

☐ Perfume Making
☐ Puppet Making

Performance & Entertainment
☐ Acting/Improv
☐ Stand-up Comedy
☐ DJ Mixing
☐ Music Production
☐ Singing/Vocal Training
☐ Songwriting
☐ Guitar/Piano/Drums
☐ Dance (Salsa, Tango, Hip-Hop, Ballroom, Swing, Belly dance)
☐ Pole Dancing
☐ Aerial Silks
☐ Trapeze
☐ Circus Skills (juggling, clowning, stilts)
☐ Magic Tricks/Illusions

Fitness & Adventure
☐ Yoga
☐ Pilates
☐ Martial Arts (Karate, Judo, Aikido, Kung Fu)
☐ Boxing/Kickboxing
☐ Archery
☐ Fencing
☐ Sword Fighting (medieval style)
☐ Rock Climbing (indoor or outdoor)
☐ Parkour
☐ Trampoline Fitness
☐ Acrobatics
☐ Roller Skating or Roller Derby
☐ Ice Skating
☐ Surfing

44

- [ ] Scuba Diving
- [ ] Snorkeling
- [ ] Kayaking
- [ ] Paddleboarding
- [ ] Horseback Riding
- [ ] Skiing/Snowboarding
- [ ] Skydiving Class (indoor wind tunnel style)

Science & Nature
- [ ] Astronomy (stargazing workshop)
- [ ] Bird Watching & Identification
- [ ] Beekeeping
- [ ] Gardening
- [ ] Hydroponics
- [ ] Bonsai Tree Training
- [ ] Mushroom Foraging
- [ ] Wild Plant Foraging
- [ ] Rockhounding & Gemology
- [ ] Meteorology Basics
- [ ] Survival Skills (fire-starting, shelter building)
- [ ] Wilderness First Aid
- [ ] Composting & Sustainability

Home & DIY
- [ ] Home Improvement (plumbing, drywall, tiling, basic construction)
- [ ] Electrical Basics
- [ ] Carpentry & Woodworking
- [ ] Welding
- [ ] Blacksmithing
- [ ] Glassblowing
- [ ] Knife Making
- [ ] Upholstery

- [ ] Interior Design
- [ ] Feng Shui Home Design
- [ ] Landscaping
- [ ] Car Repair & Maintenance
- [ ] Small Engine Repair
- [ ] Robotics & Electronics
- [ ] 3D Printing

Mind & Lifestyle
- [ ] Meditation & Mindfulness
- [ ] Breathwork
- [ ] Tai Chi / Qigong
- [ ] Philosophy Discussion Groups
- [ ] Language Classes (Spanish, French, Japanese, etc.)
- [ ] Sign Language
- [ ] Debate Club
- [ ] Chess Strategy
- [ ] Writing Workshop (poetry, novels, screenwriting)
- [ ] Journaling for Mindfulness
- [ ] Tarot Reading
- [ ] Astrology 101
- [ ] Psychic Development / Intuition Training
- [ ] Herbal Medicine & Remedies
- [ ] Aromatherapy
- [ ] Massage Therapy Basics
- [ ] Reiki or Energy Healing
- [ ] Hypnosis Training
- [ ] Personal Finance 101
- [ ] Investing & Crypto Basics
- [ ] Leadership & Coaching
- [ ] Travel Hacking (cheap flights, points, etc.

- [ ] **Take a dance lesson.** You don't need to hit the club to dance, you can take a dance class! Bonus points if you take a dancing class with a type of dancing that you both haven't tried. Just try not to step on too many toes. There are so many different dance classes from hip-hop to ballroom, there's no stopping how many different ones you can accomplish, you may even find you love interpretive dance.

TYPES OF DANCE CLASSES

Partner & Social Dances
- Ballroom (general)
- Waltz
- Foxtrot
- Viennese Waltz
- Tango (Argentine, International, Ballroom)
- Salsa
- Bachata
- Merengue
- Cha-Cha
- Rumba
- Samba
- Mambo
- Kizomba
- Zouk
- Swing
- East Coast Swing
- West Coast Swing
- Lindy Hop
- Balboa
- Hustle
- Country Two-Step
- Jitterbug
- Polka

Latin & Cultural Dances
- Flamenco (Spain)
- Sevillanas (Spain)
- Cumbia (Colombia/Mexico)
- Reggaeton (Puerto Rico)
- Bomba & Plena (Puerto Rico)
- Forró (Brazil)
- Lambada (Brazil)
- Frevo (Brazil)
- Capoeira (Brazil – martial art/dance fusion)
- Tango (Argentina)
- Cueca (Chile)
- Jarabe Tapatío (Mexican Hat Dance)
- Irish Step Dance
- Scottish Highland Dance

- English Country Dance
- Morris Dance (England)
- Tarantella (Italy)
- Greek Folk Dance (Sirtaki, Kalamatianos)
- Israeli Folk Dance (Hora)
- Bollywood Dance (India)
- Bhangra (India/Punjab)
- Kathak (India)
- Bharatanatyam (India)
- Odissi (India)
- Belly Dance (Middle East)
- Raqs Sharqi (Egyptian belly dance)
- Dabke (Lebanon/Palestine)
- African Dance (general)
- West African Drum & Dance
- Afro-Cuban Dance
- Afro-Brazilian Orixa Dance
- Polynesian Dance (Hula, Tahitian, Samoan Siva)
- Māori Haka Dance (New Zealand)
- Native American Powwow Dance

Street & Modern Dances
- Hip-Hop (general)
- Breaking (Breakdance)
- Locking
- Popping
- Krumping
- Waacking
- Voguing
- House Dance
- Shuffle Dance
- Jerkin'
- Turfing
- Litefeet

Club & Contemporary Styles
- Jazz Dance
- Contemporary Dance
- Lyrical Dance
- Modern Dance

- Postmodern/Contact Improvisation
- Dancehall (Jamaica)
- Twerking
- Reggaeton Fusion
- Pole Dance (fitness & exotic styles)
- Chair Dance
- Burlesque Dance
- Striptease Dance (sensual/fun class format)
- Heels Dance (dancing in high heels)

Traditional & Historical
- Square Dancing
- Contra Dance
- Line Dancing (country, modern pop line dance)
- Swing Era Dances (Charleston, Collegiate Shag)
- Minuet (classical European)
- Pavane (Renaissance)

- Baroque Court Dance
- Medieval Dance

Fitness & Fusion
- Zumba
- Jazzercise
- Dance Aerobics
- Dance Yoga Fusion
- Dance Meditation (Five Rhythms, Ecstatic Dance)
- Step Dance Fitness
- Dance Cardio

Performance & Theater
- Tap Dance
- Musical Theater Dance
- Broadway Jazz
- Cabaret Dance
- Showgirl Dance (Vegas style)
- Aerial Dance (on silks, hoops, trapeze)
- Acro Dance
- Fire Dance (poi, staff, fans)

☐ **Do yoga together with a twist.** Yoga and booze, yoga outside, hot yoga, naked yoga, all kinds of things you can do to make it more interesting. This is another one that is probably best done with couples that are pretty comfortable around each other. Also, it's a little on the short side. But yeah, it can be a blast to take yoga and remix it and see if you can make it a fun date activity. And, of course, the new craze of goat yoga. I am totally down for that.

YOGA TRENDS & STYLES
- **Hatha Yoga** – Slow-paced, foundational postures, great for beginners.
- **Vinyasa Flow** – Breath-to-movement sequences, energizing and fluid.
- **Ashtanga Yoga** – Structured, powerful flow with set sequences.
- **Iyengar Yoga** – Alignment-focused, often with props.
- **Kundalini Yoga** – Breath, chanting, and repetitive movements to awaken energy.
- **Yin Yoga** – Long, deep stretches held for several minutes.
- **Restorative Yoga** – Relaxation-focused, with blankets, bolsters, and pillows.
- **Power Yoga** – Strength-driven, sweaty and gym-like.
- **Bikram Yoga** – 26 poses in a heated room at ~105°F (40°C).

- **Hot Yoga (non-Bikram)** – Heated yoga flow, less rigid than Bikram.
- **Fusion & Fitness Blends**
- **Yoga Sculpt** – Yoga + weights + cardio intervals.
- **HIIT Yoga** – High-intensity intervals mixed with flows.
- **Pilates Yoga Fusion (PiYo)** – Core-heavy Pilates fused with yoga.
- **Broga** – Yoga rebranded to appeal to men, more strength focus.
- **Acro Yoga** – Partner balance-based yoga (without silks).
- **SUP Yoga** – Yoga on a stand-up paddleboard in water.
- **Snowga** – Yoga outside in the snow.
- **Doga** – Yoga with your dog (yes, that's a thing).
- **Sensory & Lifestyle Twists**
- **Goat Yoga** – Baby goats climb on you while you pose (ridiculous & adorable).
- **Beer Yoga** – Sip craft beer during poses.
- **Wine Yoga** – Same, but with vino.
- **Tequila Yoga** – You know what this is.
- **Candlelight Yoga** – Slow flow in a dark, cozy candlelit room.
- **Silent Disco Yoga** – Headphones, DJ, and flow in sync with music.
- **Glow Yoga** – Black lights + neon body paint + yoga = party.
- **Laughter Yoga** – Forced laughter exercises that turn real.
- **Naked Yoga** – Yep, just what it sounds like.
- **Couples/Tantra Yoga** – Partner-assisted, intimate stretches and breathing.
- **Music-Themed Yoga** – Beyoncé yoga, Metallica yoga, 90s hip-hop yoga.
- **Healing & Spiritual**
- **Sound Bath Yoga** – Combine postures with gongs, bowls, or chimes.
- **Chakra Yoga** – Sequences designed to "open" specific chakras.
- **Meditation + Yoga Nidra** – Guided deep rest in corpse pose.
- **Shakti Dance/Yoga Dance** – Free-form dance blended with yoga flows.
- **Pranayama Sessions** – Breathwork-heavy yoga.
- **Ayurvedic Yoga** – Customized flows based on doshas/body type.

☐ **Stretch it out in aerial yoga.** Sure, there's not much time for talking during a yoga class, but stretching your body while flying through the air in a giant hammock suspended from the ceiling will surely give you and your date something to talk about once the class is over. And if you don't end up enjoying the other person's company, at least you got a cool experience out of it.

☐ **Find some cool science experiment videos on YouTube.** Whether they fail or succeed, you are both sure to have a good time trying them out. Just make sure to go shopping ahead of time to get all the ingredients and create a playlist of stuff to try. You can both choose some videos to try before the date.

25 COOL SCIENCE EXPERIMENTS FOR COUPLES

1. **Elephant Toothpaste**. Hydrogen peroxide, yeast (or potassium iodide), dish soap = giant foamy explosion.
2. **Mentos & Coke Geyser**. Drop Mentos into soda and watch it rocket sky-high.
3. **Oobleck (Non-Newtonian Fluid)**. Cornstarch + water = weird goop that's solid when hit, liquid when still.
4. **Rainbow Milk Explosion**. Milk + food coloring + dish soap = swirling rainbow chaos.
5. **Baking Soda Volcano**. Classic: baking soda, vinegar, and food coloring erupting like lava.
6. **Glow Stick Reaction**. Break open glow sticks (safely!) and experiment with temperature effects on brightness.
7. **Invisible Ink Messages**. Lemon juice or milk on paper, revealed with heat from a candle or iron.
8. **DIY Slime**. Glue, borax (or contact solution), food coloring — endless squishy fun.
9. **Floating Paperclip**. Surface tension trick: carefully place a paperclip to "float" on water.
10. **Balloon Skewer Trick**. Push a skewer through a balloon without popping it. Physics magic.
11. **DIY Lava Lamp**. Vegetable oil, water, food coloring, and Alka-Seltzer tablets.
12. **Egg in a Bottle**. Light a flame inside a glass bottle, place an egg on top — it gets sucked inside.
13. **Dancing Raisins**. Drop raisins in soda water, watch them float up and sink down repeatedly.
14. **Magic Pepper Trick**. Sprinkle pepper on water, then dip in soapy finger — pepper flees instantly.
15. **Homemade Rock Candy**. Grow crystals from sugar water — sweet science.
16. **Vinegar & Steel Wool Battery**. Make a simple battery and light a tiny bulb.
17. **Soap-Powered Boat**. Cut a cardboard "boat," add a drop of soap at the back, and watch it zoom.
18. **DIY Hovercraft (CD + Balloon)**. CD, bottle cap, and balloon make a mini air hovercraft.
19. **Walking Water Rainbow**. Colored water "walks" through paper towels into empty cups.
20. **Corn Syrup Density Tower**. Layer liquids (honey, dish soap, water, oil, alcohol) to show density differences.
21. **Fireproof Balloon**. Fill balloon with water, hold over flame, and it won't pop.

22. **Plastic Milk (Casein Reaction)**. Vinegar + warm milk = weird moldable plastic.
23. **Dry Ice Bubbles**. Drop dry ice in water, add dish soap for huge smoke-filled bubbles.
24. **Magnetic Slime**. Slime mixed with iron filings moves when you hold a magnet.
25. **Homemade Cloud in a Jar**. Hot water, ice, and a match inside a jar creates your own little cloud.

☐ **Learn about local history and visit some historical spots.** Okay so not everyone is interested in history, but this can be a great way to learn more about your town. And you'll get to travel around to places in your town you might not have visited. You'd be surprised how much fascinating history there is in every town and city.

☐ **Learn a skill or trick that doesn't take long to learn.** There are a lot of skills or tricks that don't take long to learn. Some examples might be juggling, magic tricks, rolling a coin across your fingers, lockpicking, etc. You can find lists of things like that on Reddit and then find a how-to video on YouTube.

25 QUICK SKILLS & TRICKS

1. **Juggling 3 Balls**. Classic, awkward at first, but once you get 3 in the air it feels legendary.
2. **Coin Roll Across Fingers**. Slick little move that looks cooler than it is hard.
3. **Pen Spinning (Thumbaround)**. Desk ninja trick — spin a pen around your thumb.
4. **Card Flourishes**. Simple fan, riffle shuffle, or waterfall shuffle for poker-night flair.
5. **The French Drop (Magic Trick)**. Basic coin vanish that will fool each other instantly.
6. **Balancing a Spoon on Your Nose**. It's silly but harder than it looks — and worth the laugh.
7. **Whistling with Fingers**. That loud taxi-stopping whistle? Date-night points if you master it.
8. **Tying a Cherry Stem with Your Tongue**. Flirty, slightly risqué, and always impressive.
9. **Balloon Animal Basics**. Dog, sword, hat — doesn't take long but feels like a superpower.
10. **Rubik's Cube Beginner Method**. Learn the easy solve — suddenly you look like a genius.
11. **Speed Stacking Cups**. Plastic cup towers and pyramids — silly, but addictive.
12. **Shadow Puppets**. Learn a handful of animals (dog, rabbit, bird) to perform your own mini-show.

13. **Snap Your Fingers Loudly.** Like really loud — it's a technique, not just natural talent.
14. **Moonwalk.** The Michael Jackson move — surprisingly learnable with practice.
15. **Spin a Basketball on Your Finger.** Looks like pro-athlete stuff, but you can pick it up in an evening.
16. **Handstand (Against a Wall).** Not quite a circus trick, but fun and challenging.
17. **Yo-Yo Basics.** Walk the Dog, Rock the Baby, Elevator — easy to learn with a cheap yo-yo.
18. **Napkin Rose Folding.** Romantic little table trick, takes less than a minute.
19. **Fork Bending Illusion (Magic Trick).** Simple sleight of hand with cutlery — no actual bending required.
20. **Lockpicking (With Clear Practice Lock).** Totally legal if you use a trainer — fascinating skill to show off.
21. **Knuckle Cracking Patterns.** Weird little trick — make your joints pop in rhythm.
22. **Spinning a Coin on Its Edge.** Get it spinning perfectly and flick it into a flip.
23. **Making a Paper Crane.** Origami classic — a zen date-night activity.
24. **Palm Reading Basics.** Learn just enough to fake being a mystic.
25. **Bottle Cap Flick Trick.** Flick a bottle cap across the table with just the right snap of your fingers.

☐ **Rent / buy an instrument and learn to play it together.** If you both aren't very musically inclined, this can be really hilarious. And if one of you seems to have a knack for it, hey new instrument you can take up! It won't be hard to find some tutorials online, and you can spend as much or as little as you want for the instrument. From a kazoo or harmonica to a violin or tuba, instruments run the gamut of prices.

FUNNY & CHEAP INSTRUMENTS

- **Kazoo** – Basically humming through a party favor. Silly but addictive.
- **Harmonica** – Bluesy, portable, and perfect for dramatic train-whistle vibes.
- **Recorder** – The childhood classic every parent dreaded.
- **Ocarina** – Zelda vibes, cheap, and oddly mystical-sounding.
- **Slide Whistle** – Comedy sound effect in instrument form.
- **Ukulele** – Happy, tiny guitar with instant island energy.
- **Bongos** – Portable drums, perfect for chaotic jam sessions.
- **Tambourine** – Shake, rattle, and instantly feel like a rock star.
- **Maracas** – Rhythm made easy (and hilarious if off-beat).
- **Triangle** – One perfect "ting!" and you're the star of the orchestra.
- **Claves** – Two sticks you bang together — surprisingly satisfying.

- **Jaw Harp** – Weird twangy boing-boing sounds that never stop being funny.
- **Coconut Shells** – Technically not an instrument, but Monty Python proved otherwise.
- **Toy Keyboard** – Plays every note slightly off-pitch, guaranteed laughs.
- **Melodica** – Looks like a tiny keyboard, sounds like a wheezy accordion.
- **Egg Shakers** – Plastic eggs with beads inside, chaotic fun.
- **Plastic Bucket Drums** – Cheap, loud, and great for street-performer energy.
- **Whistle Flute (Slide Flute)** – The "whoop-whoop" cartoon sound effect.
- **Rainstick** – Shimmery rainfall in a tube, very zen until it's not.
- **Plastic Trumpet / Toy Saxophone** – Honk city. Pure chaos.

☐ **Go to a hardware store or a craft store and pick something to make together.** Another creative date idea, the sky is the limit on this one. It might help to find something that one of you wants to add to your / their house or apartment and try to make that. There are hundreds of Dollar Tree tutorials, so I suggest you watch those for some inspiration.

☐ **Educate yourselves.** If you want to use this time to "level up" your life, MasterClass has your guru for, well, everything. Learn style from Anna Wintour and look impeccable for your first date. Cook with Gordon Ramsay and wow your boo with those new knife skills. Take Billy Collins's poetry course and write each other some sonnets.

ENRICHING MASTERCLASSES FOR COUPLES

- **Gordon Ramsay Teaches Cooking** — Sharpen your knife skills, channel culinary swagger, and (hopefully) avoid setting anything on fire. A perfect kitchen date.
- **Photography by Annie Leibovitz** — Learn to take portraits that look magazine-worthy. Maybe each other's Insta feed is next-level soon.
- **Filmmaking with James Cameron** — Dive behind the scenes of cinematic masterpieces like *Titanic* and *Avatar*, then make your own epic "movie-date."
- **Acting with Helen Mirren** — Discover dramatic instincts you never knew you had—and maybe pretend you're spies or secret agents at home.
- **Screenwriting with Shonda Rhimes** — Learn to plot twists and razor-sharp dialogue; could there be a mini soap opera brewing between you two?

- **Writing with Salman Rushdie** — Get poetic, surreal, subversive. Bonus: you can write each other micro-tales or flirtatious prose.
- **Music (Tom Morello)** — Master guitar riffs and raw rock energy. You might not start a band—but might shred your way into their heart.
- **Business & Negotiation with Chris Voss** — Learn the art of persuasion (useful in arguments over who gets the last slice).
- **Mindfulness & Meditation with Jon Kabat-Zinn** — Perfect for calming post-date night brain chatter. Bonus: synchronized breathing.
- **Mindfulness + Sleep Science with Matthew Walker** — Become zen and ultra-rested—a double win in wellness.
- **Yoga Foundations with Donna Farhi** — Stretch together and laugh when someone inevitably falls over. It's both intimate and hilarious.
- **Sex & Communication with Emily Morse** — Learn how to talk about... *ahem* you-know-what. Build intimacy by leveling up the convo.
- **Mental Strength with Robin Arzón** — Build resilience, set bold goals, and maybe train for a 5K or just conquer your to-do list—together.
- **Gardening with Ron Finley** — Grow your own food and your relationship—get a green thumb and maybe feel a little revolutionary.
- **Wine Appreciation with James Suckling** — Sip and learn how to describe wine like sommeliers. Or just let the wine do the talking.
- **Dog Training with Brandon McMillan** — It's fun, useful, and adorable. Plus, future opportunities for "puppy date nights" just expanded.
- **The Art of Negotiation with Chris Voss** — Teach your brain hostage-bargaining secrets. No drama, just smarter deals—even over who washes the dishes next.
- **Persuasion with Daniel Pink** — Influence is everywhere—from flirting to business. You'll learn tricks that feel like superpowers.
- **Purposeful Communication with George Stephanopoulos** — Learn how to connect deeply, listen actively, and maybe win arguments—politely.
- **Wilderness Survival with Jessie Krebs** — Bond over building shelters, starting fires, and planning your imaginary post-apocalyptic escape.
- **Photography (Annie Leibovitz)** — Mentioned twice because consistency matters. Capture each other's essence, literally.
- **Style with Kris Jenner** — Learn how to bring out your glam duo energy. Because you two deserve to look legendary.

☐ **Drop some knowledge.** Consider yourself a life-long learner? Be a teacher too. Create a private TED Talk of your own. Choose your topic of expertise, develop a very serious slideshow, and present to each other. What could you talk about for 30 minutes without prep? Even if it is as corny as why dogs are better than cats (no offense cat people, it is 6:00 am while I write this, so my creative brain is not fully functioning.) You're an expert in something, and it's worth sharing with your date.

☐ **Learn some Tai Chi.** Relaxing but still difficult. It's great for your health and wellbeing and can make for a fun and interesting date idea. Especially if neither of you has tried Tai Chi before. There are plenty of YouTube videos, or you could see if there is a class. This is more a short date idea so try to have something else on had to do before or after.

☐ **Learn a new language together.** Sure, you could learn some of the more popular ones. But why not try an uncommon language or something like Esperanto. It would be great to have a language that you both know, but most of those around you don't.

LANGUAGES YOU COULD LEARN TOGETHER

Popular & Practical
- Spanish
- French
- Italian
- Portuguese
- German
- Dutch
- Russian
- Chinese (Mandarin or Cantonese)
- Japanese
- Korean
- Arabic
- Hindi
- Bengali
- Urdu
- Turkish
- Persian (Farsi)
- Greek
- Hebrew
- Swahili

Unique & Underrated
- Finnish
- Hungarian
- Polish
- Czech
- Slovak
- Serbian
- Croatian
- Bosnian
- Bulgarian
- Romanian
- Georgian
- Armenian
- Icelandic
- Norwegian
- Danish
- Swedish
- Estonian
- Lithuanian
- Latvian
- Basque (Euskara)
- Catalan
- Gaelic (Irish or Scottish)
- Welsh
- Maltese

African Languages
- Amharic (Ethiopia)
- Yoruba (Nigeria)
- Hausa (West Africa)
- Zulu (South Africa)
- Xhosa (South Africa, with the clicks!)
- Shona (Zimbabwe)
- Somali
- Berber/Tamazight

- Malagasy (Madagascar)

Indigenous & Rare

- Quechua (Peru/Bolivia)
- Nahuatl (Aztec language, Mexico)
- Guaraní (Paraguay)
- Mapudungun (Chile/Argentina)
- Hawaiian
- Māori (New Zealand)
- Cherokee
- Navajo
- Lakota
- Inuktitut (Inuit, Arctic Canada/Greenland)
- Sámi (Northern Scandinavia)

Ancient & Classical

- Latin
- Ancient Greek
- Sanskrit
- Old Norse
- Old English (Anglo-Saxon)
- Coptic (Ancient Egyptian Christian language)
- Aramaic (language of Jesus, still spoken by small groups)
- Akkadian (Mesopotamia, if you're *that* nerdy)

Constructed / Made-Up Languages

- **Esperanto** (made-up universal language, actually works)
- **Interlingua** (another simplified pan-European language)
- **Klingon** (Star Trek)
- **Vulcan** (Star Trek)

- **Dothraki** (Game of Thrones)
- **High Valyrian** (Game of Thrones)
- **Elvish (Sindarin, Quenya)** (Lord of the Rings)
- **Khuzdul (Dwarvish)** (Lord of the Rings)
- **Black Speech of Mordor** (Lord of the Rings — for your dark side)
- **Na'vi** (Avatar)
- **Huttese** (Star Wars, Jabba the Hutt's tongue)
- **Mando'a** (Star Wars, Mandalorian language)
- **Sith Language** (Star Wars extended lore)
- **Minionese** (Despicable Me — banana!)
- **Simlish** (The Sims)
- **Parseltongue** (Harry Potter snake speech)
- **Atlantean** (Disney's Atlantis: The Lost Empire)
- **Emoji Language** (yes, people actually try to "speak" with only emojis)
- **Toki Pona** (minimalist "language of good" with only ~120 words)
- **Pig Latin** (technically a code, but hey, it counts)
- **Ubbi Dubbi** (the Zoom kids' made-up game language)
- **Gibberish** (as in, literally adding syllables into English words)

BEST WAYS TO LEARN A NEW LANGUAGE TOGETHER

Mainstream Language Apps

- **Duolingo** – Gamified lessons, daily streaks, hilarious sentences. (You'll end up saying "the penguin drinks milk" in German, but it sticks.)
- **Babbel** – Focused on conversation and real-life phrases, less fluff.
- **Busuu** – Interactive lessons with speaking practice and feedback from native speakers.

- **Memrise** – Uses memes and spaced repetition to make vocab unforgettable.
- **LingQ** – Learn by reading & listening to real-world content (articles, podcasts, etc.).

Serious Learning Platforms
- **Pimsleur** – Audio-based learning, great for practicing in the car or while cooking together.
- **Rosetta Stone** – The OG immersion method, image-based and no English crutch.
- **Mango Languages** – Used by many libraries (often free with a card). Very structured.
- **italki** – One-on-one lessons with real native speakers over video call.
- **Preply** – Similar to italki, but with structured tutor programs.

Nerd & Niche Language Resources
- **Clozemaster** – Learn vocab in the context of full sentences.
- **Anki** – Flashcard powerhouse for custom decks (great for rare languages like Welsh or Navajo).
- **Glossika** – Repetition-based system to train fluency and pronunciation.
- **Language Reactor (Chrome Extension)** – Lets you watch Netflix/YouTube with dual subtitles.

Fun / Alternative Ways
- **YouTube Channels** – Thousands of free teachers & funny language explainers (great for niche or made-up languages).
- **Podcasts** – Coffee Break Spanish/French/German, or niche podcasts in literally any language.
- **Netflix Binge-Learning** – Watch shows dubbed in your target language with subtitles.
- **Music Playlists** – Make a shared Spotify playlist in your new language and belt it out karaoke-style.
- **Video Games in Target Language** – Switch your favorite game to the new language (Pokémon in Japanese = brain unlocked).

Constructed / Fictional Languages (For Klingon, Dothraki, Na'vi, etc.)
- **Duolingo** – Actually has Klingon and High Valyrian.
- **Memrise** – Fan-made courses for Elvish, Na'vi, even Simlish.
- **Fandom Wikis & Forums** – Deep dives with full dictionaries (LOTR Elvish, Star Wars Huttese).
- **YouTube Nerd Tutorials** – "How to curse in Dothraki" is out there, trust me.
- **Books & Dictionaries** – *The Klingon Dictionary* by Marc Okrand, Tolkien's appendices, etc.

Low-Tech DIY Fun
- Label objects in your house with sticky notes in the target language.
- Text each other ONLY in the new language for a day (even if it's nonsense).
- Pick a "word of the day" challenge and slip it into conversations.
- Create flashcards and make a drinking game out of it.

<u>Other Ideas that really need no explanation:</u>

- ☐ Attend a free class together at your local library
- ☐ Attend a talk or lecture together and discuss it afterwards
- ☐ Make up a dance together or master one
- ☐ Glass Etching or Sandblasting
- ☐ Graffiti / Street Art Workshop
- ☐ Tattoo Design Workshop
- ☐ Make Your Own Comic Book / Manga Class
- ☐ Drag Makeup & Performance Workshop
- ☐ Body & Movement Learning
- ☐ Park Dance Flashmob Class
- ☐ Fire Spinning
- ☐ Capoeira (Dance + Martial Art)
- ☐ Erotic Dance / Striptease for Couples
- ☐ Clown School
- ☐ VR/AR Creation Class
- ☐ Astronaut Training / Space Camp for Adults
- ☐ Forensics Workshop
- ☐ Cryptography Basics
- ☐ Robotics Build Class
- ☐ First Aid / CPR Certification Together
- ☐ Self-Defense for Couples
- ☐ Etiquette / Fine Dining Class
- ☐ DIY Perfume / Cologne Blending
- ☐ Knife Skills (Kitchen)
- ☐ Sound Healing / Gong Bath Training
- ☐ Astrology Birth Chart Reading Class
- ☐ Lucid Dreaming Workshop
- ☐ Shamanic Drumming or Journeying
- ☐ Tantra 101
- ☐ Mix Tape / DJ Playlist Curation Class
- ☐ Improv Comedy for Couples
- ☐ TikTok / Reels Filmmaking Class
- ☐ Escape Room Design Class
- ☐ Board Game Design Class

Nature/Exploring

- ☐ **Backyard camping or just go camping or glamping.** This one does require a tent and sleeping bags. Leave the phones in the house or the car. Tell ghost stories, look up at the stars, play cards by flashlight, talk, and enjoy the lack of distractions.

- ☐ **Try metal detecting.** This can be on the expensive side; you can get a decent entry-level metal detector for around $200. But if you calculate the cost of dinner at an upscale restaurant and a movie ticket plus snack for two, it's not that far off. And at the end of the date, you'll have a metal detector! Anyways, it can be a fun excuse to walk around and chat and maybe find some cool stuff. Just make sure to take turns.

- ☐ **Go fossil hunting.** This one depends a lot on where you live. Some places it's really easy to find fossils, some areas not so much. Look up finding fossils in your area and see where the best places are to look.

- ☐ **Buy a bunch of seeds and plant them all over in random places, see what grows over time.** Sounds weird but can be a lot of fun visiting new places and secretly or not so secretly planting seeds. It makes you look at your surroundings in a new way. Plus, it's very cool when you start seeing the plants begin to sprout and bloom.

- ☐ **Go to a botanical garden.** Quiet and peaceful, botanical gardens are great for strolling around and chatting. Walk around and enjoy all the gardening work that someone else did and be glad you don't have to deal with all that upkeep. It's a great place to talk and get to know each other. These beautiful gardens will also usually have lighting installations during the holidays that are a must see at night, which is extremely romantic.

- ☐ **Have an upscale picnic.** Location is key, so scout out a great spot at a local park. Then go all out with some wine (if they allow booze), cheese, sliced meats, French bread. Spread out a blanket on the ground or at a table, relax, and enjoy being in each other's company.

☐ **Catch a sunset.** I highly recommend scouting out a good spot ahead of time, and of course, sunsets are best enjoyed with your beverage of choice. You can do a bit of stargazing afterward too, as long as the light pollution isn't too bad.

☐ **Head to the zoo.** Zoos are great places to walk around and talk. It's casual and relaxed, and with so many animal exhibits, there is always something to talk about. Just be careful, if you date is morally opposed to zoos it might not be a good idea. Or if your local zoo is a bit run down it can be a little depressing.

☐ **Do an animal encounter at a zoo, like swimming with dolphins or hanging out with a tiger.** So, I know I already mentioned the zoo, but I thought this deserved its own spot. It can be quite expensive, but as far as date ideas go, it's something neither one of you will ever forget.

☐ **Find something touristy in your area.** Most locals never get around to doing the touristy stuff. Find out what is popular in your town on TripAdvisor and pretend to be a tourist in your own town. You can even make up fake personas if you want.

☐ **Explore a local national or state park.** Chances are that there are at least a couple of national or state parks within driving distance of you. Grab a takeout lunch and go experience what the park has to offer. There's nothing like getting out in nature to soothe the soul.

NATIONAL PARKS IN THE UNITED STATES

Alaska
- Denali National Park & Preserve
- Gates of the Arctic National Park & Preserve
- Glacier Bay National Park & Preserve
- Katmai National Park & Preserve
- Kenai Fjords National Park
- Kobuk Valley National Park
- Lake Clark National Park & Preserve

- Wrangell–St. Elias National Park & Preserve

American Samoa (U.S. Territory)
- National Park of American Samoa

Arizona
- Grand Canyon National Park
- Petrified Forest National Park
- Saguaro National Park

Arkansas
- Hot Springs National Park

California

- Channel Islands National Park
- Death Valley National Park (also Nevada)
- Joshua Tree National Park
- Kings Canyon National Park
- Lassen Volcanic National Park
- Pinnacles National Park
- Redwood National and State Parks
- Sequoia National Park
- Yosemite National Park

Colorado

- Black Canyon of the Gunnison National Park
- Great Sand Dunes National Park & Preserve
- Mesa Verde National Park
- Rocky Mountain National Park

Florida

- Biscayne National Park
- Dry Tortugas National Park
- Everglades National Park

Hawaii

- Haleakalā National Park
- Hawaiʻi Volcanoes National Park

Idaho

- Yellowstone National Park (also WY, MT)

Indiana

- Indiana Dunes National Park

Kentucky

- Mammoth Cave National Park

Maine

- Acadia National Park

Michigan

- Isle Royale National Park

Minnesota

- Voyageurs National Park

Missouri

- Gateway Arch National Park

Montana

- Glacier National Park
- Yellowstone National Park (shared with ID, WY)

Nevada

- Great Basin National Park
- Death Valley National Park (also CA)

New Mexico

- Carlsbad Caverns National Park
- White Sands National Park

North Carolina

- Great Smoky Mountains National Park (also TN)

North Dakota

- Theodore Roosevelt National Park

Ohio

- Cuyahoga Valley National Park

Oregon

- Crater Lake National Park

South Carolina

- Congaree National Park

South Dakota

- Badlands National Park
- Wind Cave National Park

Tennessee

- Great Smoky Mountains National Park (also NC)

Texas

- Big Bend National Park
- Guadalupe Mountains National Park

U.S. Virgin Islands (Territory)

- Virgin Islands National Park

Utah

- Arches National Park

- Bryce Canyon National Park
- Canyonlands National Park
- Capitol Reef National Park
- Zion National Park

Virginia
- Shenandoah National Park

Washington
- Mount Rainier National Park
- North Cascades National Park

- Olympic National Park

West Virginia
- New River Gorge National Park & Preserve

Wyoming
- Grand Teton National Park
- Yellowstone National Park (also ID, MT)

☐ **Find a place you can make a campfire and make smores.** Beers always go well with a campfire as well. There is something hypnotic about watching a fire. It makes for an easy, relaxing conversation. And who doesn't love smores? Also, sunset bonfire on the beach should be on everyone's bucket list.

☐ **Go to a plant nursery and pick out a plant or two.** You can buy a plant or tree together and take care of it or buy one for each of you. It's a great way to have a souvenir from the date. Just try not to accidentally kill it like I do most of the plants I get. Plus, nurseries have a lot of cool plants, and you can chat as you wander through all the plants.

☐ **Get wild.** Break out your favorite day-trip snacks, and load up a wildlife cam or virtual zoo tour. You can watch a baby bald eagle enjoy breakfast, or party with the polar bears at the San Diego Zoo. Looking to get wilder? Roam the woods with wolves in Minnesota or beat your chest among gorillas in the Democratic Republic of Congo.

☐ **Go on a scenic landmark crawl.** Be a tourist in your own city, but only hit up landmarks that don't charge an entrance fee, like statues, museums or other places that you'd go if you were only in town for a day.

☐ **Use just a compass and a map to get to someplace cool.** Who needs Google Maps? Go old school with a compass and map and test both of your ability to find your way to a cool destination.

☐ **Go on a scavenger hunt together.** This is a great way to get out of the house and have fun together without spending too much money. There are lots of scavenger hunt ideas online, you can make one customized for you and your partner, or there are even companies that specialize in scavenger hunts like Let's Roam.

SCAVENGER HUNT IDEAS FOR COUPLES

Nature & Outdoors Scavenger Hunt
- A heart-shaped rock
- Something that smells amazing in nature
- A feather
- A tree older than both of you combined
- A bird's nest (view from a distance!)
- A flower in your partner's favorite color
- An animal footprint in dirt or sand
- Something that feels rough, something that feels smooth
- A bug you've never seen before
- Water that reflects the sky

City / Town Scavenger Hunt
- A mural or piece of street art
- The oldest building you can find
- A street performer or busker
- Something shaped like a heart (natural or man-made)
- A landmark you've never noticed before
- A restaurant neither of you has tried
- A funny store sign
- A public bench with a plaque
- A statue or monument
- A spot with a perfect selfie backdrop

Romantic Scavenger Hunt
- A place that reminds you of your first date
- Something that represents your partner's favorite hobby
- A "hidden heart" (graffiti, leaves, cracks in the sidewalk)
- A cozy nook to sit together
- A reflection of the two of you together (mirror, window, water)
- Something that smells like love (flowers, coffee, perfume)
- A surprise treat to share (ice cream, candy, pastry)
- A place you could imagine kissing in a movie scene
- Something that makes you laugh out loud
- A sound that feels like love (birds, music, wind chimes)

Adventure & Challenge Scavenger Hunt

- Find three different shaped clouds and name them silly things
- Snap a photo of the weirdest statue or public art piece
- Do a good deed (help someone, hold a door, etc.)
- Find a sign in another language
- Trade something small with a stranger (like a pen or a coin)
- Find something older than 50 years
- Get a photo with a dog that isn't yours
- Find a hidden alley or shortcut
- Spot a license plate from another state/country
- End the hunt with a "treasure" you buy each other for under $5

Indoor / Rainy Day Scavenger Hunt

- A book title that makes you laugh
- Something with both of your initials on it
- A childhood toy (in a thrift shop or attic)
- A board game you've never played
- A candle or scent that you'd never pick but secretly like
- Something shaped like an animal
- A record or CD from the year you were born
- A quirky piece of clothing (bonus if you try it on)
- Something that feels like it belongs in a movie
- A snack with the weirdest packaging

Get the Sweetheart Scavenger Hunt Game:

https://www.etsy.com/listing/4406829002/sweetheart-scavenger-hunt-for-couples

☐ **Read up on some photography tips and go on a photography date and try to take the best photographs around town.** Just pretend like you are art students. Go around town and try to take the best pictures you possibly can with your phone camera. Get all artsy and see how it turns out. It'll be a lot of fun going from place to place scouting out shots, and you can both have fun looking over the photos at lunch or dinner or over drinks. Basically, pretend to be photographers. Everyone appreciates a good picture of themselves. And even if neither of you is a professional, that shouldn't stop you from trying to get some awesome pictures. See if you can get some photography tips online before heading out on the date.

☐ **Be local critics, go to parks or things like that and write reviews.** Become local Google Maps or Yelp stars. Go out, take some pictures, and give out some honest reviews together. If you want to save some money, go to places that are free like parks.

☐ **Do some urban exploring.** If you live in a city, there are all kinds of interesting buildings, ruins, nook and crannies, and other interesting spots perfect for urban exploration. So, if you both have a passion for exploring and live in a city, this can be a really cool date idea.

☐ **Go bird watching.** Bird watching sometimes gets called boring, but really, it's a great way to get outdoors. It gives you a reason to wander around in nature. Even if you've never done it, there are plenty of online guides out there to get started in your area. If nothing else, it's probably something the both of you have never done before.

☐ **Go on a walk through a park.** It's relaxing, it's free, it gives you plenty of time to talk. What's not to love about taking a walk in the park on a date? You could bring a frisbee, pack a lunch, and make a day of it. A lot of the other date ideas go well with a walk in the park.

☐ **Find a beautiful place to skip rocks.** This date idea is a great way to relax while still enjoying nature. You won't be doing it all day, but it's a great add-on to a trip to a park.

☐ **Go to an aquarium or aquarium store.** Name the fish and make up backstories for them. Create a little imaginary drama for them like they are finned day time soap opera characters. Or, have fun with it. Make up what type of fish they are and what they do. Their history, etc.

☐ **Star gazing road trip.** Find the area around your town with the least amount of light pollution, bring some pillows and blankets, don't forget the mosquito repellent and enjoy the night sky together. Find all the constellations or again have fun and make up your own.

THE 88 CONSTELLATIONS

Northern Hemisphere Favorites

- Andromeda
- Aquila
- Auriga
- Bootes
- Camelopardalis
- Cassiopeia
- Cepheus
- Corona Borealis
- Cygnus
- Draco
- Hercules
- Lacerta
- Leo
- Leo Minor
- Lynx
- Lyra
- Ophiuchus
- Pegasus
- Perseus
- Sagitta
- Ursa Major
- Ursa Minor
- Vulpecula

Southern Hemisphere Favorites

- Apus
- Ara
- Carina
- Centaurus
- Chamaeleon
- Circinus
- Columba
- Corona Australis
- Crux (Southern Cross)
- Dorado
- Grus
- Hydrus
- Indus
- Mensa
- Microscopium
- Musca
- Norma
- Octans
- Pavo
- Phoenix
- Pictor
- Reticulum
- Telescopium
- Triangulum Australe
- Tucana
- Volans

Zodiac Constellations *(the classic 12 plus Ophiuchus)*

- Aries
- Taurus
- Gemini
- Cancer
- Leo
- Virgo
- Libra
- Scorpius
- Sagittarius
- Capricornus
- Aquarius
- Pisces
- Ophiuchus

Other Major Constellations

- Canis Major
- Canis Minor
- Capricornus
- Crater
- Eridanus
- Hydra
- Orion
- Serpens

☐ **Plan the perfect vacation.** This works best if you share a laptop. Otherwise, you end up both looking at your phones and that's no fun. Find a country or countries to visit, choose what you want to do, pick some impressive hotels. You'll be able to see what they find fun and exciting and maybe get some more date ideas for next time.

☐ **Take a train ride somewhere.** Riding a train isn't very common in a lot of places in the USA. But there is a good chance that there is a train station in your city or town. Just make sure you'll be able to catch the train back!

TRAIN DATE IDEAS THAT DELIVER

Mystery & Dinner-Theater Train Rides

- **Murder Mystery Dinner Train (Fort Myers, FL)** – A 3.5-hour round trip across rural Florida with a live murder mystery show and a five-course dinner prepared onboard.
- **Wine Train Murder Mystery (1915 Pullman Car)** – An immersive theatrical dinner aboard a vintage car, complete with a welcome toast and multiple gourmet courses.
- **Bardstown Murder Mystery Train (Kentucky)** – A three-hour excursion with a four-course gourmet meal and onboard whodunit intrigue.
- **"Murder on the Menu" — Virginia Scenic Railway** – A three-hour, original murder mystery on wheels with beverages, entrées, and dessert included.
- **Western Maryland's Mystery Train** – Candlelit three-course dinners paired with murder mystery theatrics aboard a scenic railroad through Allegheny hills.
- **The Old Road Dinner Train (Michigan)** – Elegant four-course dining and live mystery theater through Lenawee County's serene landscape.
- **The Grand Bellevue (Theater Car Atlantic Rose)** – Interactive murder-mystery dinner in a theme-decorated theater car.

Scenic & Historic Train Journeys

- **Grand Canyon Railway** – Vintage railcars whisk you from Williams, AZ to the South Rim with live entertainment, cowboy characters, and old-west ambiance.
- **Durango & Silverton Narrow Gauge Railroad (Colorado)** – A nostalgic steam- or diesel-powered ride through the San Juan Mountains with sweeping wilderness views and themed excursions.

- **Mount Rainier Scenic Railroad (Washington)** – Heritage steam train running through forests south of Mount Rainier from Elbe to Mineral.
- **Yosemite Mountain Sugar Pine Railroad (California)** – Historic narrow-gauge steam rides through Sierra National Forest, near Yosemite's southern entrance.
- **Georgetown Loop Railroad (Colorado)** – A thrilling ascent through a looping narrow-gauge track across high trestles between Georgetown and Silver Plume.
- **Cumbres & Toltec Scenic Railroad (CO–NM)** – A heritage narrow-gauge journey over high mountain passes and gorges between Antonito and Chama.
- **Heber Valley Railroad (Utah)** – A 90-minute round-trip excursion featuring sweeping views of Timpanogos Mountain, dams, rivers, and the Provo Canyon.
- **Big South Fork Scenic Railway (Kentucky)** – Through lush countryside and historic coal-town Blue Heron; includes museum visit options.

Long-Distance Sleeper & Scenic Amtrak Routes

- **Coast Starlight** – A 34-hour journey from Los Angeles to Seattle, with coastal views, lush forests, and onboard amenities like observation cars.
- **California Zephyr** – A 52-hour sleeper train from Chicago to San Francisco through the Rockies and Sierra Nevada— epic landscapes throughout.
- **Texas Eagle** – A 65-hour ride from Chicago to Los Angeles, traversing vast Texan plains with comfortable private accommodations.
- **Cardinal** – A 26.5-hour ride from New York to Chicago via the Blue Ridge Mountains and Shenandoah Valley.
- **Rocky Mountaineer** – A luxury route through canyons, desert, and the Rockies with hotel stopovers and fine service.
- **USA Rail Pass (Amtrak)** – Offers 10 ride segments across 500+ destinations for around $500—ideal for spontaneous scenic rail adventures.

Southern & Regional Delights

- **Chattanooga's Historic Train Rides (Tennessee)** – From the Missionary Ridge local train to scenic forest routes, high tea, dinner trains, and even Pullman car lodging, these rides shine especially during fall foliage season.

☐ **Take a long walk on a virtual beach.** Using Google Maps, you can revisit a favorite place you've been, your date's old summer spot, or even give each other a tour of your childhood neighborhoods. You can even feast your eyes on global adventure by snorkeling from a resort in the Great Barrier Reef, visiting China's terra cotta warriors, hiking through Yellowstone, or exploring the International Space Station. Want to virtually explore? Check out The New York Times's The Great Empty series, capturing international hot spots in this unusual quietude.

☐ **Take a city tour.** If you live in a big city, chances are you've never played tourist there before. Grab your potential S.O. and jump on a double-decker bus for a fun date.

☐ **Stargaze at the planetarium.** There's something super romantic about staring up at the stars. But if it's too chilly outside (or light pollution makes your view not-so-pretty), take the gazing inside.

☐ **Play tourist.** This one's mostly for big city dwellers, though smaller towns have plenty of exploring to be done, too. Take the day to hit up any touristy spots that you've never seen, or revisit old favorites. It can be fun to see your city through someone else's eyes.

☐ **Go fishing.** There are so many ways to learn to fish. If you guys want a quiet peaceful day in a canoe, and just leisurely fish, it is relaxing. Or go out and deep sea fish, if you live by the ocean.

Freshwater Fishing Styles
- **Shore Fishing** – Cast from the bank of a lake, river, or pond.
- **Canoe/Kayak Fishing** – Peaceful paddling + fishing, perfect for couples.
- **Float Tube Fishing** – Sitting in a little inflatable "belly boat" and kicking around while fishing.
- **Fly Fishing** – Using lightweight flies to mimic insects, often in streams/rivers.
- **Spin Casting** – Easy beginner method with closed-face reels.
- **Baitcasting** – More advanced reels for precision casting (bass fishing favorite).
- **Drift Fishing** – Letting your bait drift naturally with the current.
- **Bottom Fishing** – Weighted bait sinks to the bottom for catfish, carp, etc.
- **Ice Fishing** – Cutting holes in frozen lakes and fishing in winter (with or without heated huts).

Saltwater Fishing Styles

- **Surf Fishing** – Standing on the beach, casting into the surf.
- **Pier Fishing** – Drop a line off a pier or dock—low effort, high fun.
- **Jetty/Rock Fishing** – Fishing from rocky shorelines (watch the waves!).
- **Inshore Fishing** – Staying near the shore, usually with light tackle.
- **Offshore/Deep Sea Fishing** – Heading out by boat for tuna, marlin, mahi-mahi, etc.
- **Trolling** – Dragging bait/lures behind a moving boat.
- **Bottom Saltwater Fishing** – Similar to freshwater bottom fishing, but for grouper, snapper, etc.
- **Reef Fishing** – Fishing around coral reefs for tropical species.
- **Shark Fishing** – From beach or boat—intense and thrilling.

Special Techniques & Fun Variations

- **Handlining** – Fishing with just a line, no rod.
- **Jug Fishing** – Floating jugs with baited lines for catfish (popular in the South).
- **Noodling** – Catching catfish with your bare hands (only for the bold!).
- **Bowfishing** – Using a bow and arrow with a line attached to shoot fish.
- **Spear Fishing** – Snorkel or scuba with a spear gun or pole.
- **Tenkara Fishing** – Japanese minimalist fly fishing (just rod, line, fly).
- **Cast Net Fishing** – Throwing a circular net into the water to trap small fish.
- **Dip Netting** – Scooping fish from the water with a net.
- **Trapping** – Using fish traps or cages (more common in survival settings).
- **Magnet Fishing** – Not fish, but treasures—dragging a magnet in rivers for "catches."

☐ **Go on a Mystery Picnic.** Part scavenger hunt, part foodie adventure, and all romance. You and your partner solve clues that lead you to hidden local gems like a bakery for fresh bread, a deli for artisan cheese, or a café for desserts, collecting picnic goodies along the way. The journey ends at a surprise location revealed only at the final clue, where you unpack your finds and enjoy a cozy picnic together. It's playful, stress-free, and turns an ordinary meal into an unforgettable shared experience.

☐ **Get lost locally, take back roads you've never taken try to find interesting stuff that isn't on Google maps.** Turn off the GPS and see if you can get yourself lost in your hometown. Going down roads you've never been down can feel like an adventure, and you never know what hidden gems you might find.

☐ **Find places that are supposedly haunted in your area and visit them at night.** If one of you is easily scared, this might not be the best date idea. But if you are both into horror movies and enjoy a good scare, this can be a lot of fun. Old abandoned buildings are the best.

☐ **Find somewhere you can feed the ducks together.** Note: it's better for the ducks if you avoid bread and feed birdseed or grapes instead.

Extra Nature & Exploring Ideas

☐ **Go Foraging Together** – Hunt for edible mushrooms, berries, or wild herbs (with a guidebook or local expert).

☐ **Tubing or Lazy River Float** – Rent tubes and drift down a river with snacks and drinks.

☐ **Go Geocaching** – Use an app to find hidden treasures (real-world treasure hunt with GPS).

☐ **Visit a Waterfall** – Hike to one, or plan a road trip specifically around waterfall-hopping.

☐ **Rent ATVs or Dirt Bikes** – Explore trails with a little adrenaline rush.

☐ **Try Horseback Trail Riding** – Scenic and romantic, especially if you've never done it before.

☐ **Go Whale Watching (or Dolphin Tour)** – If you're near the coast, nothing beats spotting sea life together.

☐ **Hot Air Balloon Ride** – Romantic and unforgettable, especially at sunrise or sunset.

☐ **Take a Ferry Ride** – Short, scenic boat trips give you the magic of being on the water without a big commitment.

☐ **Zip Lining in the Forest** – Thrilling way to see nature from a new perspective.

☐ **Berry or Apple Picking** – Seasonal, sweet, and perfect for a cute couple's photo op.

☐ **Visit a Lighthouse** – Many are open to the public and come with epic views.

☐ **Go Stargazing with a Telescope** – Planetariums are nice, but a real telescope in a dark field is magical.

☐ **Go Sandboarding or Sledding on Dunes** – If you're near a desert or sandy coast, this is hilarious fun.

☐ **Do a Riverboat or Lake Cruise** – Scenic, slow, and often with dinner/drinks.

- ☐ **Try Rockhounding / Gem Mining** – Some places let you sift for gems or fossils.
- ☐ **Snowshoeing or Cross-Country Skiing** – Winter-friendly alternative to hiking.
- ☐ **Explore Tide Pools** – Check out marine life in rocky coastal pools at low tide.
- ☐ **Take a Night Hike** – Some parks offer guided moonlight or glowworm hikes.
- ☐ **Wildlife Safari Drive** – Some wildlife parks have drive-through safaris (lions and giraffes included).

Other Ideas that really need no explanation:

- ☐ Laze around in a field
- ☐ Rent scooters and cruise around town
- ☐ Go to a natural spring.
- ☐ Take a walk through a rainforest
- ☐ Get fish and chips by the water
- ☐ Visit the countryside and enjoy the road trip
- ☐ Head to the beach
- ☐ Go hunting together
- ☐ Go to a garden center together and pick out some plants or houseplants

Sports/Adventurous/ Water Activities

☐ **Hit up a go-kart track.** Tons of fun even though it can be a little expensive. I've never met anyone who went around a go-kart track and was bored doing it. Sure, it won't last all day, but it's a fantastic add-on activity. Just remember to keep it fun and not too competitive.

☐ **Go sky diving or bungee jumping or a simulation of both.** Sure, it'll be expensive. But it'll definitely be a date that you'll both remember for a long time. Just make sure that both of you are game, if your partner isn't into it, don't pressure them to do it.

☐ **Go ziplining.** Always nice to do something that gets the heart pumping.

☐ **Do some geocaching.** It's like hiking plus surprise presents! It can be a lot of fun searching for the geocache together, and you might just visit some remarkable places neither of you has been before. The best apps for that are: Geocaching by Groundspeak, C:Geo, Cachly, Cache Maid, and Looking 4 Cache Pro.

☐ **Go bowling.** There is a bowling alley in almost every town and city. Chances are you haven't been bowling for a while. Go give it a shot. If there is an extreme difference in skills you might not want to keep score, maybe just make it a learning session.

BOWLING GAMES & VARIATIONS
Classic Styles
- **Ten-Pin Bowling** – The standard game you'll find in almost every U.S. bowling alley: 10 pins, 2 balls per frame.
- **Nine-Pin Bowling** – Found in parts of Europe and Texas, uses 9 pins in a diamond formation.
- **Five-Pin Bowling** – Canadian favorite: 5 shorter pins, smaller balls, and a scoring system up to 450.
- **Candlepin Bowling** – Popular in New England & Canada: very thin pins and handheld-sized balls. Players get 3 rolls per frame.
- **Duckpin Bowling** – Shorter, squat pins with small balls you can palm. Quirky and harder than it looks.

- **Kegel (Nine-Pin Skittles)** – Traditional European style: pins set in different formations with unique scoring.
- **Petanque-Style Bowling (Skittles)** – Old-school pub version played in the UK with wooden pins and balls.

Party & Date-Friendly Twists

- **Cosmic / Glow Bowling** – Blacklights, neon pins, music, and sometimes even smoke machines.
- **Bowling with a Twist** – Set challenges for each frame (e.g., bowl left-handed, granny-style, backward, or on one leg).
- **Obstacle Bowling** – Add chairs, cones, or random objects to make the lane trickier.
- **Partner Bowling** – One person does the approach, the other releases the ball. Chaos guaranteed.
- **Speed Bowling** – You each roll as fast as possible, no waiting turns.
- **Blindfold Bowling** – One player is blindfolded, the other gives directions.
- **Extreme Spin Bowling** – Only spin throws allowed (hook, curve, or granny spin).
- **Bowling Poker** – Each strike/spare earns a card; best poker hand at the end wins.
- **Truth or Dare Bowling** – Miss a spare, you get a dare. Get a strike, you give one.

Outdoor / Alternative Bowling

- **Lawn Bowling (Bowls)** – Played on grass with biased (curved) balls aiming for a smaller target ball ("jack").
- **Bocce** – Italian ball-throwing game, kind of a cousin to bowling.
- **Skittles (Outdoor Pub Bowling)** – Pins set up outdoors or in rustic alleys, common in the UK.
- **Ice Bowling** – Yes, some rinks or winter festivals set up frozen alleys.
- **Beach Bowling** – Dig a trench "lane" in the sand, use a volleyball or weighted ball, and improvise pins.

Arcade & Digital Spin-Offs

- **Bowling Arcade Games (like Skee-Ball or VR Bowling)** – Fun twist if you're somewhere without lanes.
- **Wii Bowling (or Switch Bowling)** – Still iconic for couples who want the bowling vibe at home.
- **VR Bowling** – Many VR arcades now feature hyper-realistic bowling simulators.

☐ **Go horseback riding.** Another one that can get a little expensive. But it's not a standard date idea, and if you or your date has never tried horseback riding, it's something you won't forget.

☐ **Go to the nearest amusement park or water park.** Amusement parks and water parks are always a blast, so if you've got one not too far away give it a go. It's, of course, better if you can do it on a weekday, but if you both work all week, weekends are doable as well.

☐ **Go rock climbing.** Another fun physical activity you can do together. It won't be an all-day thing, but it's great for a short date or as an add-on or back-up date.

☐ **Play a sport or activity you're both terrible at or have never tried.** Think table tennis, tennis, badminton, volleyball, or even a silly game of basketball or strip horse. Sand volleyball with beers after is always a win. Badminton sets are cheap and great for the park, giving you just enough physical challenge to have fun without highlighting big differences in skill.

☐ **Play pinball or go to an arcade for a short, high-energy date.** It's not usually a full-date idea unless you both love pinball, but it's great for friendly competition. Try beating a high score together, bounce between machines, play Skee-Ball, and don't skip air hockey. Many cities have arcade bars, which make it easy to keep things casual and fun. Just avoid going ultra-competitive. It's not the best spot for deep conversation, but it's always a good time.

☐ **Make a list of missions and see how many you can complete.** Think: buy ice cream from a truck, find three pay phones, get a bull's-eye, jump over four benches. It's totally adaptable and only as fun as you make it. Randomness is the whole point.

MISSION IDEAS FOR COUPLES
Food & Drink Missions
- Order the weirdest item at a diner or food truck.
- Buy a drink with an ingredient you've never tried.
- Find a restaurant with a neon sign and take a picture in front of it.
- Share one giant dessert at a random café.
- Ask a barista to make you a "surprise drink" and drink it no matter what.

City & People Missions

- Find someone wearing the same color as you and ask for a selfie.
- Spot three different types of hats in the wild.
- Find a street performer and tip them together.
- Wave at a stranger until they wave back.
- Ask someone for directions to a place you already know.

Funny Physical Missions

- Do a cartwheel (or attempt one) in a public park.
- Jump over three benches in a row.
- Get a bullseye at a dart board or arcade game.
- Take turns piggyback racing across a parking lot.
- Recreate a cheesy rom-com pose (like a dip-kiss) in a public place.

Shopping & Object Missions

- Find a rotary phone.
- Locate a $2 bill.
- Buy the cheapest thing in a thrift shop.
- Snap a picture of cowboy boots.

Pop Culture / Random Missions

- Spot a mural or graffiti with a face on it.
- Take a photo pretending to be a movie poster.
- Find three pay phones (or what's left of them).
- Do an "album cover" pose in front of a brick wall.
- Find a license plate from a state/country you've never been to.

Romantic / Couple Missions

- Kiss in front of a fountain.
- Leave a sticky note with a compliment for a stranger.
- Take a shadow selfie holding hands.
- Serenade each other with a random song lyric in public.
- Write your names in chalk somewhere safe.

Get the Full Mission Accomplished Game:

https://www.etsy.com/listing/4407260277/mission-accomplished-couples-game

☐ **Jump in the water.** This one is kind of seasonally dependent. Going swimming in the winter is not so fun. But there are usually indoor pools as well that you can try. Just make sure your date likes swimming / can swim. You can hit up a lake, community pool, or even buy some cheap kiddie pools.

☐ **Go Jogging.** If you are both into fitness and jogging, a jog can be a great way to bond over something you both love. But this suggestion really only works if you are both into jogging. If just one of you is, or if neither of you is, you might give this idea a pass.

☐ **Play some mini golf.** Chances are you haven't done putt-putt in quite a while, but it can be a lot of fun as long as you don't take it too seriously. Never take putt-putt too seriously, it would be way too frustrating. And with a name like putt-putt, it's okay to be a little silly.

☐ **Rent a boat.** For this one, a body of water is a must. But most towns or cities have a few lakes around. And there is a good chance someone is renting out things that float. So, go out on the water and have a good time. There are so many different boats to try out.

FUN BOATS TO RENT OR TRY

- **Speedboat** – Fast, splashy, thrill-seeker vibes.
- **Sailboat** – Classic, romantic, and perfect if you want to learn a skill together.
- **Paddleboat (Pedal Boat)** – Those little two-seaters with foot pedals, great for laughs on a lake.
- **Rowboat** – Old-school, slow, romantic — cue the notebook vibes.
- **Kayak** – Solo or tandem, calm lakes or exciting rivers.
- **Canoe** – A little more space than kayaks, great for couples with snacks and gear.
- **Bicycle Boat / Water Bike** – Literally a bike that pedals on water.
- **Pontoon Boat** – The party boat! Flat, spacious, and perfect for picnics on the water.
- **Houseboat** – Overnight floating date idea, complete with beds, kitchens, and decks.
- **Yacht (Charter)** – Luxe option if you want to go all out.
- **Fishing Boat** – Smaller motorboats designed for casting and chilling.
- **Jon Boat** – Flat-bottom boat, super steady and easy for beginners.
- **Catamaran** – Twin-hull sailboat, smooth and spacious.

- **Trimaran** – Three-hulled boat, very stable, often used for sport sailing.
- **Raft (Inflatable or Whitewater)** – Lazy float trip or adrenaline-pumping rapids.
- **Dragon Boat** – Team paddling experience, fun for group dates.
- **Gondola** – Venetian romance if you can find one (some U.S. cities even have gondola rentals!).
- **Pedal Kayak (with fins)** – Kayak with pedals instead of paddles.
- **Hovercraft Boat** – Rare, but if you can find rentals, it's futuristic fun.
- **Glass-Bottom Boat** – Great for sightseeing fish and reefs.
- **Submarine Tour Boat** – In some tourist areas, you can rent/ride a mini-sub.
- **Outrigger Canoe** – Hawaiian-style canoe with stabilizers.
- **Inflatable Dinghy** – Fun, silly, and cheap to rent.
- **Banana Boat Ride** – Inflatable "banana" towed by a speedboat for pure chaos.
- **Jet Ski / Personal Watercraft** – Not a boat technically, but always a fun rental option.

☐ **Go ice skating.** An indoor rink or if it is winter at a frozen pond, this is a great date idea. It helps if you're both terrible or both good. If you're good and your date isn't, teach them how.

☐ **Rent motorized scooters and zip around town.** I would recommend those stand-up scooters/skateboards where you have the controller in your hand. A load of fun and a great way to get around. Stop at whichever shops look exciting and make a day of it.

☐ **Rent bikes and go on a bike trip together.** A lot of cities now have bikes you can borrow, and even if yours doesn't, there is a good chance your local bike shop rents out bikes. Riding a bike around is fun, and even if it's a bit difficult to chat while riding, you can also talk when you stop for breaks.

☐ **Shooting range, archery, ax throwing.** Hit stuff with other stuff! Whether it's a shooting range, archery range, or ax throwing range, it can be a ton of fun if you've never tried it. And if you have tried it, you can always try to do better this time! This is another one that might be a little expensive but can definitely be memorable.

TARGET HITTING SPORTS

- **Knife Throwing** – Similar to axes, but smaller and requires finesse.
- **Dart Throwing** – Bar classic, can be casual or super competitive.

- **Spear Throwing (Atlatl or Javelin)** – Old-school hunting vibes or track & field style.
- **Blowgun Shooting** – Yes, there are ranges for this, and it's surprisingly addictive.
- **Slingshot Shooting** – Childhood energy, but with real targets.
- **Paintball** – Shoot each other with paint pellets, tactical + hilarious.
- **Airsoft** – Similar to paintball but with realistic pellet guns.
- **Laser Tag** – Less mess than paintball, all the running-around fun.
- **Clay Pigeon Shooting (Skeet/Trap Shooting)** – Shotguns and flying clay targets.
- **Crossbow Shooting** – A medieval step up from archery.
- **Bocce / Lawn Bowling / Petanque** – Tossing weighted balls toward a target ball.
- **Curling** – Shuffle big stones on ice toward a target circle.
- **Axe Golf / Knife Golf (Target Courses)** – Some ranges set up "courses" with multiple targets.
- **Hatchet Golf (Canadian twist)** – A variation of throwing axes at target holes.
- **Snowball Target Throwing** – Winter version of target fun.
- **Frisbee Golf (Disc Golf)** – Throw discs at baskets on outdoor courses.
- **Hammer Toss (Strongman-style or fun fairground style)** – Heaving heavy things as far as possible.
- **Cabers / Log Toss (Scottish Games)** – Extreme version: throw whole logs.
- **Tomahawk Throwing** – Lighter axe variant with more flips.
- **Throwing Stars (Shuriken)** – Martial arts ranges sometimes allow this.
- **Balloon Dart Carnival Games** – Simple, goofy, and nostalgic.
- **Virtual Gun Ranges / VR Shooting Sims** – No real weapons, just fun high-tech targeting.

☐ **Take to the skies.** This one is expensive and if one of you has a fear of flying definitely give this one a miss. But if you are up for spending the coin and enjoy a trip through the skies, this can be a ton of fun.

WAYS TO FLY TOGETHER

- **Helicopter Tour** – City skylines, waterfalls, canyons, or coastlines. Short but thrilling.
- **Hang Gliding** – Run off a hill, soar like a bird. Equal parts terrifying and exhilarating.
- **Paragliding** – Similar to hang gliding but with a parachute wing. Can often do tandem rides.

- **Skydiving** – The ultimate adrenaline. Tandem skydives are common first-timer options.
- **Indoor Skydiving (Wind Tunnel)** – All the thrill of free-fall, none of the fear of jumping from a plane.
- **Glider Plane Ride (Soaring)** – Silent, engine-free flights that ride thermal currents. Peaceful and surreal.
- **Small Plane Tour** – Rent a Cessna or similar through a local flight school for a personal sightseeing flight.
- **Ultralight Aircraft** – Open-air flying machine, like sitting on a powered kite. Wildly fun.
- **Gyrocopter Ride** – Quirky cross between a helicopter and a plane. Super maneuverable.
- **Seaplane Ride** – Take off/land on water, often in scenic places like Alaska or the Caribbean.
- **Zip Lining (Sky Trekking)** – Not quite "flight," but you'll be soaring over valleys and forests.
- **Parasailing** – Get towed by a speedboat while floating high under a parachute. Perfect beach date.
- **Wing Walking** – Old-school daredevil adventure — stand strapped to the wing of a biplane while it flies.
- **Aerobatic Biplane Ride** – Stunt planes doing flips, loops, and dives. Pure adrenaline.
- **Helium Balloon Cluster Ride** – Like *Up* the movie, rare but real — strapped to giant balloons.
- **Drone VR Flight Experience** – Strap into a VR headset and fly a drone POV for a high-tech flight.

☐ **Play disc golf.** This hobby often gets overlooked, but it's fun and relatively cheap to start. And most towns and cities have a disc golf course. It's a fun way to spend the afternoon and gives you something to do while you are getting to know each other.

☐ **Go to a roller-skating rink.** Chances are you have a roller rink in your town and chances are you haven't visited it in a very long time. So, head on over, lace up, and see how much you remember about skating.

☐ **Darts or pool.** Hit up a bar that has darts or pool and give it a go. There are lots of dart and pool games to try, so look up the rules for a game none of you has played and try it out. You might find you like pool or darts, or you might just head back to the bar. Either way, a win!

CLASSIC BAR GAMES FOR COUPLES

- **Darts** – From 301 and 501 to Cricket, always a crowd favorite.
- **Pool / Billiards** – 8-ball, 9-ball, cutthroat, or even snooker if you want to go fancy.
- **Foosball** – Table soccer, fast-paced and competitive.
- **Shuffleboard (Table or Floor)** – Slide pucks down a smooth board, aiming for points.
- **Air Hockey** – Gliding puck chaos — perfect for smack talk.
- **Skee-Ball** – Arcade-style rolling balls into rings for points.
- **Arcade Basketball / Pop-A-Shot** – Hoop-shooting frenzy on a timer.
- **Pinball Machines** – Retro, flashy, and addictive.
- **Ring Toss / Hook & Ring (a.k.a. Tiki Toss)** – Swing a ring on a string to hook it — sounds simple, maddeningly hard.
- **Cornhole (Bean Bag Toss)** – Common in outdoor beer gardens.
- **Beer Pong** – Cups, ping pong balls, and strategy (or chaos).
- **Flip Cup** – Drinking game staple, race to flip the cup upside down.
- **Giant Jenga** – Oversized wooden blocks and suspenseful crashes.
- **Connect Four (Giant or Tabletop)** – Bar-sized versions are surprisingly fun.
- **Quarters** – Bounce a coin into a cup (old-school drinking game).
- **Dominoes** – Classic game of tiles and strategy.
- **Card Games** – Poker, blackjack, or even Uno at a casual bar.
- **Trivia Nights** – Brainy bar fun — sometimes competitive, sometimes just funny.
- **Golden Tee (Golf Arcade)** – Spinning ball controls your golf swing.
- **Ring Toss Carnival Style** – Bottles, rings, and the illusion you'll win every time.
- **Dice Games (Liar's Dice, Bar Dice)** – Quick and easy to play with drinks.

☐ **Go paintballing.** So, this one might be a bit intense if they've never been paintballing. If you have never tried it, go for it. It's a blast. Just make sure you are okay with a little bit of stinging pain. Be on the same team though, no need to make your date mad by peppering them with paintballs.

☐ **Find the nearest small stream, make small boats, and then race them down the stream.** If you bring along a picnic, you can make a day of it. Of course, this one is very weather dependent so you'll have to decide if it will be a nice day out. But even if the weather is bad, we have plenty of other date ideas that are great for inside dates as well.

☐ **Pick out workout videos on YouTube and do them together.** Definitely better if you both are into fitness and working out. Doesn't really work so well if neither of you is into fitness or if only one of you is.

☐ **Learn the rules of a sport you don't know much about and watch a game together.** You can either watch the sport at a sports bar if there is a game going on or just watch some old games on the internet. There are tons of great sports out there that you've probably never even heard of.

SPORTS TO LEARN & WATCH TOGETHER
Popular but Often Overlooked

- **Rugby** – Two teams carry, pass, and kick an oval ball across a field, aiming to score in the "try zone." Like a mix of soccer + football, but rougher.
- **Cricket** – English favorite: bat-and-ball game where teams take turns batting and fielding; games can last hours to days.
- **Lacrosse** – Played with long sticks and small nets at the end, teams pass and shoot a small rubber ball into goals.
- **Field Hockey** – Like ice hockey, but on grass with curved sticks and a hard ball.
- **Water Polo** – Soccer-meets-basketball in a swimming pool. Players tread water the entire game.
- **Handball** – Fast-paced sport where players throw a ball into the opponent's goal; popular in Europe.
- **Badminton** – Lightweight rackets and a "birdie" (shuttlecock), more intense than it looks.
- **Table Tennis (Ping Pong)** – Small paddles, lightweight ball, quick reflexes.

Unique or Regional Sports

- **Hurling (Ireland)** – Ancient stick-and-ball game played with a flat stick ("hurley") and a small ball ("sliotar"). Fast and physical.
- **Gaelic Football (Ireland)** – Mix of soccer, rugby, and basketball. Players kick or hand-pass a ball to score.
- **Kabaddi (India, Bangladesh, etc.)** – Tag meets wrestling: one player chants "kabaddi" while trying to tag opponents without being tackled.

- **Sepak Takraw (Southeast Asia)** – Volleyball but using only feet, knees, chest, and head to hit a rattan ball over a net.
- **Bandy (Scandinavia/Russia)** – Ice hockey's cousin, played with a ball instead of a puck, on a field the size of a soccer pitch.
- **Australian Rules Football** – Played on oval fields with oval ball; players kick and punch-pass to score between massive goalposts.
- **Bossaball (Spain/International)** – Volleyball played on trampolines with music and acrobatics.
- **Underwater Hockey (Octopush)** – Players push a puck across the bottom of a swimming pool with small sticks while holding their breath.
- **Underwater Rugby** – Similar concept, but played in deep pools with goals at the bottom.
- **Buzkashi (Afghanistan, Central Asia)** – Players on horseback compete to drag a goat carcass into the goal circle (ancient, brutal sport).
- **Calcio Storico (Italy)** – Historic mix of rugby, soccer, and wrestling played in Florence; famously violent.
- **Hornussen (Switzerland)** – Players hit a small puck (the "hornuss") with a long stick, and opponents try to stop it midair with paddles.

Quirky & Fun to Learn
- **Curling** – Sliding heavy stones on ice toward a target, teammates sweep to guide it. Surprisingly strategic.
- **Disc Golf (Frisbee)** – Golf, but with frisbees thrown into metal baskets.
- **Ultimate Frisbee** – Teams pass a frisbee down the field to score in end zones.
- **Quidditch (Muggle Quidditch)** – Inspired by Harry Potter: players run with brooms between their legs, mixing rugby, dodgeball, and tag.
- **Pickleball** – A mash-up of tennis, ping pong, and badminton, hugely popular lately.
- **Roller Derby** – Skaters race around a track trying to lap the other team while blocking and checking.
- **Spikeball (Roundnet)** – Small trampoline net in the middle; teams bounce the ball back and forth, fast-paced beach favorite.
- **Korfball (Netherlands)** – Like basketball but with mixed-gender teams and slightly different hoops.
- **Polo** – Players on horseback hit a small ball with long mallets into the opposing team's goal.
- **Canoe Polo** – Same, but played in kayaks!

Wild & Obscure
- **Cheese Rolling (UK)** – Competitors chase a rolling wheel of cheese down a steep hill. Chaos guaranteed.
- **Wife Carrying (Finland)** – Men race while carrying their wives (or partners) through an obstacle course.

- **Toe Wrestling (UK)** – Exactly what it sounds like: players lock toes and wrestle.
- **Chess Boxing** – Alternates rounds of boxing and speed chess until one player wins by checkmate or knockout.
- **Giant Pumpkin Kayaking** – Racing across water inside hollowed-out giant pumpkins.
- **Extreme Ironing** – People iron clothes in bizarre locations (cliffs, rivers, mountains). Yes, it's real.
- **Zorbing** – Rolling downhill inside a giant inflatable ball.
- **Snow Polo / Camel Polo** – Regional polo variations on snow or with camels.

☐ **Rent a convertible sports car or luxury car and cruise around all day.** This is another one that is on the expensive side. Just make sure to check the weather before you get the convertible.

☐ **Cheer on your favorite sports team.** You can watch at a bar or at a stadium. Either way, you will bond over your shared love of sports.

☐ **Go apple picking.** Seasonal-specific activities are like limited-edition dates: You can only participate in them during certain times, which makes them all the more special.

☐ **Create your own Amazing Race.** Set up mini challenges, clues, and checkpoints that lead you across town or through a full scavenger-hunt-style adventure. Each stop needs a task — solve a puzzle, eat something weird, take a photo at a landmark, or complete a goofy dare to earn the next clue. End at a "pit stop" like a picnic, a dinner reservation, or ice cream on a park bench. It's playful, competitive, and can be as simple or elaborate as you want.

AMAZING RACE DATE CHALLENGE IDEAS
Food & Drink Challenges
- Eat something spicy (hot wings, jalapeños, or wasabi).
- Order and finish a food item you've never tried before.
- Share a milkshake without using your hands.
- Blindfold taste test (guess 3 flavors correctly to move on).
- Pick up a picnic item at a deli to use at the final pit stop.

Physical Challenges
- Jump rope 50 times in a row.
- Do a cartwheel (or attempt one).
- Climb a set of stairs or a hill together and take a selfie at the top.
- Run a relay around a park bench or fountain.
- Balance something (like a book) on your head while walking a distance.

Puzzle / Brain Teaser Challenges
- Solve a riddle or trivia question to unlock the next clue.
- Do a crossword or word search with a hidden keyword.
- Assemble a mini puzzle (jigsaw or tangram).
- Decode a message written in emojis.
- Complete a math challenge (fun, not boring like use birthdays as a code).

City & Exploration Challenges
- Take a photo with a stranger wearing the same color as you.
- Find a mural or street art piece and recreate it as a pose.
- Spot a license plate from another state.
- Locate a landmark and take a "tourist selfie."
- Buy something under $2 from a convenience store.

Romantic / Cute Challenges
- Write each other a love note in under 2 minutes.
- Take a shadow selfie holding hands.
- Find something heart-shaped (graffiti, leaves, rocks).
- Serenade each other in public with one line from a random song.
- Hug for a full 60 seconds before moving on.

Random / Fun Dares
- Get a stranger to high-five you.
- Record a silly TikTok dance together.
- Pretend to be tourists and ask someone for directions to a place you already know.
- Recreate a movie scene in public (Titanic arms, Dirty Dancing lift, etc.).

Final Pit Stop Ideas:
- A hidden picnic spot.
- A restaurant you already booked in secret.
- An ice cream shop.
- A romantic lookout point.
- Your living room decorated with candles & dessert waiting.

EXAMPLE AMAZING RACE DATE

Clue #1: "Your journey begins where the beans are roasted. Find the spot where caffeine dreams are toasted."

→ Go to a local coffee shop.

Challenge: Blindfold taste test. One of you orders two mystery drinks, the other has to guess at least one flavor correctly to earn the next clue.

Clue #2: "Find a wall that's alive with color. Strike a pose and capture the art."

→ Head to a mural or piece of street art nearby.

Challenge: Recreate the mural with your own bodies (take a silly photo).

Clue #3: "Numbers unlock the way ahead. Add your birthdays together and find the sum."

→ The answer equals the dollar amount you must spend at a convenience store.

Challenge: Buy *exactly* that amount (no more, no less): snacks, drinks, whatever fits.

Clue #4: "Find the water that reflects the sky. Your final stop is where ripples meet romance."

→ Local fountain, pond, or lakeside spot.

Final Pit Stop: Spread out your purchased snacks, sit together by the water, and celebrate your finish line with a mini picnic.

Get The Great Date Race Game:

https://www.etsy.com/listing/4407838884/the-great-date-race-for-couples

☐ **Compete in your own Olympic games.** Make mini-games like sock-slide races, paper airplane javelins, water balloon tosses or blindfold drawing contests. Keep score like real Olympians. Add an opening ceremony with snacks as the "torch," play epic music and crown the winner with a homemade medal. It's playful, ridiculous, and a perfect way to spark laughter while testing each other's skills.

HOW TO DO YOUR OWN COUPLE'S OLYMPICS

1. **Pick Events:** Choose 5–10 mini-games, silly challenges, or sporty activities. Mix physical, funny, and creative so no one has the unfair advantage.
2. **Keep Score:** Use a notebook or phone to tally points. Gold = 3 points, Silver = 2, Bronze = 1.
3. **Add Flair:** Play the Olympic theme music, make "country flags" (even if it's Team Couch vs. Team Fridge), and do an opening ceremony (parade into the backyard with snacks).
4. **Celebrate:** End with a "medal ceremony," maybe the winner gets a massage, picks the movie, or chooses the next date.

EXAMPLE EVENTS FOR A COUPLE'S OLYMPICS

- **Sock Slide Race** – Slide across the kitchen floor in socks, furthest wins.
- **Pillow Javelin** – See who can throw a pillow the farthest.

- **Water Balloon Toss** – Whoever lasts longest without dropping wins.
- **Push-Up Challenge** – Most in one minute takes the medal.
- **Spoon Egg Relay** – Balance an egg/ping pong ball on a spoon and race.
- **Cup Stacking Sprint** – Stack and unstack 10 cups as fast as possible.
- **Blindfold Drawing** – Draw each other while blindfolded; funniest wins.
- **Chopstick Challenge** – Move 20 small objects (like marshmallows or M&Ms) from one bowl to another with chopsticks.
- **Paper Airplane Throw** – Distance + accuracy = points.
- **Couple's Trivia** – Answer questions about each other, fastest right answer scores.
- **Mini Track & Field** – 20-yard dash, long jump over a blanket, or a frisbee discus throw.
- **Balance Battle** – Stand on one leg, hands on hips, whoever lasts longest wins.

   Bonus twist: Make each event themed after a "real" Olympic event but with a goofy household spin (like "Couch Diving" = best belly flop onto cushions).

☐ **Running Obstacle Courses.** Obstacle course races are the grown-up version of playground fun, with a whole lot more sweat. They're built to test endurance, teamwork, and sheer determination, but couples can treat them as a playful challenge instead of a competition.

Examples of Obstacle & Fun Runs:

- **Tough Mudder** – A classic mud run filled with crawling, climbing, and team challenges.
- **Spartan Race** – Endurance-based obstacles like rope climbs, spear throws, and wall jumps.
- **Color Run** – A 5K where volunteers throw colored powder at you as you pass, ending in a rainbow mess.
- **Bubble Run** – Foam and bubbles everywhere—more like a party than a race.
- **Zombie Run** – Dash through a course while "zombies" chase you for your flags.
- **Foam Fest** – Inflatable obstacles, foam pits, and mud combined for messy fun.
- **Rugged Maniac** – 25+ obstacles including fire jumps, water slides, and climbing walls.
- **Warrior Dash** – Shorter, beginner-friendly mud obstacle course with fire and mud pits.
- **Inflatable Obstacle Runs** – Bouncy castles stretched into a race course.
- **Glow Run / Neon Dash** – Night runs with glow sticks, neon paint, and dance party vibes.

☐ **Do a real triathlon.** The classic swim-bike-run combo is intense, but training together can be an amazing bonding experience. Start with a shorter sprint triathlon and work your way up to the full ironman distances. Crossing the finish line side by side is unforgettable.

☐ **Do a funny triathlon.** If endurance sports aren't your style, flip the script and invent your own goofy triathlon instead. Pick three challenges that are totally unserious like ice cream eating + mini golf + karaoke, or video games + Nerf gun shootout + racing grocery carts through the parking lot. It doesn't matter what the events are as long as they're competitive and ridiculous. Bonus points if you award medals (or milkshakes) to the winner.

FUNNY TRIATHLON IDEAS FOR COUPLES

1. **Foodie Triathlon**
   a. Eat something spicy (like a hot wing or pepper)
   b. Speed-eat a donut without using your hands
   c. Blind taste test — guess the food flavor
2. **Bar Crawl Triathlon**
   a. Darts (hit at least 20 points)
   b. Pool (sink 3 balls)
   c. Karaoke challenge (one song each)
3. **Backyard Triathlon**
   a. Water balloon toss until one pops
   b. Sack race with pillowcases
   c. Three-legged race
4. **Netflix & Chill Triathlon**
   a. Speed-binge (watch anew show and describe the plot)
   b. Trivia quiz about each other's favorite shows
   c. Movie quote battle (name the film first)
5. **Arcade Olympics**
   a. Skeeball high score
   b. Air hockey match
   c. Dance Dance Revolution round
6. **Game Night Triathlon**
   a. Beat each other at Connect Four
   b. Fastest Jenga tower collapse
   c. Uno — first to lay down all cards
7. **Sweet Tooth Triathlon**
   a. Ice cream sundae speed-build
   b. Chocolate taste test (guess the brand)
   c. Cookie-decorating contest
8. **Beach Triathlon**
   a. Frisbee accuracy throw
   b. Sandcastle speed-build
   c. Tug-of-war in the surf

9. **Carnival Triathlon**
   a. Ring toss
   b. Balloon dart throw
   c. Funnel cake speed-eating
10. **Coffee Shop Triathlon**
    a. Order each other the weirdest drink
    b. Latte art attempt (with foam or whipped cream)
    c. Trivia round: guess facts about coffee
11. **Lazy Sunday Triathlon**
    a. Nap time — who can stay still longest
    b. Pancake flipping contest
    c. Board game speed round
12. **Grocery Store Triathlon**
    a. Race to find the cheapest item in a random aisle
    b. Grab three items to make a funny meal
    c. Shopping cart obstacle course in the lot
13. **Romantic Triathlon**
    a. Write a 2-line love poem
    b. Slow dance for 2 minutes in public
    c. Take a shadow selfie kiss
14. **Nerd Triathlon**
    a. Solve a Rubik's Cube (or try)
    b. Trivia questions (sci-fi, fantasy, or superheroes)
    c. Best dramatic reading of a comic book line
15. **Festival Triathlon**
    a. Photo scavenger hunt (find a hat, animal shirt, & a balloon)
    b. Win a small prize at a booth
    c. Eat something fried you've never tried
16. **Sports Bar Triathlon**
    a. Trivia on a random sport you don't know
    b. Predict the score of the game (closest wins)
    c. Shoot paper balls into a trash can like basketball
17. **Throwback Triathlon**
    a. Play hopscotch
    b. Jump rope 50 times
    c. Race to blow the biggest bubblegum bubble
18. **Travel Triathlon**
    a. Try a dish from a country you've never visited
    b. Learn 5 phrases in a new language
    c. Take a photo imitating a travel ad pose
19. **Winter Triathlon**
    a. Snowball target toss (or balled-up socks indoors)
    b. Build the fastest mini snowman (or pillow fort)
    c. Hot chocolate chug

20. **Summer Triathlon**
    a. Slip n' slide race
    b. Popsicle-eating contest
    c. Best cannonball into a pool
21. **Pet Triathlon**
    a. Teach a pet a trick (or attempt)
    b. Race to clean up toys faster
    c. Costume challenge — dress them in something silly
22. **Party Store Triathlon**
    a. Pick the funniest balloon
    b. Wear 3 costume props at once
    c. Record a 30-second TikTok using store props
23. **TikTok Triathlon**
    a. Recreate a viral dance
    b. Lip sync battle
    c. Try a trending food hack and rate it
24. **Road Trip Triathlon**
    a. Car karaoke
    b. Spot the weirdest roadside sign
    c. Drive-thru ordering challenge (order for each other)
25. **Anything-Goes Triathlon**
    a. Thumb wrestling
    b. Rock, paper, scissors — best of 7
    c. Chug a glass of water without stopping

Get the Full Date Night Triathlon:

https://www.etsy.com/listing/4405909321/date-night-triathlon-101-fun-printable

☐ **Enjoy some active two-person games and sports together.** Sometimes the best dates are the ones that get you moving, laughing, and maybe a little competitive. Two-person games and sports are perfect because they're simple, flexible, and all about you and your partner. Whether you're volleying back and forth, running around a field, or chasing a frisbee in the park, it's an easy way to bond, burn some energy, and maybe discover a new shared hobby. The beauty is you can keep it as casual or as intense as you want, just don't forget to celebrate the winner with ice cream afterward.

Two-Person Games & Sports Ideas

- Tennis
- Pickleball
- Racquetball
- Squash
- Badminton
- Ping-Pong (Table Tennis)
- Frisbee / Ultimate Frisbee (just 1-on-1 version)
- Croquet
- Bocce Ball
- Horseshoes
- Cornhole (bean bag toss)
- Ladder Toss
- Paddleball (beach paddle game)
- Spikeball (roundnet, works with 2 players taking turns)
- Handball
- Paddle Tennis
- KanJam (disc throwing game)
- Beach Volleyball (play in pairs, just back and forth)
- Hacky Sack
- Catch (with a baseball, football, or glove)
- Frisbee Golf (discs, 2-player course)

Extra-Cool Additions

Winter & Ice Adventures
- ☐ Snowboarding or skiing (if you already ski, try switching gear with each other)
- ☐ Sledding or tubing down a big hill
- ☐ Snowshoeing date through the woods
- ☐ Ice fishing together in a hut
- ☐ Build an epic snow fort or have a snowball fight

Extreme / Thrill Adventures
- ☐ Whitewater rafting (different classes of rapids, from fun to insane)
- ☐ Canyoneering (climbing, rappelling, swimming through canyons)
- ☐ Cliff diving (if safe/local)
- ☐ Sandboarding or dune bashing (if you're near a desert)
- ☐ Indoor skydiving obstacle races (wind tunnel with challenges)

Unique Competition Ideas
- ☐ Escape room race (who solves more puzzles faster)
- ☐ Trampoline park obstacle course
- ☐ Dodgeball (find an adult rec league or trampoline park version)
- ☐ Nerf gun arena battle
- ☐ Foam sword fighting (LARP or just pool noodles in the park)

Water Fun Not Yet Covered
- ☐ Go water skiing
- ☐ Wakeboarding (like water skiing but on a board)
- ☐ Kneeboarding (easier version of water skiing)
- ☐ Windsurfing or kiteboarding
- ☐ Cliffside rope swing into a lake
- ☐ Lazy river tubing day trip

Adventure Vehicle Fun
- ☐ ATV / Quad biking through trails
- ☐ Jet boat ride (fast turns on rivers, like in New Zealand)
- ☐ Snowmobile adventure
- ☐ Segway tours (funny and surprisingly challenging)

Silly / Festival-Style Sports
- ☐ Inflatable gladiator joust (giant padded sticks)
- ☐ Mechanical bull riding at a bar or fair
- ☐ Bubble soccer (play soccer while inside a giant inflatable ball)
- ☐ Giant hamster ball racing (zorbing on a track)
- ☐ Human foosball (you strap in like real foosball players)

Other Ideas that really need no explanation:

- ☐ Do a surfing lesson together
- ☐ Spend the day at the local pool
- ☐ Go on a motorbike ride
- ☐ Go skinny-dipping
- ☐ Go snorkeling
- ☐ Pick a sport you know nothing about and go to a game
- ☐ Chill out in a flotation tank
- ☐ Visit a high-ropes course
- ☐ Have a water balloon or water gun battle, or just a water fight in general.
- ☐ Book a horse and carriage ride
- ☐ Go to a monster truck rally
- ☐ Play really big chess
- ☐ Go to the batting cages
- ☐ Go to a local baseball game or go to a Savana Bananas game if they come to your area.
- ☐ Go scuba diving
- ☐ Go paddleboarding

Mini Adventures & Road Trips

☐ **Take the Scenic Train Ride.** Find a short regional line with panoramic views and make it your movie moment on rails.

☐ **Mapless Adventure.** Pick a direction, start driving, and let intuition (and road signs) guide the day.

☐ **Haunted Road Trip.** Visit the creepiest spots within 100 miles: abandoned hotels, ghost bridges, and graveyards.

☐ **Historical Marker Hunt.** Stop at every random roadside plaque and learn strange local lore.

☐ **Secret Picnic.** Each of you secretly picks a spot within an hour's drive; flip a coin to choose.

☐ **Sunrise-to-Sunset Challenge.** Leave before dawn, chase daylight all day, and end with the sunset in a new place.

☐ **Alphabet Drive.** Find towns or attractions starting with each letter A–Z over a few months of mini-trips.

☐ **Mystery Gas Station Game.** Pull over at the next station, grab one snack and one drink the other has to try.

☐ **Waterfall Chase.** Map every waterfall nearby and try to see them all in one weekend.

☐ **Lighthouse Loop.** Drive the coast and stop at every lighthouse you find; bonus points for climbing to the top.

☐ **Tiny Town Tour.** Visit the smallest towns within 200 miles and rate their diners.

☐ **Abandoned Places Expedition.** Take photos of forgotten buildings before they're gone. Make up a history of these buildings and film it like it's the top news story.

☐ **Cave Crawlers.** Explore a local cave or cavern, bonus if you end with flashlights and echoes of laughter.

☐ **Bridge Hopping.** Cross every major bridge in your region in one day. Or map prettiest bridges like you're in a Nicholas Sparks movie.

☐ **Vintage Route Adventure.** Follow an old highway or trade route and stop wherever nostalgia hits.

☐ **Random City Generator.** Use an online wheel to pick your next destination; no vetoes allowed.

☐ **Scavenger Drive.** Make a list of absurd items and find them all before sunset.

The Madness Menu

1. A pink car
2. A windmill (real or decorative)
3. A yard flamingo
4. A sign with a typo
5. A payphone that still works
6. A mural of someone you've never heard of
7. A house with Christmas lights up in the wrong season
8. A goat on something that's not the ground
9. A license plate from a faraway state
10. A handwritten "No Trespassing" sign
11. A bathtub in a yard
12. Someone selling produce out of their trunk
13. A road sign with an animal crossing symbol
14. A drive-thru you've never noticed before
15. A mannequin outside a store
16. A boat that's nowhere near water
17. A mailbox shaped like something ridiculous
18. A sign with your initials on it
19. A cat in a window
20. An old gas station with a retro sign
21. A giant flagpole
22. A random swing set in an empty field
23. A tree covered in something unnatural (lights, shoes, ribbons)
24. A car wash with neon lights
25. A license plate that spells an actual word
26. An animal crossing the road (bonus if it's weird)
27. A local business with a pun for a name
28. A house painted an outrageous color
29. A person walking an unusual pet
30. A closed store that still has "Open" signs up
31. A scarecrow that's clearly not seasonal
32. A road named after food (Maple, Peach, Bacon, etc.)
33. A random tiny library box
34. A vehicle with more stickers than paint
35. A shoe on the side of the road (just one)
36. A statue you've never noticed before
37. A "Welcome to [City]" sign in terrible condition

38. A giant inflatable of anything
39. A water tower with graffiti
40. An abandoned shopping cart
41. A license plate with your birth month
42. A place that sells both tacos and tires
43. A pay-to-use binocular viewer
44. A truck with hay bales
45. A stop sign covered in stickers
46. A building shaped like an animal or object
47. A mailbox covered in vines
48. A random chair sitting by itself outdoors
49. A business that's inexplicably still open
50. A road that suddenly turns into dirt

☐ **Farmstand Crawl.** Drive country roads and stop at every fruit stand or market you see.

☐ **Diner Diaries.** Visit three different diners in one day: breakfast, lunch, and pie stop, and rank them.

☐ **Antique Trail.** Hit as many antique stores as possible; find something weird for under $10 each.

☐ **Retro Motel Night.** Skip the resort, stay at a vintage roadside inn with neon signs and 60s energy. Think *Schitt's Creek* energy.

☐ **State Line Selfie Quest.** Drive to where two or three states meet and take a "borderline couple" photo.

☐ **Old Movie Road Trip.** Visit filming locations from a favorite classic or cult film. Or, visit restaurants, landmarks, or oddities featured on your favorite shows.

☐ **Microbrewery Map.** Plot every small brewery within 100 miles and hit three in a day (responsibly).

☐ **Camping Lite.** Pitch a tent in the backyard or nearby campsite, bring gourmet snacks, and pretend you're off-grid.

☐ **Deserted Beach Day.** Find a remote coastline or lake nobody visits and claim it as "your beach."

☐ **Sunset Summit.** Pick a hill or lookout point and climb it for the sunset; thermos of wine optional.

☐ **Seasonal Loop.** Do the same mini-road trip each season and compare how it transforms.

☐ **Vintage Car Rental.** Rent a classic car for the day: convertible, jeep, or muscle car and cruise like it's 1975.

☐ **Lost Town Trek.** Research a defunct mining or boomtown and see what's left.

☐ **Hot Springs Hunt.** Find hidden or natural hot springs within a few hours' drive.

☐ **Tunnel Tour.** Drive through or walk to the most cinematic tunnels in your area. Bonus if you shout to hear the echo.

☐ **Small Airport Café.** Have lunch while watching tiny planes take off; surprisingly romantic and cinematic.

☐ **Historic Train Station Crawl.** Visit old depots turned cafés or museums and imagine the travelers who passed through.

☐ **Night Drive with No GPS.** Navigate only by road signs and intuition. Turn the headlights and music up.

☐ **Wildflower Trail.** Hunt for the best bloom spot in spring and make it your seasonal tradition.

☐ **Ferry Adventure.** Find the nearest ferry, drive onboard, and explore whatever's on the other shore.

☐ **Tiny Zoo or Animal Rescue Visit.** Support small rescues or sanctuaries. Feed llamas or walk goats.

☐ **Mountain Pass Challenge.** Pick a nearby scenic byway or pass and conquer it together.

☐ **Hidden Cemetery Picnic.** Peaceful, a little gothic, strangely grounding.

☐ **Local Legends Route.** Visit spots tied to urban myths: haunted roads, alien sightings, miracle springs.

☐ **Rainy Day Drive.** Wait for a storm, grab coffee, and go driving just to listen to the rain hit the windshield.

☐ **Random Airbnb Night.** Pick a nearby listing with a unique vibe (tiny home, treehouse, yurt) and book it for one night.

☐ **Secret Postcard Mission.** Send postcards to yourself from every mini-adventure with the date and one memory.

Stay At Home

☐ **Choose a series of movies you'll both enjoy, and have a daylong movie marathon in your PJs.** This is a pretty chill date idea for those who like staying at home.

Action & Adventure Series

1. The Lord of the Rings + The Hobbit
2. The Matrix Trilogy (+ Matrix Resurrections if you're brave)
3. The John Wick Series
4. The Mission: Impossible Series
5. The Indiana Jones Series
6. The James Bond Films (pick an actor era!)
7. The Jason Bourne Series
8. The Die Hard Series
9. The Mad Max Series (+ Fury Road)
10. The Fast & Furious Series

Sci-Fi & Fantasy

11. Star Wars Saga (Originals, Prequels, Sequels, or all)
12. The Marvel Cinematic Universe (choose a character arc, like Iron Man or Avengers)
13. The Harry Potter Films (+ Fantastic Beasts spin-offs)
14. The Hunger Games Series
15. The Divergent Series
16. The Twilight Saga
17. The Chronicles of Narnia
18. The Dune Series (1984 + 2021 + sequels when out)
19. The Avatar Films (so far 2, but more coming)
20. The Jurassic Park / Jurassic World Series

Animated & Family-Friendly

21. The Toy Story Films
22. The Shrek Films (+ Puss in Boots spin-offs)
23. The Frozen + Tangled + Disney Princess marathon
24. The Minions / Despicable Me Series
25. The Incredibles + Pixar superhero-themed films
26. The Kung Fu Panda Series
27. The Cars Films (+ Planes spinoffs if you want)
28. The Ice Age Series
29. The Finding Nemo + Finding Dory + Pixar undersea set
30. The Monsters, Inc. + Monsters University

Superhero Universes

31. The Dark Knight Trilogy (Christopher Nolan's Batman)
32. The Batman Anthology (Tim Burton + Schumacher films)

33. The Spider-Man Series (Tobey, Andrew, Tom — pick one run or marathon all)
34. The X-Men + Deadpool Films
35. The Deadpool + Logan mini-set
36. The Captain America Trilogy (leading into Avengers)
37. The Thor Series
38. The Guardians of the Galaxy Trilogy
39. The Doctor Strange + Multiverse arc
40. The Black Panther + Wakanda Forever

Comedy & Feel-Good
41. The Hangover Trilogy
42. The Anchorman Films
43. The Legally Blonde Films
44. The Mean Girls (+ spiritual successors like Easy A, Clueless)
45. The Bridget Jones Trilogy
46. The Pitch Perfect Trilogy
47. The 21 & 22 Jump Street films
48. The Zombieland Duo
49. The Bill & Ted Trilogy
50. The Austin Powers Trilogy

☐ **Watch a movie you've both seen a bunch and try to make memes from it.** There are so many memes from movies and shows. Pick a movie that you both love and see what kind of memes you can pull from it. Post them up in Reddit. Who knows, you might get a few upvotes and people might use or adapt your meme.

☐ **Write a story together.** This is another date idea that is a little bit short but is still pretty fun. Get a piece of paper, you write two sentences of a story then pass it to them. Then they write two sentences. And then you write two sentences, they write two sentences, and so on. The story gets pretty crazy pretty quickly.

25 PROMPTS FOR WRITING A STORY TOGETHER
- A raccoon in a Hawaiian shirt just knocked on your door asking for a cup of sugar.
- You wake up in a parallel universe where pizza is used as currency.
- On your first day as a superhero, your only power is making people sneeze.
- A cat inherits a billion-dollar company and makes you its personal assistant.
- The mayor has just announced that ducks will now run the city council.
- You find a mysterious remote that pauses time... but only when someone sneezes.

- The last slice of pizza is speaking to you. It doesn't want to be eaten.
- An alien lands in your backyard but refuses to leave until it learns salsa dancing.
- You've been mistaken for the royal heir of a tiny country that only exists on Thursdays.
- A time traveler shows up from the year 3025, but they only came back to return a library book.
- You're cursed to turn into a chicken every time someone compliments your shoes.
- The GPS in your car suddenly develops a personality and refuses to take you home.
- Your new roommate turns out to be Bigfoot, and he won't stop borrowing your shampoo.
- A villainous goose has stolen the Declaration of Independence, and you're the only one who can stop it.
- You order a latte, but the barista writes a prophecy on your cup instead of your name.
- The moon calls you on the phone to complain about Earth's noise.
- Your pet goldfish just challenged you to a duel… and it's winning.
- A mysterious door appears in your kitchen, leading directly to a Taco Bell in another dimension.
- You accidentally buy a haunted blender that won't stop making margaritas.
- A genie grants you three wishes, but only for things you don't actually want.
- You're hired as a dragon babysitter, but the dragon insists it's actually your boss.
- Every time you sneeze, a new celebrity shows up in your living room.
- The internet has vanished, and the only website left is your old MySpace page.
- A talking squirrel offers you $10,000 to help him plan a bank heist.
- You find a button that says "Do Not Press"… and your partner presses it anyway.

Get the Once Upon a Date Game:

https://www.etsy.com/listing/4407954769/once-upon-a-date-storytelling-game-250

☐ **Host trivia night.** Remember Sporcle, the online trivia platform that made a big splash about a decade ago? We're ready for a comeback. Whether you're naming candy bars or listing out all the presidents in record time, you'll learn a lot about your date in the process.

☐ **Netflix party and chill.** We've already binged numerous shows from making Breaking Bad a success to Squid Game. Grab your favorite pillows to create a cozy tucked-in vibe, pick a movie, and set up a Netflix Party.

NETFLIX GAMES FOR COUPLES

Roulette & Randomizers
- **Netflix Roulette** – Use a spinner/wheel or online generator to pick a random show/movie (no backing out!).
- **Shuffle Challenge** – Close your eyes, scroll, and click—whatever it lands on, you watch.
- **Alphabet Game** – Watch something starting with each letter of the alphabet over multiple date nights.

Drinking / Snack Games
- **Sip & Spot** – Take a sip every time a cliché happens (car chase, awkward kiss, dramatic pause).
- **Snack Attack** – Assign snacks to recurring tropes (eat popcorn when someone gasps, candy when a new character enters).
- **Character Shots** – Choose a character; drink/snack whenever they appear or say their catchphrase.

Prediction Games
- **Next Line Guessing** – Pause before a big line and try to guess what comes next.
- **Plot Twist Wager** – Each of you predicts how the episode will end. Whoever's closest wins.
- **Character Fate Bets** – Pick who's most likely to die, betray, or fall in love next.

Interactive Play-Alongs
- **Scene Reenactments** – Pause and act out a line before letting it play.
- **Emoji Recaps** – Only describe the last scene using emojis and see if your partner gets it.
- **Improv Subtitles** – Mute and dub your own dialogue for 1 minute.

Competitive Mini-Games
- **Bingo Boards** – Make Netflix Bingo with squares like "awkward silence," "car explosion," "bad CGI," or "flashback."

- **Trivia Breaks** – After an episode, quiz each other on details (character names, locations, etc.).
- **Skip-Intro Reflex** – First to grab the remote when "Skip Intro" pops up wins a point.

Romantic / Cute Twists
- **Compliment Rule** – Each time you pause, say one thing you like about the other.
- **Kiss Cue** – Whenever there's a kiss onscreen, you have to kiss too.
- **Love or Roast** – After each episode, give a loving compliment or a funny roast about each other's taste.

☐ **Tap your inner sommelier.** Just shy of stomping grapes in the tub, you can get close to vineyards from your couch. The Sonoma County Vintners have this handy list of wines you can order direct to home. On date night, you can create your own tasting notes (with coaching from this Wine Folly blog). Not confident in guiding your own tasting skills? Invite Emma Swain, the CEO of St. Supery, to walk you through the wine-tasting experience she hosted on Zoom. Don't forget your own virtual Zoom background of a vineyard for the full feel on your date.

☐ **B.Y.O. Brunch for a boozy drag show.** Order takeout brunch or make your own mimosas at home, then head out to a local drag show or livestream one together. Cheer, tip, and toast to pure, unapologetic joy.

☐ **Take a deep breath over meditation and tea.** Join a guided meditation with MyWellBeing. For a quick grounding exercise, you can walk through together anytime. Anna Murphy, an executive coach in Chicago, recommends a 5-4-3-2-1 check-in: List five things you see, four that you feel, three that you hear, two that you smell, and one that you taste. Once you've hit the zen zone, make a cup of tea and discuss how you're both feeling.

☐ **Get some space.** Channel your inner Ariana Grande and take a trip that's out of this world. Explore NASA's virtual exhibits, tour the International Space Station through the Space Center Houston app, or visit a local planetarium and stargaze together.

☐ **Virtual tours.** An easy way to travel without leaving the couch. You and your date can explore famous landmarks, museums, cultural sites, and even Broadway shows from home. Wander the Louvre, roam Machu Picchu, or stream a musical together. It's affordable, awe-inspiring, and a unique way to share a one-of-a-kind date night.

VIRTUAL TOURS TO TRY

Museums & Art Galleries

☐ The Louvre (Paris, France) – Tour Egyptian Antiquities, Michelangelo's works, and the Galerie d'Apollon.

☐ The British Museum (London, UK) – Explore the Rosetta Stone, Egyptian mummies, and more via Google Arts & Culture.

☐ The Metropolitan Museum of Art (New York, USA) – A deep dive into 5,000 years of art.

☐ The Vatican Museums & Sistine Chapel (Rome, Italy) – View Raphael's Rooms and Michelangelo's masterpiece ceiling.

☐ Guggenheim Museum (New York, USA) – Virtual stroll through its unique spiral galleries.

☐ Van Gogh Museum (Amsterdam, Netherlands) – Discover hundreds of works from the artist's life.

☐ Uffizi Gallery (Florence, Italy) – Renaissance gems like Botticelli's *The Birth of Venus*.

☐ Rijksmuseum (Amsterdam, Netherlands) – Rembrandt, Vermeer, and Dutch Golden Age treasures.

☐ Smithsonian National Museum of Natural History (Washington D.C., USA) – Dino fossils, gems, and immersive halls.

☐ Museum of Modern Art (New York, USA) – Contemporary art icons.

Historic Landmarks & Sites

☐ The Great Wall of China – Walk along this ancient wonder virtually.

☐ Machu Picchu (Peru) – 360° views of the ancient Inca citadel.

☐ Pyramids of Giza (Egypt) – Explore inside tombs and temples.

☐ Petra (Jordan) – Roam the rose-red city carved into cliffs.

☐ Colosseum (Rome, Italy) – Step inside the gladiator arena.

☐ Taj Mahal (India) – Sunrise and sunset views of this world wonder.

☐ Eiffel Tower (Paris, France) – Interactive climb to the top.

☐ Stonehenge (England) – Explore the mysterious stone circle.

☐ Angkor Wat (Cambodia) – Tour the vast ancient temple complex.

☐ Easter Island (Chile) – Up-close with the Moai statues.

Zoos & Aquariums

☐ San Diego Zoo (USA) – Live cams of pandas, koalas, and polar bears.

☐ Georgia Aquarium (USA) – Whale sharks, beluga whales, and penguins.

- ☐ Monterey Bay Aquarium (California, USA) – Jellyfish, sharks, sea otters, and more.
- ☐ Smithsonian's National Zoo (Washington D.C., USA) – Panda cam is legendary.
- ☐ Houston Zoo (USA) – Giraffes, gorillas, and elephants.

Space & Science
- ☐ NASA Virtual Tours – Tour the Johnson Space Center, Hubble mission control, and International Space Station.
- ☐ International Space Station (ISS) – Explore modules and astronaut living quarters.
- ☐ Mars Rover Experience – See Mars through NASA's rover footage.
- ☐ CERN (Switzerland) – Walk inside the world's largest particle physics laboratory.
- ☐ Smithsonian Air & Space Museum (USA) – From Apollo 11 to the Wright brothers' plane.

Performances & Culture
- ☐ Broadway HD – Stream Broadway classics like *Cats*, *Les Misérables*, and *Phantom of the Opera*.
- ☐ The Globe Theatre (London, UK) – Watch Shakespeare plays filmed in the historic replica theater.
- ☐ The Bolshoi Ballet (Moscow, Russia) – Legendary ballet performances available online.
- ☐ Metropolitan Opera (New York, USA) – Free nightly streams of iconic operas.
- ☐ Berlin Philharmonic (Germany) – Digital concert hall with stunning symphonies.

Nature & Adventure
- ☐ Yellowstone National Park (USA) – Virtual geysers, hot springs, and landscapes.
- ☐ Grand Canyon (USA) – 360° hikes and overlooks.
- ☐ Yosemite National Park (USA) – Explore waterfalls, cliffs, and meadows.
- ☐ Great Barrier Reef (Australia) – Dive underwater to view coral and sea life.
- ☐ Northern Lights (Aurora Borealis) – Live cams from Norway, Finland, and Canada.

☐ **Virtual Reality.** Whether you're hoping to turn your living room into a match arena or fly through fantasy worlds from your couch, VR games offer an immersive escape and a fantastic shared experience.

TOP VR GAMES OF 2025 (CRITIC AND PLAYER FAVORITES)

According to recent expert roundups, 2025's must-play VR titles span genres from narrative-heavy shooters to relaxing rhythm games:

- **Half-Life: Alyx** — A transformative VR shooter with gripping story and stellar immersion
- **Resident Evil 4 VR** — A nerve-wracking remake that intensifies every moment
- **Superhot VR** — Stylish gameplay where time only moves when you do
- **Walkabout Mini Golf** — A calm, clever spin on mini-golf in diverse and whimsical courses
- **No Man's Sky VR** — Epic, freeform universe exploration in virtual reality
- **Tetris Effect: Connected** — Hypnotic visuals and rhythm-based gameplay elevate a classic
- **Wands Alliances** — Cast spells in a steampunk VR dueling shooter
- **Batman: Arkham Shadow, Astro Bot Rescue Mission, Alien: Rogue Incursion**—VR takes on these franchises feel especially vivid
- **Skyrim VR** — Explore Tamriel like never before
- **Beat Saber** — Dance-saber rhythm game that's still on top of the VR physical fun leaderboard
  Best for PlayStation VR2 (PSVR2) Owners
  TechRadar highlights standout titles leveraging PSVR2's haptics and power :
- **Gran Turismo 7 VR** — Full cockpit racing bliss
- **Resident Evil Village** — Horror amplified in VR
- **The Walking Dead: Saints & Sinners** — Survival horror at its most immersive
- **Horizon: Call of the Mountain** — A flagship exclusive for VR adventure
- Others: *Puzzling Places, Kayak VR, Tetris Effect, Beat Saber, Pistol Whip, Pavlov, Hitman: World of Assassination*

Multiplayer & Social VR Highlights

Looking for co-op or just playful competition? From Meta Quest libraries, some favorites include:

- **Walkabout Mini Golf VR** — Great multi-course mini-golf charm
- **Rec Room** — Social hub with tons of mini-games
- **Arizona Sunshine** — Gory zombie survival, best in co-op
- **Carly and the Reaperman** — Puzzle-solving duo mode
- **Population: One** — Battle royale across VR platforms
- **Cook Out** — Fast-paced cooking chaos
- **Star Trek: Bridge Crew** — Ergonomic teamwork in space
- **Zenith: The Last City** — Expansive VR MMORPG

- **Warplanes: WW1 Fighters** — Aerial dogfight nostalgia
- **Gorilla Tag** — Ridiculously fun social VR tag game with arm-powered locomotion

Notable VR Adventures & RPGs
Broader titles that shine in VR fidelity and storytelling:
- **Asgard's Wrath 2** — A sprawling action-RPG with Norse and Egyptian myth mashups, often called "VR's Zelda"
- **Assassin's Creed Nexus VR** — Stealth and melee in gritty VR format with Ezio, Connor, and Kassandra
- **Homeworld: Vast Reaches** — Space RTS refined for VR interaction
- **Just Dance VR** — A full physical dance party in VR form

Upcoming Titles to Watch
2025 is bursting with new games across all major platforms:
- **The Midnight Walk, MADiSON VR, Slender: The Arrival VR**, and more PSVR2 exclusives
- **Vestiges: Fallen Tribes, Silent North, Exer Gale, Loop One Done, Pedal Rebel VR** — playful, social VR prototypes from Meta's showcase
- And long roster of releases like **Aces of Thunder, Arken Age, Roboquest, Dungeons of Eternity**, plus sports, strategy, horror, and fantasy concepts

☐ **Build a Slip 'N Slide.** A summer must: Set up a Slip 'N Slide in your backyard. Not only is this silly date a sure-fire hit, but it's a refreshing way for the two of you to cool off in the summer heat.

☐ **Have an Instagram date.** Does your boo love racking up likes on the 'Gram? Juice up your phones and head out in search of inspiration. You might find yourselves drawn to a park you never noticed before, or a part of the city where the graffiti is super-photogenic. Take tons of selfies so that you have your own Instagram trail of the date.

☐ **Buy and read some comic books together.** Again, both of you will at least have to have a passing interest in comic books. But if you both do, it can be neat to start a new series that you haven't read before. Try to pick one that both of you don't know much about. That way, you can both experience it with fresh eyes. Or hang out at the comic book store and maybe learn some history.

☐ **Pillow fort party.** Just like what it sounds, make a pillow fort together. And now that you are adults, you can make it even more amazing than the ones you made as a kid. Once inside, do whatever you want, watch a movie, have drinks and chat, snuggle, do some gaming, whatever floats your collective boats! Also, don't forget to do a pillow fight in your underwear, so cute!

☐ **Turn Your Living Room into the Main Stage.** Queue up a live concert stream, local artist session, or an old festival performance and make a night of it. Dress for the part: glitter, fringe, flower crowns, whatever makes you feel unreasonably famous. Turn up the lights, pour something strong, and dance like you're front row without worrying about the line for the bathroom.

☐ **Stay In, Go Global: Virtual & At-Home Date Experiences.** You don't need to leave your couch to explore, compete, or spark romance, virtual date experiences are everywhere, from interactive challenges to streaming performances. Whether you're looking to cozy up or go virtual-adventuring, there's something for every couple who's staying in.

Digital At-Home Date Packs — Delivered Fun
- **AmazingCo's At-Home Activity Date Night**. A digital experience with 9 interactive, relationship-building challenges—think "Guess That Tune," origami frog races, armchair travel trivia, and more. Delivered via a link on your preselected date, this pack guides you through 2–3 hours of fun, friendly competition, complete with conversation prompts and optional scoring.
- **AmazingCo's Foodie Date Night**. A 2–3 hour foodie-filled experience including cooking, tasting challenges, trivia, and creative mini-quests— all done from home with minimal supplies required.
- **AmazingCo's Romantic Date Night**. A cozy, connect-focused option featuring puzzles, games, and prompts designed to spark intimate conversation and laughter. These packs are great if you want a pre-made, smoothly guided evening without the prep work.

Other Engaging Virtual Date Ideas
From cultural exploration to interactive games, here are fresh and interactive ways to bring the spark to your screen:
- **Virtual Cooking Challenges** — Choose a recipe, shop for ingredients, and cook while video-chatting. A delicious and collaborative way to play chef together.

- **Online Game Nights & Trivia** — Team up for trivia, online board games, or virtual escape rooms—great for long-distance or house-hold date nights.
- **Live Performances & Streaming Events** — Watch concerts, theater, or comedy shows online via platforms like Bandsintown, Tiny Desk (Home) Concerts, or Broadway stream services.
- **Creative Collaborations**
  o **Paint & Sip Sessions** — Join online painting classes or follow YouTube art tutorials together.
  o **Make a Vision Board** — Craft your future together using magazines, a poster board, and shared dreams as the guide.
- **Go on a Virtual Tour** — From museums to natural wonders and operas, explore the Louvre, Taj Mahal, or live opera streams — all from home.
- **Personality & Conversation Games** — Ask "36 Questions That Lead to Love," play "Virtual Q&A," or use conversation card decks to spark intimacy.
- **Surprise Dinner Delivery** — Send your partner a surprise meal and enjoy it "together" over video.
- **Tarot & Mystery Room Adventures** — Dive into virtual escape rooms or schedule a tarot reading to share a unique, interactive experience.

☐ **Board Games.** Obviously, I would list all board games when you are bored. See what I did there?

Classic & Timeless
- Chess
- Checkers (Draughts)
- Backgammon
- Go
- Dominoes
- Mahjong
- Snakes & Ladders (Chutes & Ladders)
- Ludo / Parcheesi

Family Game Night Staples
- Monopoly
- Clue (Cluedo)
- Scrabble
- Trivial Pursuit
- The Game of Life
- Sorry!
- Risk
- Battleship

Party & Group Favorites
- Pictionary
- Charades (board/card versions)
- Taboo
- Scattergories
- Cranium
- Balderdash
- Apples to Apples
- Cards Against Humanity (technically card-based, but party classic)
- Telestrations
- Codenames
- Outburst

Date-Friendly / 2-Player Greats
- Connect Four
- Jenga
- Othello (Reversi)
- Mancala

- Hive
- Jaipur
- Patchwork
- Onitama
- Stratego

Modern Strategy Board Games (Huge hits in board game cafés)
- Catan (Settlers of Catan)
- Ticket to Ride
- Carcassonne
- Pandemic (co-op, save the world together)
- Azul
- Splendor
- 7 Wonders
- Dominion
- Wingspan
- Agricola
- Scythe
- Gloomhaven
- Terraforming Mars

Cooperative Adventures (work *with* each other)
- Forbidden Island
- Forbidden Desert
- Betrayal at House on the Hill
- Arkham Horror
- Eldritch Horror
- Mansions of Madness
- Decrypto

- Sherlock Holmes Consulting Detective
- Chronicles of Crime

Silly / Quick Fun
- Exploding Kittens
- Sushi Go!
- Unstable Unicorns
- Throw Throw Burrito
- Taco Cat Goat Cheese Pizza
- Joking Hazard
- Don't Get Got
- One Night Ultimate Werewolf
- Coup
- Secret Hitler

Heavy Thinkers (for hardcore game nights)
- Twilight Struggle
- Diplomacy
- Eclipse
- Brass: Birmingham
- Puerto Rico
- Ark Nova
- Spirit Island
- Through the Ages

Artsy / Offbeat Board Games
- Dixit
- Mysterium
- Concept
- Wavelength

☐ **Card Games**. Just as same as board games. I am going to list all of them. It is good to learn.

Timeless Classics
- Poker (Texas Hold 'Em, Omaha, 7-Card Stud, 5-Card Draw)
- Blackjack (21)
- Baccarat
- Solitaire (Klondike, Spider, FreeCell, Pyramid, TriPeaks)
- War
- Go Fish
- Old Maid

- Crazy Eights
- Rummy (Gin, Indian, Contract)
- Hearts
- Spades
- Bridge
- Euchre
- Pinochle
- Whist
- Canasta

107

Party & Social Card Games

- Uno
- Phase 10
- Skip-Bo
- Apples to Apples (card version)
- Cards Against Humanity
- Exploding Kittens
- Unstable Unicorns
- Sushi Go!
- Taco Cat Goat Cheese Pizza
- Fluxx
- The Mind
- Spot It! / Dobble
- Love Letter
- Coup
- One Night Ultimate Werewolf
- Werewolf / Mafia
- Secret Hitler

Casino / Gambling Favorites

- Texas Hold 'Em
- Omaha Poker
- 7-Card Stud
- Caribbean Stud Poker
- Pai Gow Poker
- 3-Card Poker
- Casino War
- Keno (card-based variant)

Traditional / Cultural Card Games

- Durak (Russia)
- Skat (Germany)
- Belote (France)
- Scopa (Italy)
- Briscola (Italy)
- Tarabish (Canada)
- President / Asshole (US/International)
- Kemps (France/US)
- Cuarenta (Ecuador)
- Truco (Argentina, Uruguay, Brazil)
- Mus (Spain/Basque)
- Hanafuda (Japan – e.g., Koi-Koi)

- Daihinmin / Daifugō (Japan)
- Teen Patti (India, "Indian Poker")
- Andar Bahar (India)
- Seep (India/Pakistan)
- Ganjifa (India, historic painted cards)
- Tien Len (Vietnamese climbing game)
- Big Two (China/Hong Kong, a.k.a. Deuces)

Trick-Taking Games (Like Hearts/Spades style)

- Pitch
- 500
- Oh Hell!
- Bid Euchre
- Kaiser
- Pepper
- All Fours

Couple / Date-Friendly Simple Games

- Speed
- Slapjack
- Egyptian Rat Screw
- BS (a.k.a. I Doubt It)
- Gin Rummy
- Cribbage (needs board + cards)
- Casino-style 31
- Memory (Concentration)
- Ninety-Nine
- Fan Tan

Modern Designer Card Games (Board-game crossover style)

- Dominion (deck-building OG)
- Arkham Horror: The Card Game
- Marvel Champions: The Card Game
- KeyForge
- Gloom
- Hanabi (cooperative fireworks game)

- The Resistance (social deduction)
- Bang! (wild west shootout)
- Illusion (optical trick card game)
- Red7
- For Sale

☐ **Best & Worst Movies of the Year You Were Born.** Pop some popcorn, pour a drink, and take a trip back in time. Look up the year you were born and find the highest-rated (or Oscar-winning) movie and the lowest-rated box office flop from that year. Then watch them back-to-back. The "best" will make you feel like your year produced cinematic genius, while the "worst" will remind you how far Hollywood will go to make a buck. It's hilarious, nostalgic, and a great way to see what the world was watching when you first showed up. Bonus points if you dress in outfits from that era or add in a playlist of hit songs from the same year.

BEST & WORST MOVIES OF THE YEAR YOU WERE BORN
1950
- *Best:* **Sunset Boulevard** – A dark, biting Hollywood noir classic with unforgettable lines.
- *Worst:* **Rocketship X-M** – Low-budget, scientifically laughable sci-fi that aged terribly.

1951
- *Best:* **A Streetcar Named Desire** – Marlon Brando's smoldering performance defined a generation.
- *Worst:* **Bedtime for Bonzo** – Ronald Reagan + a chimpanzee... enough said.

1952
- *Best:* **Singin' in the Rain** – Joyful, dazzling, maybe the best musical ever made.
- *Worst:* **Bela Lugosi Meets a Brooklyn Gorilla** – Painful comedy, poor Lugosi deserved better.

1953
- *Best:* **From Here to Eternity** – Academy Award winner with iconic beach kiss scene.
- *Worst:* **Glen or Glenda** – Ed Wood's bizarre "docu-drama" about gender identity, unintentionally camp.

1954
- *Best:* **On the Waterfront** – Brando's "I coulda been a contender" still echoes.
- *Worst:* **The Silver Chalice** – A biblical flop so bad Paul Newman apologized for it.

1955
- *Best:* **Rebel Without a Cause** – James Dean defined teen angst forever.
- *Worst:* **Son of Sinbad** – A cheesy sword-and-sandal mess, pure kitsch.

1956

- *Best:* **The Ten Commandments** – DeMille's biblical spectacle, over-the-top but glorious.
- *Worst:* **Fire Maidens from Outer Space** – Awkward aliens + bad sets = sci-fi disaster.

1957

- *Best:* **12 Angry Men** – Brilliant ensemble drama that redefined courtroom storytelling.
- *Worst:* **Plan 9 from Outer Space** – Ed Wood's infamous turkey, often crowned "worst ever."

1958

- *Best:* **Vertigo** – Hitchcock's hypnotic masterpiece of obsession and mystery.
- *Worst:* **The Blob** – Beloved as camp now, but critics panned it as silly nonsense.

1959

- *Best:* **Ben-Hur** – 11 Oscars, epic chariot races, Hollywood at full grandeur.
- *Worst:* **The Tingler** – William Castle's horror gimmick fest, pure schlock.

1960

- *Best:* **Psycho** – Hitchcock shocked the world with the shower scene and redefined horror.
- *Worst:* **The Leech Woman** – A laughably bad sci-fi/horror about eternal youth gone wrong.

1961

- *Best:* **West Side Story** – A soaring musical that swept the Oscars.
- *Worst:* **The Beast of Yucca Flats** – Starring Tor Johnson, possibly the dullest monster movie ever.

1962

- *Best:* **Lawrence of Arabia** – Epic, poetic, and visually breathtaking.
- *Worst:* **The Wild Women of Wongo** – Colorful costumes couldn't save this incoherent tropical fantasy.

1963

- *Best:* **8½** – Fellini's dazzling masterpiece about creativity and identity.
- *Worst:* **The Creeping Terror** – "Monster" looks like a parade float covered in carpet scraps.

1964

- *Best:* **Dr. Strangelove** – Kubrick's razor-sharp satire on nuclear war.
- *Worst:* **Santa Claus Conquers the Martians** – Famously ridiculous holiday sci-fi trash.

1965

- *Best:* **The Sound of Music** – Julie Andrews twirling into film immortality.
- *Worst:* **Frankenstein Meets the Space Monster** – Title says it all: pure Z-grade nonsense.

1966

- *Best:* **The Good, The Bad, and The Ugly** – Leone's spaghetti western opera.
- *Worst:* **Manos: The Hands of Fate** – The reigning king of so-bad-it's-good cinema.

1967

- *Best:* **The Graduate** – Dustin Hoffman + Simon & Garfunkel = a cultural landmark.
- *Worst:* **They Saved Hitler's Brain** – A laughable mess about Hitler's head surviving postwar.

1968

- *Best:* **2001: A Space Odyssey** – Kubrick's sci-fi revolution, equal parts dazzling and confounding.
- *Worst:* **The Astro-Zombies** – Awful costumes, nonsense plot, cult infamy.

1969

- *Best:* **Midnight Cowboy** – The only X-rated film to win Best Picture, raw and groundbreaking.
- *Worst:* **They Came to Rob Las Vegas** – Ambitious heist flick turned tedious bore.

1970

- *Best:* **Patton** – Sweeping biopic with George C. Scott's powerhouse performance.
- *Worst:* **Trog** – Joan Crawford's last film, battling a caveman in a rubber suit.

1971

- *Best:* **A Clockwork Orange** – Kubrick's violent, satirical classic.
- *Worst:* **Dracula vs. Frankenstein** – A sloppy, bargain-bin monster mash.

1972

- *Best:* **The Godfather** – Mafia masterpiece, one of the greatest films ever made.
- *Worst:* **The Thing with Two Heads** – Ray Milland's head grafted onto a Black man's body. Enough said.

1973

- *Best:* **The Exorcist** – Horror landmark that made audiences faint in theaters.
- *Worst:* **The Swinging Cheerleaders** – Exploitative, zero-plot sports comedy.

1974

- *Best:* **Chinatown** – Neo-noir brilliance from Polanski and Nicholson.
- *Worst:* **Zardoz** – Sean Connery in a red diaper-sling. Surreal, unintentionally hilarious.

1975

- *Best:* **Jaws** – Spielberg created the summer blockbuster.
- *Worst:* **At Long Last Love** – Bogdanovich's all-sung musical flop.

1976

- *Best:* **Rocky** – Underdog story that became the people's champ.
- *Worst:* **The Food of the Gods** – Killer giant animals terrorize people with bad effects.

1977

- *Best:* **Star Wars** (later retitled *A New Hope*) – Sci-fi changed forever.
- *Worst:* **Exorcist II: The Heretic** – Infamous mess, nearly killed the franchise.

1978

- *Best:* **Grease** – John Travolta + Olivia Newton-John = pop culture phenomenon.
- *Worst:* **Sgt. Pepper's Lonely Hearts Club Band** – Bee Gees + Peter Frampton = trainwreck.

1979

- *Best:* **Apocalypse Now** – Coppola's masterpiece of war, madness, and cinema excess.
- *Worst:* **Caligula** – Historical epic turned pornographic chaos.

1980

- *Best:* **The Empire Strikes Back** – Darker, deeper, and the best *Star Wars* ever made.
- *Worst:* **The Gong Show Movie** – A self-indulgent flop no one asked for.

1981

- *Best:* **Raiders of the Lost Ark** – Indiana Jones swings onto the big screen. Instant legend.
- *Worst:* **Heaven's Gate** – Bankrupted United Artists, 5+ hours of misery.

1982

- *Best:* **E.T. the Extra-Terrestrial** – Spielberg makes the whole world cry with a glowing finger.
- *Worst:* **Inchon** – Overblown war drama that cost $46 million and made… $5 million.

1983

- *Best:* **Return of the Jedi** – Ewoks aside, a triumphant end to the trilogy.
- *Worst:* **Jaws 3-D** – Plastic sharks lunging into the camera. Painful.

1984

- *Best:* **Ghostbusters** – Who ya gonna call? Comedy, horror, and sci-fi in one perfect mix.
- *Worst:* **Bolero** – Bo Derek's "erotic" disaster, infamous for all the wrong reasons.

1985

- *Best:* **Back to the Future** – Time-travel magic, DeLorean dreams, cultural phenomenon.
- *Worst:* **Gymkata** – A gymnast uses martial arts in a spy movie.

1986

- *Best:* **Platoon** – Oliver Stone's searing Vietnam war drama.
- *Worst:* **Howard the Duck** – George Lucas' WTF moment with a creepy duck-man.

1987
- *Best:* **The Untouchables** – De Palma's stylish gangster epic with Sean Connery stealing scenes.
- *Worst:* **Ishtar** – Infamous desert comedy that became Hollywood's punchline.

1988
- *Best:* **Die Hard** – Bruce Willis redefined the action hero barefoot in a skyscraper.
- *Worst:* **Mac and Me** – Shameless McDonald's/Pepsi commercial disguised as an E.T. rip-off.

1989
- *Best:* **Batman** – Tim Burton + Jack Nicholson = gothic blockbuster perfection.
- *Worst:* **Star Trek V: The Final Frontier** – "What does God need with a starship?" Exactly.

1990
- *Best:* **Goodfellas** – Scorsese's masterpiece. "As far back as I can remember, I always wanted to be a gangster…"
- *Worst:* **Troll 2** – Famously terrible, with no trolls in it.

1991
- *Best:* **The Silence of the Lambs** – Hannibal Lecter and fava beans.
- *Worst:* **Nothing But Trouble** – A Dan Aykroyd fever dream with prosthetics from hell.

1992
- *Best:* **Unforgiven** – Clint Eastwood's gritty anti-western.
- *Worst:* **Stop! Or My Mom Will Shoot** – Sylvester Stallone vs. a nagging mom… who wins? No one.

1993
- *Best:* **Jurassic Park** – Spielberg made dinosaurs real. Childhoods changed forever.
- *Worst:* **Super Mario Bros.** – The infamous, cursed video game adaptation.

1994
- *Best:* **Pulp Fiction** – Tarantino rewrote cinema with burgers, briefcases, and dance moves.
- *Worst:* **North** – Roger Ebert: "I hated this movie. Hated hated hated hated it."

1995
- *Best:* **Toy Story** – Pixar's game-changer. First full CGI movie and still magical.
- *Worst:* **Showgirls** – Sleazy Vegas "satire" that tanked careers but gained cult status.

1996
- *Best:* **Fargo** – "Oh yah, real good then." Dark comedy perfection.
- *Worst:* **Kazaam** – Shaquille O'Neal as a rapping genie in a boombox. Enough said.

1997

- *Best:* **Titanic** – James Cameron made history sink, and everyone cried.
- *Worst:* **Batman & Robin** – Bat-nipples. Ice puns. The death of a franchise.

1998

- *Best:* **Saving Private Ryan** – That opening D-Day sequence? Still unmatched.
- *Worst:* **Godzilla (U.S. version)** – A giant iguana and Matthew Broderick mumbling about "science."

1999

- *Best:* **The Matrix** – "What if I told you…" cinema changed forever with bullet time.
- *Worst:* **Wild Wild West** – Giant mechanical spider. Will Smith still apologizes for it.

2000

- *Best:* **Gladiator** – Russell Crowe yelling "Are you not entertained?!" made us all entertained.
- *Worst:* **Battlefield Earth** – John Travolta's Scientology-fueled space flop.

2001

- *Best:* **The Lord of the Rings: The Fellowship of the Ring** – Middle-earth began, and nerd culture won.
- *Worst:* **Freddy Got Fingered** – Tom Green screaming "Daddy, would you like some sausage?" Enough said.

2002

- *Best:* **The Lord of the Rings: The Two Towers** – Helm's Deep. Need I say more?
- *Worst:* **Swept Away** – Madonna + Guy Ritchie = cinematic shipwreck.

2003

- *Best:* **The Lord of the Rings: The Return of the King** – 11 Oscars, flawless victory.
- *Worst:* **Gigli** – Bennifer 1.0… and the most mocked flop of the decade.

2004

- *Best:* **Eternal Sunshine of the Spotless Mind** – Love, memory, heartbreak — and Jim Carrey *serious*.
- *Worst:* **Catwoman** – Halle Berry won an Oscar AND a Razzie in the same year. Iconic.

2005

- *Best:* **Batman Begins** – Nolan resurrected Batman from Bat-nipple hell.
- *Worst:* **Son of the Mask** – Proof Hollywood hates fun.

2006

- *Best:* **The Departed** – Scorsese finally got his Oscar. "I'm not the rat!"
- *Worst:* **Basic Instinct 2** – Sharon Stone came back… nobody asked for it.

2007

- *Best:* **No Country for Old Men** *or* **There Will Be Blood** (cinema gods spoiled us that year).
- *Worst:* **Norbit** – Eddie Murphy in fat suits again. The early 2000s were unkind.

2008

- *Best:* **The Dark Knight** – Heath Ledger's Joker. Still unmatched.
- *Worst:* **The Love Guru** – Mike Myers killed his career with this one.

2009

- *Best:* **Inglourious Basterds** – Tarantino rewrote WWII with cinema and flamethrowers.
- *Worst:* **Dragonball Evolution** – Anime fans still haven't forgiven Hollywood.

Extra Stay-at-Home Date Ideas You Could Add

- ☐ **Cook-Off Challenge** – Pick one ingredient (like eggs, chocolate, or hot sauce) and each make a dish. Judge on creativity and taste.
- ☐ **Blindfolded Taste Test** – Try random foods blindfolded and guess what they are.
- ☐ **Karaoke Night** – DIY karaoke using YouTube lyric videos, or apps like Smule.
- ☐ **At-Home Escape Room Kits** – Printable or boxed kits let you solve mysteries without leaving the living room.
- ☐ **DIY Spa Night** – Face masks, bathrobes, foot baths, candles — go full relaxation mode.
- ☐ **Mixology Night** – Compete to make the best new cocktail using whatever you've got at home.
- ☐ **Art Swap** – Draw or paint portraits of each other (good or bad, it's funny either way).
- ☐ **Video Game Night** – From Mario Kart to Just Dance, pick co-op or versus games.
- ☐ **Theme Night** – Pick a country (Italy, Japan, Mexico) and cook food, play music, and dress in theme.
- ☐ **Home Planetarium** – Get a star projector or use an app to turn your ceiling into the night sky.
- ☐ **Build LEGO or Models Together** – Either freestyle or follow a kit (bonus: blindfold one builder while the other gives instructions).
- ☐ **Dream Vacation Planning** – Pick a place you want to visit and plan the trip as if it's happening tomorrow.
- ☐ **Photo Album Night** – Go through old photos together, make a scrapbook, or create a joint digital album.
- ☐ **Improv Night** – Play improv prompts (like "Whose Line Is It Anyway") or try comedy skits.
- ☐ **Pet Training Date** – If you have a pet, teach them a new trick together.

☐ **Make a Vision Board** – Combine goals, magazine cutouts, and dreams on a big poster.

☐ **DIY Science Night** – Try simple at-home experiments (volcano, oobleck, balloon rockets).

☐ **Poetry Slam** – Write silly or romantic poems for each other and perform them dramatically.

☐ **Board Game Building** – Invent your own board game together and playtest it.

Other Ideas That Really Need No Explanation:

☐ Visit your favorite book store, or have a cozy reading day at home
☐ Put together the ultimate song playlist
☐ Play bingo
☐ Make your own waterpark in the backyard
☐ Play some poker!
☐ Babysit together
☐ Deck the house in fairy lights for zen ambiance!
☐ Throw a garden party for two
☐ Hit a morning movie - or watch it in bed!
☐ Redecorate a room in your house or paint a room
☐ Go happy hour hopping, or enjoy an at-home bar crawl instead!
☐ Have a staycation at home
☐ Play Guitar Hero or other interactive video games together.
☐ Watch early morning cartoons and make breakfast together.
☐ Give each other a foot soak, pedicure, and foot massage using fancy lotions. Or do the whole shebang with massage oil and have a complete pamper night.
☐ Play Mad Libs together.
☐ Go "eyebombing"
☐ Plan a total surprise date for your partner. Then switch roles next time.
☐ Build a blanket fort and watch movies in your PJs.
☐ Do a book club together
☐ Read each other's favorite books or your favorite children's books
☐ Have a dance off
☐ Make a parody song together

Power Couple Energy

☐ **Go donate blood together.** This one is a much shorter date idea, but it could easily be added to another date idea. It's definitely not a typical date idea, but giving blood is an awesome thing to do, so why not do it together?

☐ **Go to a local fundraising event.** Do a little good on your date and have fun in the process. There are always groups running fundraising events, and they can be a lot of fun.

☐ **Volunteer somewhere.** Loads of places are looking for volunteers. Have a volunteer date night, and you'll be doing something awesome while getting to spend time with your date. You can always volunteer at a soup kitchen or homeless shelter. My favorite is playing with the dogs at the animal shelter.

☐ **Find a public place with a lot of litter and clean it up.** Similar to the volunteering or giving blood, this one is really uncommon for a date idea. And you have to make sure your date will be into it. But if you are both up for it, cleaning up a public space can be a rewarding way to spend the afternoon.

☐ **Bring your significant other to work day.** This one is kind of a weird date, and it definitely depends on where you work. But with a lot of workplaces, you can show your SO around, and they can see what you do most days. Plus, a lot of workplaces have some great perks you can take advantage of for a date! This is probably best done on your day off but might be cool depending on the job.

☐ **Go to a local fundraising event**. Charity 5Ks, gala dinners, trivia nights, or community raffles. These events let you have fun while knowing your ticket is making a difference.

☐ **Volunteer somewhere**. Soup kitchens, homeless shelters, food pantries, or animal shelters are always in need of helping hands. Bonus points if you pick a cause you're both passionate about.

☐ **Find a public place with a lot of litter and clean it up**. Grab gloves, trash bags, and maybe a speaker for music. Make it fun and rewarding by seeing the immediate difference you create.

☐ **Bring your significant other to work day**. This one depends on your workplace, but sometimes sharing your professional world can make for a unique and personal "philanthropy" twist.

☐ **Design Your Dream Business Together.** Create a pretend (or real) startup: name, product, logo, mission. You'll learn who's the visionary and who's the operator real fast.

☐ **Record a Podcast Episode Interviewing Each Other.** Ask deep, raw, and hilarious questions about success, fears, and love. Bonus: listen back a year later.

☐ **Set Yearly Goals and Vision-Board It Out.** Glass of wine, stack of magazines, and a joint Pinterest board. Manifestation is sexier when shared. I know you were worried, but I got inspirational journals too.

Pick up any of my inspirational therapy books at my website.

https://yourdatingunexpert.com/paperback-payback#inspirational-therapy

☐ **Do a Mini "CEO Day."** Book a café corner or coworking space. Bring laptops, coffee, and ambition. Plan your empire, quarterly review style.

☐ **Train for a 5K Together.** Morning jogs, matching playlists, and a finish-line selfie that says, "We don't chase, we pace."

☐ **Take a Leadership Workshop Together.** Learn communication, emotional intelligence, or breaking through blockages as a duo. You'll use it more than you think.

☐ **Host a Charity Event.** Throw a small dinner or online fundraiser for a cause you both care about. Nothing hotter than shared purpose.

☐ **Launch a Joint Social Media Page.** Chronicle your goals, adventures, or passion project. It's the digital version of planting a flag together.

☐ **Book a Couples Branding Photoshoot.** Power outfits, sleek poses, professional lighting. Capture your "we mean business" energy.

☐ **Start a Mini Investment Club.** Research stocks, crypto, or startups and invest tiny amounts together. It's like fantasy football for your future.

☐ **Attend a Networking Event as a Power Duo.** Walk in like you're co-founders of your own life. Handshakes, inside jokes, mutual hype.

☐ **Mentor Someone Together.** Take a younger couple or aspiring entrepreneur under your wing. Leave a legacy early.

☐ **Start a Side Hustle.** Print-on-demand, Etsy shop, or YouTube channel, doesn't matter. The shared grind builds loyalty.

☐ **Book an Inspirational Speaker or Summit Weekend.** Attend together and debrief over cocktails about what inspired you most.

☐ **Plan a Future-You Retreat.** Choose a location, set 5-year goals, and act like you already made it. Dress the part, live the vibe.

☐ **Take a Financial Wellness Course.** Learn investing, budgeting, and generational wealth, the sexiest kind of security.

☐ **Write a Couples Mission Statement.** Why you're together, what you're building, what you stand for. Corporate romance at its best.

☐ **Adopt a Cause.** Animal rescue, ocean cleanup, literacy program. Make it *your* shared contribution.

☐ **Read a Business or Mindset Book Together.** Trade insights like love notes. Debate chapters over dinner.

Top Picks by Industry Leaders

1. **Blue Ocean Strategy** – *W. Chan Kim & Renée Mauborgne*. Learn how to stop competing and start creating uncontested market space. Revolutionary for both business and life design. (My personal favorite.
2. **Atomic Habits** – *James Clear*. Small, consistent actions create massive transformations. Ideal for couples building habits together.
3. **The 7 Habits of Highly Effective People** – *Stephen R. Covey*. A foundational mindset manual on integrity, synergy, and leadership, basically couple's therapy disguised as productivity.

4. **Think and Grow Rich** – *Napoleon Hill*. The OG mindset book. Vision, persistence, and faith in action.
5. **Start with Why** – *Simon Sinek*. Because the most magnetic leaders and relationships know their why.
6. **The Mountain Is You** – *Brianna Wiest*. Emotional intelligence meets personal accountability. A must-read for anyone ready to stop self-sabotaging success.
7. **The 4-Hour Workweek** – *Tim Ferriss*. Redefine success, income, and freedom. Learn to automate your life and live intentionally, together.
8. **Daring Greatly** – *Brené Brown*. Vulnerability as strength. Essential for couples who lead with courage instead of perfection.
9. **You Are a Badass at Making Money** – *Jen Sincero*. Rewire your mindset about wealth and worth. Funny, sharp, and totally affirming.
10. **The Subtle Art of Not Giving a F*ck** – *Mark Manson*. Clarity through chaos. Learn what actually matters and stop wasting energy on what doesn't.
11. **Leaders Eat Last** – *Simon Sinek*. Build trust, empathy, and resilience in teams and relationships.
12. **The E-Myth Revisited** – *Michael E. Gerber*. Why most small businesses fail and how to fix it. Perfect if you're building something from scratch together.
13. **The Millionaire Fastlane** – *MJ DeMarco*. A blunt, modern look at how to build real wealth through leverage and mindset shifts.
14. **Deep Work** – *Cal Newport*. Master focus in a distracted world. It's productivity therapy for the ambitious.
15. **The One Thing** – *Gary Keller & Jay Papasan*. Learn to cut through the noise and focus on what drives everything else.
16. **The Alchemist** – *Paulo Coelho*. A poetic fable about purpose and destiny. Read it when you need reminding that you're on the right path.
17. **The Psychology of Money** – *Morgan Housel*. How emotion, ego, and behavior shape financial outcomes. The truth behind every "money argument."
18. **Can't Hurt Me** – *David Goggins* A wake-up call in book form. Discipline, grit, and self-mastery, no excuses.
19. **The 48 Laws of Power** – *Robert Greene*. Dark, strategic, and deeply human. Read together and debate every chapter like a power couple book club. (He also has another one of my ultimate favorites, *The Art of Seduction.*)
20. **Girlboss** – *Sophia Amoruso*. An unapologetic take on female entrepreneurship, hustle, and reinvention.
21. **Good to Great** – *Jim Collins*. Why some companies and people break through and others don't. Data meets destiny.
22. **The Power of Now** – *Eckhart Tolle*. Presence as a business and spiritual edge. For couples balancing ambition with peace.
23. **The War of Art** – *Steven Pressfield*. Creativity, resistance, and the courage to finish what you start.

24. **The Richest Man in Babylon** – *George S. Clason.* Ancient wisdom on wealth that still beats most modern advice.

25. **The Big Leap** – *Gay Hendricks.* Break through your "upper limits" and learn to expand into success without self-sabotage.

26. **How to Win Friends and Influence People** – *Dale Carnegie.* The timeless classic on empathy, influence, and connection. If every couple read this, half of modern arguments wouldn't exist. (And, round it off with my second favorite.)

☐ **Redesign Your Home Office.** Vision boards, plants, matching chairs. Productivity is better when it looks good.

☐ **Start a "Wins" Journal.** Every day, jot down what you both accomplished. Review it monthly, champagne optional.

☐ **Pitch Each Other Your Dream Projects.** Five-minute elevator pitch style. Then help each other refine the idea like real partners.

☐ **Create a Couples Budget.** Sexy? Not yet. Empowering? Always. Align money goals and you'll never argue about them again.

☐ **Learn a Power Skill Together.** Coding, photography, copywriting, anything that builds both confidence *and* opportunity.

☐ **Design a Personal Brand Kit.** Colors, fonts, aesthetic, how you show up in the world as a pair.

☐ **Do a "Philanthropy Challenge."** Pick a cause and raise or donate a set amount by month's end. Get creative with how you make it happen.

☐ **Write Each Other LinkedIn Recommendations.** Compliment their professional side, it's like flirting in corporate.

☐ **Plan a Dream Real-Estate Tour.** Visit open houses, pretend you're shopping for your future mansion. Manifestation, but make it Zillow.

☐ **Create a Shared Bucket List.** Add 50 goals that blend adventure and ambition. Cross off one each month.

☐ **Volunteer-Vacation Together.** Travel somewhere meaningful and help a local community. Change scenery *and* lives.

☐ **Start a Shared Blog or Newsletter.** Write about what you're learning, doing, or building together. Modern power couples publish.

☐ **Plan a "Quarterly Review" Date.** Coffee, notebooks, no distractions. Reflect, adjust, celebrate, repeat.

☐ **Build a Passion Project.** It could be a podcast, cookbook, or docuseries, something that uses both of your strengths. I love a true crime, lol…that could be gold, I don't think a couple has done that yet. I just may have given you a million-dollar idea.

☐ **Do a Social Media Detox Together.** One week offline to reset focus and intimacy. Track how your energy shifts.

☐ **Take a Public-Speaking Challenge.** Toastmasters, open-mics, or pitching contests. Push each other out of comfort zones.

☐ **Plan a Community Give-Back Day.** Organize friends to volunteer together. You two are the ring-leaders, obviously.

☐ **Train for a Charity Race or Walk.** Choose a cause close to your hearts and raise awareness together.

☐ **Film a "Future Us" Video.** Record where you are now and what you want to become. Watch it every anniversary. Or, manifestation, record as your future self. The future self of where you want to be at in a year, and then watch it next year.

☐ **Join a Mastermind Group.** Surround yourselves with other ambitious duos. Steel sharpens steel.

☐ **Build a Shared Morning Routine.** Wake up early, work out, plan, and affirm together. Discipline is intimacy.

☐ **Write a Joint Letter to Your Future Selves.** Seal it for five years. You'll be shocked how much you grew.

☐ **Create a Couple's Charity Fund.** Pledge a small percent of income toward doing good, together.

☐ **End the Month with a Celebration Dinner.** Dress up, review your wins, and toast to your evolving empire.

Fresh Additions for Extra Impact

☐ **Host a Charity Garage Sale.** Clean out your closets together and donate proceeds to a cause you care about.

☐ **Adopt a Family for the Holidays.** Buy gifts or essentials for a struggling family through a charity program.

☐ **Sponsor a Child or Animal.** Many organizations let you write letters, send packages, and truly connect.

☐ **Bake Sale for a Cause.** Bake together and sell goodies to donate profits.

- [ ] **Plant Trees or Join a Community Garden**. Grow something that gives back to everyone.
- [ ] **Virtual Volunteering**. Tutor kids online, read to the blind, or support nonprofits with skills from home.
- [ ] **Donate Hair Together**. Locks of Love and similar groups accept donations to make wigs for cancer patients.
- [ ] **Make Care Packages**. Assemble hygiene kits for shelters, or snack packs for delivery drivers and mail carriers.
- [ ] **Fundraise Creatively**. Set up a trivia night, karaoke livestream, or online raffle for a charity.
- [ ] **Support a Crisis Hotline or Awareness Walk**. Join local efforts for causes like mental health, suicide prevention, or domestic violence awareness.
- [ ] **Pet Fostering**. Foster a cat or dog together. It's temporary, adorable, and makes a difference.
- [ ] **Random Acts of Kindness Day**. Pick a day to pay for coffee, hand out flowers, or write anonymous love notes around town.
- [ ] **Charity Craft Night**. Make blankets, cards, or hats to donate.

Other Ideas That Really Need No Explanation:

- [ ] Donate to a local charity
- [ ] Order takeout and support local small businesses
- [ ] Help make someone else's day by doing something kind together
- [ ] Visit a nursing home
- [ ] Visit a children's hospital with toys
- [ ] Write letters together to the military
- [ ] Bring meals to your local fire department

Concert/Festivals/ Events

☐ **Watch a movie in the park or at a drive-in movie theater.** If there are no drive-ins in your area, make your own. Buy some snacks, find somewhere scenic to park, grab a tablet, put it on the dash.

☐ **Go to a local festival or fair.** If you live in a smaller town, there might not be so many festivals. But if you live in a bigger city, there are festivals of some type almost every month. Have a look at a city calendar and see if there is a fun festival.

☐ **Hit up an art museum.** Whether you are both into art or not, an art museum can be a quiet place to walk around and have a conversation. If one or both of you are into art, you can talk about the paintings and what you think of them. If you both aren't into art, you can always play "pretend to be an expert" and make up things about the paintings and sculptures. Consistently good for a laugh.

☐ **Go see some live standup comedy.** Not the best place for conversation, but hopefully you'll both get some good laughs at the show. And as long as you both have fun on the date, that's what's important.

☐ **See a play or musical.** Support your local theater scene and check out a play. You won't be able to talk during the play, but then again you can't talk during movies either. And whether it's good or bad, you'll still have something to talk about afterward. It's a great spin on the traditional dinner and a movie.

☐ **Go to one of those dinner theater/murder mystery places.** Nothing like dinner and a show. It can be a bit expensive, but if you don't mind spending a bit more, it can make for a fun and exciting date idea.

☐ **Hit up a local artist art gallery.** Most towns and cities have at least one art gallery for one or more local artists. Go check it out and pretend you are art critics. If there is more than one art gallery, you can hop from one to the other and get an idea of the art scene in your neck of the woods.

☐ **Find a nearby quirky museum.** There are so many small quirky museums. There might just be a few in your city or town or at least not too far away. They can make for fun road trip destinations and can be a lot of fun to walk through and check out all the unique exhibits

☐ **See a local band.** It's always great to support local music, and you never know, you might find your next favorite band. It's not really conducive to conversation, but if you are both into music, it can be a great way to spend the evening.

☐ **Go to a car show.** This one can be kind of hit or miss depending on how much you both like cars. But even if you both aren't super into cars, it's a good excuse to walk around and talk. Plus, if you both have never been to a car show, it might be a cool new experience.

☐ **See what events are happening at the local university or college.** Chances are they'll have talks, events, fundraisers, etc. that you can pick and choose from. Unless you are going to college, it's unlikely that you'd think to check your local university or college for something to do. But most of them have lots of things going on all month that are open to the general public.

☐ **Go to a science center if your city has one.** Science centers are usually filled with all kinds of fun, hands-on activities. You might think that they are mostly for kids, but what are adults? Kids who got taller. It'll be fun and exciting. Plus, you'll both have lots to talk about, and you both might just learn something new.

☐ **Go to an author reading.** Bookstores and libraries regularly host author readings, and they're almost always free. It's a fun way spend an afternoon and stay on the pulse of the literary community. Plus, it'll give you something to talk about later.

☐ **Try your hands at movie / Halloween makeup and watch horror movies.** Go to the local party store, buy some fake blood or Halloween makeup. Spend some time putting it on together then curl up on the couch and have a scary movie marathon. If you love, love, love horror and want a deep dive, get my book *The Anthology of Cinema: Horror.*

https://amzn.to/4qQGW7X

☐ **Go to a town hall meeting or another local political session.** Local politics has a big impact on your daily life and can be a form of politics you can actually make a difference in. Even if it's just a local town hall meeting or a vote on some local decision. Go check it out. It may be a bit of a dull date, but it's probably a date idea you've never done!

☐ **Find a Free Concert.** No matter where you live, you can usually find a free concert or two, even if it's not an artist from Spotify's Best New Music playlist. Plan a date around it and see if you two can't find a new tune to be your song. Levitt Pavilion always has great free music every summer.

FREE CONCERT VENUES & SERIES
- Levitt Pavilion Arlington, TX
- Levitt Pavilion Dayton, OH
- Levitt Pavilion Denver, CO
- Levitt Pavilion Los Angeles, CA
- Levitt Pavilion San Jose, CA
- Levitt Pavilion Fort Lauderdale, FL
- Levitt AMP Stevens Point, WI (Pfiffner Pioneer Park)
- Levitt AMP Sheboygan, WI (Downtown summer series)
- Concerts on the Square, Madison, WI (Wisconsin Chamber Orchestra)
- River Rhythms, Milwaukee, WI (Pere Marquette Park)
- Levitt Pavilion SteelStacks, PA (Bethlehem)
- Levitt Pavilion Westport, CT

☐ **Go to an open mic night. Bonus points if one or both of you gets up on stage.** This one can be a bit hit or miss because at some open mic nights, it's a little challenging to have a conversation with all the noise. But you'll definitely have something to talk about afterward, and if one / both of you gets up on stage, it'll surely be a memorable evening.

☐ **Visit a food truck festival.** Go around from truck to truck and rate your favorites. If the winning truck has a standalone restaurant, then you already have an idea for date two!

☐ **Check out a live music venue.** Concerts can be tough for a first date, but a smaller venue makes it easier to mingle between sets.

If this truly is your first date and you need help with questions, visit my Etsy shop!

https://www.etsy.com/shop/YourDatingUnExpert

☐ **Instrumental music.** Pure sound without words. Whether it's a solo pianist filling a quiet hall or a small ensemble weaving melodies together, instrumental concerts let you focus on the music itself— textures, rhythms, and moods that feel universal. It's an intimate, emotional experience perfect for slowing down and listening deeply.

☐ **Symphonies.** Big, bold, and sweeping. A symphony concert brings together dozens of musicians to create a massive wall of sound that can move you from goosebumps to tears in a single movement. From Beethoven to modern composers, symphonies are timeless nights out that feel both classy and powerful.

☐ **Orchestras.** Think of orchestras as the engine behind many grand musical experiences: symphonies, concertos, and film scores all rely on them. Seeing a full orchestra live is breathtaking: violins, brass, woodwinds, percussion all layered together. If you've ever wanted to feel the sheer force of live music, this is it.

☐ **Operas**. Where drama meets music at full volume. Operas combine powerful singing, live orchestra, elaborate costumes, and larger-than-life stories: romance, betrayal, triumph, tragedy. Even if you don't understand the language, the emotion comes through loud and clear. It's one of the most passionate live experiences you can share.

OTHER MUSIC EXPERIENCES

☐ **Choirs & Vocal Ensembles** – From gospel choirs to chamber choirs, nothing beats the power of voices blending in harmony.

☐ **Chamber Music Concerts** – Small, intimate groups (like string quartets or piano trios) that feel deeply personal.

☐ **Jazz Clubs** – Smooth, improvisational, and often candlelit—perfect for late-night vibes.

☐ **Blues Bars** – Raw, soulful performances in intimate venues.

☐ **Rock Concerts** – Arena-sized energy with singalongs and lighters in the air.

☐ **Indie Gigs** – Discover up-and-coming bands in smaller, cozier venues.

☐ **Folk & Acoustic Nights** – Storytelling through music, often unplugged and stripped down.

☐ **World Music Festivals** – From African drumming circles to sitar recitals, global sounds can be unforgettable.

☐ **Electronic Music Shows** – High-energy DJ sets, laser lights, and beats you feel in your bones.

☐ **Experimental/Avant-Garde Music** – Offbeat, strange, but sometimes magical explorations of sound.

☐ **Musical Theatre Performances** – Broadway or local productions full of song and story.

☐ **Ballet Performances** – Music and dance woven together in timeless classics or modern pieces.

☐ **Film Score Concerts** – Symphonies performing famous soundtracks (think Star Wars or Harry Potter live with orchestra).

☐ **Silent Disco** – Everyone wears headphones and dances to their own beat—fun, quirky, and surprisingly intimate.

☐ **Street Performances & Busking** – Impromptu music in parks or subways; discover hidden gems together.

☐ **Cultural Festivals** – Celebrate music from specific traditions: mariachi, flamenco, klezmer, gamelan, etc.

☐ **Karaoke Nights** – Whether at a bar or private room, it's fun, loud, and hilarious.

- [ ] **Battle of the Bands** – See local groups compete for glory and bragging rights.
- [ ] **Acoustic Coffeehouse Shows** – Low-key, cozy, and perfect for a relaxed night.
- [ ] **Outdoor Summer Concerts** – Lawn chairs, picnic baskets, and live music under the stars.
- [ ] **Marching Bands** – Catch one at parades, college games, or festivals for big brassy energy.
- [ ] **Drum Circles** – Interactive, primal, and community-driven music experiences.
- [ ] **Music Workshops** – Learn instruments, songwriting, or even beatboxing together.
- [ ] **Immersive Music Events** – Think candlelight concerts or projection-mapped venues where visuals meet sound.

Other Ideas That Really Need No Explanation:

- [ ] Go to the local town/city show
- [ ] Visit a jazz club
- [ ] Order tickets to a film festival
- [ ] Go to exhibits like the Van Gogh or the Alice in Wonderland Experience.
- [ ] Go to dance recitals
- [ ] Music festivals
- [ ] Look up City Guides on ticket websites.

Crafting/Hoarding/ Creative Projects

☐ **Buy a load of modeling clay and see what you can make.** This is a bit of a short activity, but it's great for something to do at the park or as an evening activity at home with some wine. Let out your inner artist and make some hilarious creations.

☐ **Buy some cheap watercolor paint, get a drawing pad, do portraits of each other or dueling landscapes.** A great idea if you are both horrible at painting or are both aspiring painters. If one of you is way better than the other, it might not be the best choice. If you are both horrible at painting, it can be a hilarious way to spend a date. And if you are both good at painting, you get to connect over your love of art. Another great idea that goes along with this is to paint each other. There was this famous painter who laid out a huge canvas and threw colors on two people, their mission was to then have sex on the canvas and see what they created. Seems cool, but I guess you don't have to go to those lengths if you don't want to.

☐ **Paint and build a model you are both interested in.** Any Walmart or Target will have quite a few models for you to choose from. Pick something you both like and try painting and gluing it together. If you both enjoy it and it turns out well, maybe you found a new hobby. If it turns out terribly, at least you both can have a laugh, and you have a good story. You know like a model airplane, or a car, or whatever maybe even a dinosaur, I don't know, whatever trips your fancy.

☐ **Buy some Lego kits and put them together.** First off, your date has to like Legos. But if they do, it can be fun picking one out together and then putting it together. Perfect for a coffee shop or a trendy bar.

☐ **Give graffiti a shot but in a legal way.** Watch some tutorials online, then head to the hardware store. Grab a piece of plywood or particle board and some spray cans, and you are off to the races. You could also cut some stencils if you wanted to go that route. Use the particle board or the plywood as your canvas and have fun.

☐ **Antique shop creativity.** Make up histories for the items, buy old photos and make up identities and maybe put them in a photo album, buy an old appliance or machine and try to use it, restore an old piece of furniture. Antique stores have a lot of neat stuff in them. You'll both probably come home with some neat trinkets or decorations for your house. Plus, you get to guess what some of the old tools/appliances were used for. Lots to talk about and check out in antique stores.

☐ **Find a project on Pinterest or Instructables and make it together.** This works well because it gets you both working together. And once you've finished the project, you can look with pride on your creation or if it's less than perfect, you can always have a good laugh. Plus, there are so many projects out there you are sure to find one that both of you are excited about doing.

☐ **Origami somewhere nice.** Even if you've never tried origami, it's something you can pick up and start learning. It's a lot more fun with some beautiful scenery. Find yourselves someplace nice and fold away.

☐ **Paint some pottery.** There are quite a few places, usually at a mall, where you can go and paint some pottery. Then they fire them, and you've got a souvenir from your date!

☐ **Get some coloring books and color.** This one is on the super relaxed side. It'll give you lots of time to talk and can be quite soothing. Just make sure it's something your date will enjoy. You can do it at a park or at a coffee shop.

☐ **Budget mad scientist/inventor.** Assign yourselves a budget of 10 or 20 dollars. Then go to Walmart or the Dollar Store and see what awesome contraption you can cobble together using only the things you bought with your budget. Creativity meets crafts. It's cheap, fun, and you'll probably get a good story out of it!

☐ **Get some sidewalk chalk and get creative.** Cheap, fun, and good for a laugh. It's more fun than you'd expect making the concrete and asphalt your canvas, even if you are both terrible at drawing.

☐ **Make a time capsule.** This is another unique date idea that will be interesting to some and boring to others. So, make sure you are both game. After you make sure it's something you are both interested in, get yourselves a waterproof container and fill it with all kinds of cool stuff. Then find some random place to bury it.

☐ **Go to a science center if your city has one.** Science centers are usually filled with all kinds of fun, hands-on activities. You might think that they are mostly for kids, but what are adults? Kids who got taller. It'll be fun and exciting. Plus, you'll both have lots to talk about, and you both might just learn something new.

☐ **Build and launch a rocket.** They are less expensive than you might imagine, and they can be fun to put together. But the real fun part is when you launch them. They are a great project to work on together, and you both can share in the experience of launching it.

☐ **Do an Arduino or Raspberry Pi project together.** This one is definitely a bit technical, but it's easier than you might think. There is a ton of documentation out there to help you along and plenty of sample projects to choose from. Perfect if you both like tinkering.

☐ **Brainstorm a new product or business.** Yeah, so this is kind of a weird one. It sounds super boring but can actually be a lot of fun if you both get into it. That being said, you and your date need to be relatively creative to pull it off. But if you do, you can find out a lot about the other person, what they like, what their skills are, and who knows you might come up with a business idea you would like to try.

☐ **Get stuff done date.** Okay so this sounds horrible, but it actually can be fun, and it's definitely productive. Oh, and it's meant mostly for couples who live together. Find some chores or stuff you can do together, blast some music, and open up a bottle of wine or a few beers. It's a way to make getting stuff done a little more fun, and you get to spend some time together. Like paint or redecorate a room.

☐ **Make matching t-shirts.** You can either get iron on ones, or you can get a company to print the designs on a shirt and send them to you. But the fun part is designing your shirts. Making them as ridiculous as possible. If neither of you has done much digital design, I would recommend checking out Canva for putting the images together.

☐ **Make masks.** Most craft stores will carry some type of blank masks, but if they don't, there is always Amazon. Then just get together hang out and decorate your masks. You can both do your own thing or have them based on a theme. Whatever works for both of you. Don't worry if they turn out horrible, that's part of the fun. Make sure to get some photos together after you finish!

☐ **Take turns drawing a picture.** One person draws one part, and then the other does the next part. Or if you want a really interesting picture, one person draws until a timer runs out and then the next person goes.

☐ **Make a collage.** Test your artist prowess by making a collage, it takes a while and provides you both with a lot of time to chat and get to know each other. Plus, it pairs pretty well with drinks.

☐ **Make flip books.** This is another creative date idea that might not fill a full evening, but it is a great way to spend time together doing something creative. It'll take the pressure off talking by giving you both something to do, and at the end, you'll have a fun flip book. You could even put them together so that where one leaves off the other person's begins.

☐ **Get lyrical and write an original song, bonus points if you can also bust out a tune for it and sing it together.** This is a date idea that can be done at a bar or coffee shop, at least the writing can be, you might want to do the actual singing somewhere else. It can be a blast collaborating and is a great way to get creative. Just make sure to have fun with it and don't take it too seriously.

☐ **Take some trial fitness classes.** Most fitness places have trial classes for free. Give one or two of them a shot. It'll make for a lively date, and you might even find a class that you are really into.

☐ **Make some YouTube videos, whether they be instructional, funny, or whatever.** Having a common goal or task can be a great way to have a date. And what better than to make goofy videos to put on YouTube. Even if you don't end up posting the videos, it can be a lot of fun making them together and then looking over them.

☐ **Make slow motion videos with your phone.** Most cell phones these days have a slow-motion feature on them. You would be surprised how cool everyday stuff looks when you smash it or crush it. You could also do some stunts. A full grown adult trying to do something they used to do all the time as kids can be pretty hilarious. Just make sure not to get injured.

☐ **Attempt to learn calligraphy.** So, attempt is the key word here. You first few tries will probably be a bit laughable, but it's easy to start because there are plenty of video tutorials online and beginner pens aren't crazy expensive. So, give it a shot, be patient, and just remember failures can be as fun or more fun than successes.

☐ **Invite a guest storyteller.** You've been swapping stories for a few phone calls, maybe it's time to turn to the storytelling experts. The Moth, a globally renowned event series and podcast, features live vignettes of real human experiences. You'll laugh, tear up, and have some new content for your endless phone calls with your virtual lover. You can "buy tickets" by making a gift via the Moth website, and send your date a calendar invite for showtime.

☐ **Do a themed photo shoot (professional or amateur).** Time to get all dressed up and get goofy. You could stick with one theme or try a few themes. Professional photoshoots are always great, but this one works just as well with cell phone cameras.

☐ **Write letters to folks who might want them or folks who don't.** Are you both passionate about something? Write a letter to someone who might be able to do something about it. Love a celebrity or musician? Write them a fan letter. Write a bunch of letters to a bunch of people. Your local representative, celebrities, companies, prisoners, random pen pals in different countries. People underestimate the power of a handwritten letter. You might even hear back from them!

☐ **Take a painting class.** The couple who crafts together, stays together. Right?

☐ **Go to a poetry reading.** Not someone who can muster up sweet nothings on your own? Let someone else come up with the romantic words to set the mood.

<u>Other Ideas That Really Need No Explanation:</u>

- ☐ See a fortune teller
- ☐ Do a live drawing class
- ☐ Draw pictures (or caricatures!) of each other.
- ☐ Buy an inexpensive face painting kit and paint each others' faces (now this is a selfie opportunity!)
- ☐ Make a ridiculous video on your smartphones, using one of the many apps available.
- ☐ Design and build a gingerbread house together.
- ☐ Build or paint a simple piece of furniture together.
- ☐ Do a photo shoot together with ridiculous outfits and crazy poses.

Shopping/Browsing

☐ **Play tour guide and take them to your favorite spots.** By being a tour guide, you can share some of the places you really enjoy and see if they enjoy the same types of things you do. Plus, you are already familiar with the place so you can show them around and make sure they get the best experience possible.

☐ **Do a pub crawl, coffee shop crawl, thrift store crawl, or any other type of crawl you want.** Pick a theme, plot some of them on a map, and go! Works well with some of the other date ideas like renting scooters or bikes to ride around town.

☐ **Take a mini road trip to someplace not too far away.** Research what there is to do in a town close by and choose something you both will be interested in. It's like a super mini vacation to a nearby city.

☐ **Go to Target or Walmart, buy cheap RC cars, then race/crash/destruction derby them.** There are all kinds of fun things you can do. Set up courses and jumps. Race them. Play tag with them. Cheap is key though. Some of the RC cars can get crazy expensive.

☐ **Play fake tour guide/art expert.** Go to a museum or historical location. Pretend to be the tour guide or expert and make up outrageous "facts" about the art or the history of the area for your date. Then switch roles. Bonus points if you pick up random people for your tours.

☐ **Drive around looking for yard sales and see if you can find any cool stuff.** It's like treasure hunting! You can find out what kind of stuff they are into and maybe find some super cool things for yourself. Plus driving around looking at random people's stuff leads to some funny conversations.

☐ **Go to an old cemetery and look at the graves.** So, this is definitely not everyone's idea of a good date. And it really should not be your first or second date. It's much better for couples who have been together for a while. But a lot of people enjoy the peaceful nature of graveyards and guessing at the stories from the gravestones or trying to find the oldest graves.

☐ **Go to a flea market.** Going to a flea market can yield some interesting treasures. You'll always see something unexpected at a flea market. And you can chat about the items and vendors you see.

☐ **Get lost locally, take back roads you've never taken try to find interesting stuff that isn't on Google maps.** Turn off the GPS and see if you can get yourself lost in your hometown. Going down roads you've never been down can feel like an adventure, and you never know what hidden gems you might find.

☐ **Go to an auction.** There are all kinds of auctions going on at any point in time. See if you can find an interesting one near you. You don't need to buy anything, but it can be fun to bid on stuff together. Just getting out and doing something different can be a lot of fun.

☐ **Try on ridiculous clothing/outfits you would never normally wear.** The mall or a thrift store is the perfect place to do this. It can get hilarious really quick. And who knows, you might find that you look terrific in an entirely different style than you usually rock. Then, are you ballsy enough to go out for a night on the town with that outfit? I think so!

☐ **People watch at a crowded location.** Sitting in a crowded place takes the pressure off having a conversation. You can just chat idly about this or that. Or you can discuss the people passing by and what their lives might be like. This one is really dependent on the person. Some people love sitting and people watching, and some don't. One fun thing to do is create imaginary and fantastical backstories for the people you are watching.

☐ **Go to the nearest airport and get to where you can watch planes take off.** You'll have to find somewhere that isn't unbelievably noisy. I don't want you all to be losing your hearing. But if you can find a great spot, it really is neat to see these giant tubes of metal defying gravity.

☐ **Find an interesting neighborhood or suburb and walk and talk.** Whether it's a super wealthy area or a historic district, find a cool neighborhood and walk around. You'll be surprised at all the details you pick while walking that you might not normally see while driving.

☐ **Visit an outdoor market.** Whether it's a flea market or a farmer's market, wandering from booth to booth is a fun way to get to know one another.

☐ **Browse a bookstore.** Books are the ultimate conversation starters, so you'll probably have tons to chat about. Bonus: Most shops have coffee spots, so you can discuss your finds over a brew, too.

Other Ideas to do in a bookstore

☐ **Bookstore Confessions.** Meet at a bookstore, each pick a book that says something about you: past, present, or future. Trade and explain your choices over coffee.

☐ **Bookstore Date with a Twist.** Pick a book you think the other would secretly love but never admit to.

☐ **Bookstore Scavenger Hunt.** Set a timer and find the weirdest, sexiest, or most random titles for each other to read aloud.

☐ **Blind Grab at a Bookstore.** Buy the first book you touch without looking.

☐ **HomeGoods/TJ Maxx/Ross Madness.** Head to HomeGoods and take turns filming each other describing the most absurd, unnecessary item you can find. Think "a winter coat, like with buttons, like a puff jacket…for your wine bottle. (Yes, those exist.)" Your partner's job? Deadpan reply, "Oh, I think we have that and in an array of fabulous colors." It's equal parts improv, inside joke, and couple's therapy disguised as retail chaos.

Other Ideas That Really Need No Explanation:

☐ Get lost in IKEA
☐ Go coupon shopping for activities
☐ Take a long walk to dinner
☐ Take a chopper ride
☐ Visit an odd, unusual or quirky tourist attraction together. Check out Atlas Obscura for some really unique sites!
☐ Window shop together.
☐ Take a day trip together and explore the next town over.

Budget or Challenge Dates

☐ **$10 Thrift-Store Outfit Date.** Each of you gets ten bucks to build the other's look. Model your finds like it's Paris Fashion Week on clearance.

☐ **Dollar Tree Cooking Challenge.** Shop only at a dollar store. Anything edible is fair game. The meal might be tragic or genius.

☐ **Free Date Marathon.** Spend an entire day together without spending a cent. Walks, window-shopping, library visits, people-watching. Creativity = currency.

☐ **The $5 Night Showdown.** Who can plan the better date with only five dollars? Loser does dishes.

☐ **Barter Date.** Trade skills or favors with friends for your outing: photos, massages, pet-sitting, so your night out costs nothing.

☐ **Coin-Flip Adventure.** Let a single coin decide every choice, left or right, sweet or salty, stay or go in. Fate's your chauffeur.

☐ **Park Picnic Remix.** Bring whatever's already in your fridge, even if it's cereal and pickles. Make it look intentional.

☐ **Drive-In DIY.** Project a movie on your garage or a sheet outside. Popcorn mandatory, ticket price zero.

☐ **Coupon Night.** Use only coupons or reward points for dinner, dessert, and gas. Make it a sport.

☐ **Garage Sale Scavenger Hunt.** With ten dollars each, find the funniest or most random treasure before noon.

☐ **Mystery Ingredient Cook-Off.** Each pick one random pantry item; both must use both ingredients somehow.

☐ **DIY Photo Booth.** Hang a bedsheet, grab your phone's timer, and stage a full couple shoot. Free glamour, priceless chaos.

☐ **Recycled Gift Exchange.** Find something in your house you no longer want and re-gift it dramatically.

☐ **Thrift-Flip Challenge.** Buy one old object and transform it into art or décor before next week's date.

☐ **Board-Game Borrow.** Borrow games from friends or the library and host a mini-tournament with ridiculous prizes.

☐ **Neighborhood Talent Show.** Perform songs, jokes, or poems for each other, bonus points if neighbors join in.

☐ **Farmers Market Face-Off.** With fifteen bucks total, buy ingredients for a single dish. Cook, then judge like *MasterChef*.

☐ **$20 Gas-Tank Getaway.** Fill up with twenty bucks and drive until half the tank's gone. Whatever town you reach = the adventure.

☐ **Upcycle Night.** Use scrap fabric, cardboard, or jars to make something "sellable." Loser has to list theirs online.

☐ **Streaming-Only Supper.** Cook a meal entirely from recipe videos you find that night. No repeats allowed.

☐ **Potluck with Strangers.** Each invite one friend, but don't tell the other who. Everyone brings a cheap dish. Chaos ensues.

☐ **Zero-Waste Day.** Try to generate no trash for 24 hours. Bond over creative problem-solving and smug eco-bragging rights.

☐ **Garage Band Jam.** Download free music apps and create a song using only virtual instruments.

☐ **Dollar-Menu Taste Test.** Hit three fast-food places and rank each dollar-menu item like food critics.

☐ **Home-Movie Festival.** Film short clips throughout the week on your phones, then premiere them with popcorn.

☐ **Plant-Swap Stroll.** Exchange cuttings or seeds with neighbors. Build your couple garden from freebies.

☐ **Sidewalk Chalk Art Date.** Compete to draw each other's portraits on the driveway. Winner gets bragging rights till it rains.

☐ **Coffee-Shop Camp-Out.** Buy one drink, stay for hours, and co-write something: a story, business plan, or bucket list.

☐ **Budget Travel Night.** Spin the globe, land on a random country, and recreate it with whatever's already in your pantry.

☐ **Tiny Gourmet.** Only eat foods that cost under a dollar but plate them like fine dining.

☐ **$10 Decor Makeover.** Redecorate a corner of your home using thrift finds, candles, and creativity.

☐ **Public Transportation Adventure.** Ride the bus or subway to the last stop just to see what's there.

☐ **Window-Shopping Wish List.** Visit luxury stores and pretend you're rich. Assign each other imaginary budgets.

☐ **Cook-What-You-Have Night.** No grocery run allowed. Invent a dish from whatever's at home.

☐ **Free Museum Day.** Hunt down a free-entry day or community event and play culture critics.

☐ **BYO Movie Snacks.** Sneak homemade treats into the theater. Compare snack smuggling strategies.

☐ **Street-Performer Safari.** Walk downtown and tip every performer with spare change. Rate the acts. If there are no street performers in your town, guess what, you will be the street performer and perform in your downtown area.

☐ **Park Workout Date.** Create a mini fitness circuit using benches, steps, and playground gear. End with smoothies.

☐ **Compliment Cards.** Write five compliments each on scrap paper and hide them for the other to find through the week.

☐ **Garage-Sale Flip.** Buy one strange item and resell it online for profit.

☐ **Rainy-Day Race.** When it rains, set a timer and see who can find the best indoor free activity nearby.

☐ **DIY Wine Tasting.** Grab the cheapest bottles you can find and host a blind taste test. Pretend to be sommeliers.

☐ **Cooking with YouTube Chefs.** Randomly pick a recipe video by scrolling eyes-closed. Whatever appears = dinner.

☐ **Handmade Gift Exchange.** Create small crafts or love notes with materials you already own.

☐ **Picnic Under the Stars.** Free, eternal, and better than any restaurant. Bring leftover dessert and wish lists for life.

Get to Know Each Other/ Favorites/ Nostalgia

☐ **Redo a field trip you enjoyed as a kid.** We all took field trips as a kid. But when have you taken one as an adult? Go get in touch with your inner elementary school self and relive an awesome field trip from the past.

☐ **Make a bucket list, talk about all the things you put on yours, steal good ideas and brainstorm ideas together.** This is a great "get to know you" date idea. You can find out more about their goals and aspirations and see if they match or complement your own. It's a perfect activity for a coffee shop.

☐ **Buy a puzzle and hit a coffee shop.** Like the coloring date idea, this one is really relaxing. And there is a lot of time to talk and get to know each other. You just have to make sure that your date likes puzzles rather than finding them dull. Or do one at home with wine and put together a custom photo puzzle.

☐ **Pretend to be an ultra-wealthy couple, test drive expensive cars or go to open houses.** It can be a lot of fun pretending to be someone else. You can make up fake names and backstories for yourselves as well. See how well you can pull it off.

☐ **Read One Another's Tarot Cards.** Even tarot newbies will enjoy a date spent deep-diving into how to read tarot or oracle cards. You might be surprised what you two learn about one another in the process!

☐ **Spend a Night at The Museum.** Look online for times that local museums offer free admission (Pro tip: It's usually in the evening!) and roam around with your special someone, picking out your favorite pieces or exhibits.

☐ **Play Truth Or Dare.** Revisit the infamous childhood game of Truth or Dare by walking around town taking turns asking each other the age-old question. You'll learn tons about each other and have a total blast! Play the same game at home with a more scandalous twist, if you dare.

☐ **Share Embarrassing Photos.** Headgear, frizzy hair and some freaky-looking sweaters? Check! Collect some old photos, be they funny baby pics or cringy high school grad pics, and trade them with your date. Not only will it provide some good laughs, but it will keep the conversation flowing and help you both see different sides of one another.

☐ **Join a fun interesting meetup together.** There are a lot of meetups these days, and they cover almost every interest. Find one that you think you'll both find interesting and give it a shot. You can search for meetups in "your town/city" on Google or see what meetup.com has to offer. Plus, you might meet some of your new best friends.

☐ **Power out date night.** Pretend like there is no power and no charge in your devices. Party like it's 1799! Break out the candles and pull out some card or board games or whatever you usually do when the power goes out. If you are up for it, tell ghost stories. Who didn't love Are You Afraid of the Dark?

☐ **Find your new favorite show.** Before the date, both of you should scout out a few candidates, then watch an episode or two together and decide yay or nay. If you both give an enthusiastic yay, it's binge time! This is another that works best with couples that have been together for a while. Go all out with Russian Roulette-style of have Netflix pick it for you with their random button.

☐ **Listen to a podcast or audiobook together someplace nice.** This is definitely not everyone's idea of a great date, but a lot of people might enjoy being with the person they love, in a nice location, listening to a good book or podcast. Then if you want some talking time, you can always pause and discuss the book or podcast. A great idea if you are on a road trip as well.

☐ **Go to your local library, rent a book, take turns reading to each other and use character voices.** With this one, the sillier it is, the more fun it is. Find an interesting fictional book and create some bombastic character voices. You can take turns reading, or each of you does a character. Look through very old newspapers or magazines at the library. Some folks will find this to be super boring, and some will find it extremely interesting. It all depends on the person. But it can be really interesting to find out what people 70 or 80 years ago were concerned or interested in. You'll probably find that there are a lot of parallels to today's news. Plus, old ads are really cool. Just remember when you are going through them not to get too loud.

- [ ] **Get a couple's massage.** This is one of the more expensive ideas on this list, but they are a great way to relax together and have some downtime. Afterward, I'd have something relaxing planned like sitting on a bench near a lake or river to continue that chill vibe.

- [ ] **Take turns listening to each other's favorite songs.** This date idea works really well for those couples who love music. You can introduce each other to awesome music. Nothing bonds people faster than sharing in something that you both love.

- [ ] **Movies from your childhood night.** Find some movies that had a big impact on both your childhoods, pop some popcorn, and enjoy your trip down memory lane. It will be a great way to connect on some common ground, and you might be surprised at all the things you don't remember about your favorite childhood movies.

- [ ] **A book club for two.** Each of you picks a short story, novella, or graphic novel for the other to read, and then you get together on the date and discuss them over drinks. This one is an excellent idea if you are both into books. But I wouldn't suggest it unless you are both avid readers. If someone doesn't read much, it might make them feel like they are preparing for a book report.

- [ ] **Test your cosmic compatibility.** Whether you swear by your horoscope or think it's hooey, embrace the cosmic bizarreness of the times by reading your horoscopes to each other. What definitely describes you and what doesn't?

- [ ] **Plan a day trip.** This is a great idea for someone who you know as a friend, but want to get to know in a more romantic way. Head out of town for a ski or beach trip, and enjoy some one-on-one time.

☐ **Get deep.** Maybe you're a big Brene Brown fan, or you're just running low on ways to get deeper while distanced. "The 36 Questions That Lead to Love", published in 2015, is the best conversational road map to connect with your virtual date. Find out their dream superpower, gaze into their eyes, and start to envision what your future partnership might look like. Romantic, intellectual, and inspiring, this exercise is a must for all couples from fifth date to 50 years together. Figure out each other's love language Get the book and read it to each other and take the quiz together.

☐ **Learn to Zentangle Together.** Set up a cozy space with pens, paper, and a playlist you both love. Follow a short Zentangle tutorial or create your own flowing patterns. It's part art, part meditation, and all about relaxing side by side while your designs slowly take shape.

Other Ideas That Really Need No Explanation:

☐ Climb a tree (and unleash your inner child)
☐ Play a game from your childhood
☐ Interview each other
☐ Visit your grandparents - or give them a call if this is safer
☐ Have a country-themed date night
☐ Have dinner at a themed restaurant
☐ Go for a swim and sauna
☐ Relax at the spa
☐ Get back in touch with your inner child and finger paint together.
☐ Plan a future date you can go on together with a strict budget limit ($5, $10).
☐ Build a campfire together and enjoy sitting by it and talking. Roast marshmallow or hot dogs.
☐ Play old-fashioned playground games together: jacks, 4-square, hopscotch.
☐ Watch each other's favorite childhood movies, indulging in favorite childhood snacks while you do.

Deep Connection

Because connection doesn't happen on command, it's built in the quiet moments, the weird questions, and the vulnerability that sneaks up when you least expect it. These are the dates that make you remember why you liked each other in the first place.

☐ **The 36 Questions Night.** Take turns asking each other the famous "36 Questions to Fall in Love." Add a glass of wine, low lighting, and no distractions. The vulnerability gets real by Question 20.

Set I

1. Given the choice of anyone in the world, whom would you want as a dinner guest?
2. Would you like to be famous? In what way?
3. Before making a telephone call, do you ever rehearse what you are going to say? Why?
4. What would constitute a "perfect" day for you?
5. When did you last sing to yourself? To someone else?
6. If you were able to live to the age of 90 and retain either the mind or body of a 30-year-old for the last 60 years of your life, which would you want?
7. Do you have a secret hunch about how you will die?
8. Name three things you and your partner appear to have in common.
9. For what in your life do you feel most grateful?
10. If you could change anything about the way you were raised, what would it be?
11. Take four minutes and tell your partner your life story in as much detail as possible.
12. If you could wake up tomorrow having gained any one quality or ability, what would it be?

Set II

13. If a crystal ball could tell you the truth about yourself, your life, the future or anything else, what would you want to know?
14. Is there something that you've dreamed of doing for a long time? Why haven't you done it?
15. What is the greatest accomplishment of your life?
16. What do you value most in a friendship?
17. What is your most treasured memory?
18. What is your most terrible memory?
19. If you knew that in one year you would die suddenly, would you change anything about the way you are now living? Why?
20. What does friendship mean to you?
21. What roles do love and affection play in your life?

22. Alternate sharing something you consider a positive characteristic of your partner. Share a total of five items.

23. How close and warm is your family? Do you feel your childhood was happier than most other people's?

24. How do you feel about your relationship with your mother?

Set III

25. Make three true "we" statements each. For instance, "We are both in this room feeling ..."

26. Complete this sentence: "I wish I had someone with whom I could share ..."

27. If you were going to become a close friend with your partner, please share what would be important for him or her to know.

28. Tell your partner what you like about them; be very honest this time, saying things that you might not say to someone you've just met.

29. Share with your partner an embarrassing moment in your life.

30. When did you last cry in front of another person? By yourself?

31. Tell your partner something that you like about them already.

32. What, if anything, is too serious to be joked about?

33. If you were to die this evening with no opportunity to communicate with anyone, what would you most regret not having told someone? Why haven't you told them yet?

34. Your house, containing everything you own, catches fire. After saving your loved ones and pets, you have time to safely make a final dash to save any one item. What would it be? Why?

35. Of all the people in your family, whose death would you find most disturbing? Why?

36. Share a personal problem and ask your partner's advice on how he or she might handle it. Also, ask your partner to reflect back to you how you seem to be feeling about the problem you have chosen.

☐ **Memory Lane Drive.** Take a drive and show each other meaningful places from your past: childhood home, old hangout, favorite restaurant. Tell the stories that shaped you.

☐ **Love Letter Trade.** Write each other letters. No phones, no texts, not even ChatGPT, just old-school honesty with your old noggin. Read them aloud or swap and read privately. Either way, it's intimacy in ink.

☐ **Dream Mapping.** Grab a poster board and map out your dreams, five years from now, one year from now, or just next weekend. It's half therapy, half time travel.

☐ **Truth or Truth.** Skip the dares. Just ask each other increasingly real questions, the kind that make you pause before answering. ("What part of yourself are you still learning to like?")

50 Connection Question Examples

1. What part of yourself are you still learning to like?
2. When do you feel most misunderstood?
3. What's the worst advice you've ever followed?
4. Who was your "almost," and do you still think about them?
5. What emotion do you hide most often?
6. What's one thing you pretend not to care about but secretly do?
7. When was the last time you felt genuinely proud of yourself?
8. What do you envy in other people that you wish came naturally to you?
9. What's a truth you outgrew?
10. Who taught you how to love and who taught you how *not* to?
11. When did you first realize love wasn't always safe?
12. What story about yourself do you keep repeating that's no longer true?
13. What kind of pain makes you shut down the fastest?
14. What's one mistake you'd make all over again?
15. What's your emotional "flight pattern?" Do you run, numb, or fight?
16. Who do you become when you're scared?
17. What compliment do you never believe, even when it's true?
18. When did you last cry and pretend you didn't?
19. What do you wish someone had taught you sooner?
20. What part of your childhood still leaks into your adult relationships?
21. What's your emotional blind spot?
22. What version of yourself do you hide when you like someone?
23. What's something you'd never post online but wish people knew?
24. What memory would you erase if you could and what would that cost you?
25. What's one pattern you can't seem to break?
26. What scares you more — being loved too much or not enough?
27. What's the lie you tell yourself to stay comfortable?
28. Who brings out your worst self, and why do you let them?
29. What's something you've forgiven but not forgotten?
30. What part of your story still feels unfinished?
31. When's the last time you sabotaged something good?
32. What's your biggest fear about being truly seen?
33. What's one apology you owe yourself?
34. What kind of love feels the most foreign to you?
35. What's one truth about you that people never guess?
36. When did you last feel like the villain?
37. Who would you call if everything fell apart at 3 a.m.?
38. What's something that used to define you that no longer does?

39. What's your emotional love language, not what you say, but what you *do* when you care?
40. When's the last time you lied to protect someone's feelings?
41. What belief do you hold that constantly gets tested?
42. What's your secret addiction not a substance, but a pattern?
43. When do you feel most powerful?
44. What's one thing you've never told your parents?
45. What memory do you revisit when you need to remember who you are?
46. What kind of peace are you chasing right now?
47. What's the hardest thing to forgive yourself for?
48. What's one truth about love you didn't believe until it happened to you?
49. When did you realize you were done with pretending?
50. What would you want someone to understand about you before they love you?

☐ **The "What If" Game.** Ask ridiculous hypotheticals and meaningful ones alike. "What if we met in another life?" "What if money didn't exist?" It's equal parts philosophy and flirting.

50 Questions for Inspiration

1. What if we met ten years earlier, would we still have liked each other?
2. What if you could relive one day exactly as it happened, which one?
3. What if every person you ever loved showed up in one room, who would you talk to first?
4. What if you could read minds for one hour, who's the first person you'd listen to?
5. What if you had to describe yourself with no words, how would you show who you are?
6. What if the version of you from five years ago could see you now, would they be proud or shocked?
7. What if heartbreak was the price of creativity, would you still choose to love?
8. What if you could erase one memory, would you, or do you need the lesson?
9. What if every lie you ever told appeared tattooed on your skin, what would show first?
10. What if you woke up tomorrow and your life was completely different, what's the first thing you'd check for?
11. What if love really did have an expiration date, how would you spend the time left?
12. What if you had to choose between peace and passion, which would you keep?
13. What if the person who hurt you most showed up to apologize, would you let them?

14. What if you had to start your life over with only the lessons, not the memories, what would you rebuild first?
15. What if money didn't exist, what would you actually do with your days?
16. What if your younger self could ask you one question, what would it be?
17. What if your soulmate was nothing like your type?
18. What if every decision you ever made was filmed, would you watch it?
19. What if you could send one text to your 80-year-old self, what would you ask?
20. What if love was a limited resource, would you spend it carefully or recklessly?
21. What if you could time travel to any moment in history, but only as an observer?
22. What if someone handed you a folder with the truth about everyone you know, would you open it?
23. What if your favorite memory fades completely unless you tell someone, who would you tell?
24. What if every time you kissed someone, they could see your last heartbreak?
25. What if you only had one year left to live, what would you finally stop pretending to care about?
26. What if you could live inside any movie for a week, which would you choose?
27. What if you were invisible for one day, where would you go first?
28. What if you could meet one person from the past, who, and what would you ask?
29. What if you had to teach a class on love, what would the first lesson be?
30. What if you could trade places with anyone for 24 hours, who gets your life?
31. What if you could know one secret, but it changes how you see everything?
32. What if you fell in love with someone you could never touch, would words be enough?
33. What if you could undo one "no," what would it change?
34. What if every person came with a soundtrack, what would yours sound like right now?
35. What if your biggest fear came true, would you survive it or become it?
36. What if your dreams were memories from another life, what do you think you've already lived?
37. What if every thought you had for a day came true, how chaotic would it get?
38. What if you had to live one week completely offline, what would you fill it with?
39. What if your ex wrote a book about you, what would the title be?

40. What if you had to describe love without using the word *love*, what would you call it?
41. What if every person you meet is a mirror, who are you attracting lately?
42. What if happiness was a skill, not a feeling, would you practice it?
43. What if you could see ten years into your future, would you look?
44. What if everything that ever went wrong was secretly for you, not against you, would that change how you feel about the past?
45. What if every time you told the truth, it cost you something, would you still be honest?
46. What if your biggest heartbreak was actually your initiation?
47. What if the universe was trying to get your attention, what sign would finally make you listen?
48. What if you met the person you were meant to be *before* you were ready, would you let them go or learn fast?
49. What if you had to love yourself out loud, not just in your head, what would it sound like?
50. What if everything you've ever wanted showed up right now, could you actually handle it?

50 Questions - Flirty Edition

1. What if we had met on vacation, would we have still come home?
2. What if every time you kissed someone, you saw their favorite memory, would you still kiss me?
3. What if we were the last two people on earth, who'd go insane first?
4. What if we had to fake-date for a month, how long before it stopped feeling fake?
5. What if every time we touched, we had to say what we were thinking, would you still touch me?
6. What if your ex showed up right now, would you pull me closer or play it cool?
7. What if the way someone looked at you could give you chills, would I be in danger?
8. What if I dared you to tell me your most distracting thought right now, would you do it?
9. What if we were trapped in an elevator for two hours, how would you kill the time?
10. What if every kiss revealed a secret, would you still want one?
11. What if we had to go on a date with no talking, how would you make me laugh?
12. What if I could hear your internal monologue for five minutes, would I blush or laugh?
13. What if every time you lied, your shirt disappeared, how honest would you be?

14. What if we switched lives for a day, what's the first thing you'd do as me?

15. What if I said I could tell what kind of kisser you are just by looking, want me to prove it?

16. What if you had to flirt using only movie quotes, which one would you choose first?

17. What if we had to reenact a romantic scene from a film, which one are you picking?

18. What if your love life had a title, would it be a rom-com, thriller, or horror?

19. What if I told you I can always tell when someone's thinking about me, what should I be feeling right now?

20. What if I asked you to text me something you'd never say out loud, would you?

21. What if you had to plan a spontaneous date tonight, where would we end up?

22. What if every time you complimented someone, you had to mean it, what's yours for me?

23. What if we had to share a bed but couldn't touch, who'd break the rule first?

24. What if your phone screen showed your most recent thought, should I be worried?

25. What if we kissed right now and the world glitched, would you risk it?

26. What if someone could only fall in love with your voice, what would you whisper first?

27. What if you could pause time for one hour, what would you do with me frozen next to you?

28. What if I could read your mind for ten seconds, how long before you looked away?

29. What if we woke up married in Vegas, would you panic or make breakfast?

30. What if your favorite scent suddenly smelled like me, what memory would it pull up first?

31. What if we had to confess a crush to someone tonight, would you pick truth or dare?

32. What if you could see someone's chemistry with you as a color, what color are we?

33. What if we had to take a shot every time we made eye contact, how drunk would we be?

34. What if I told you the way you laugh is my favorite sound, what would you do with that power?

35. What if you could only flirt through text for 24 hours, how would you keep me hooked?

36. What if I asked you to tell me a secret that would change how I see you, what would it be?
37. What if we had to go skinny dipping to save the world, would humanity survive?
38. What if your favorite song came on right now, would you dance with me or just watch?
39. What if someone described their perfect night, and it sounded exactly like this?
40. What if I could only say yes for the next hour, what would you ask me to do?
41. What if we swapped phones for ten minutes, would I be entertained or traumatized?
42. What if your body could talk, what would it say to me right now?
43. What if your lips had to tell a story before you kissed, what would yours be about?
44. What if I said I already know what you're thinking, would you deny it?
45. What if we got caught in the rain, would you run or pull me closer?
46. What if every time we laughed, it counted as foreplay, how far along are we?
47. What if you had to send one flirty text that would never be read aloud, what would you write?
48. What if we played Truth or Dare right now, which one would you secretly hope I pick?
49. What if the lights went out right this second, what happens next?
50. What if this was the beginning of our favorite story, how would you want it to start?

    *If you are getting a little frisky, you can see the next chapter 😊

☐ **Life Timeline Project.** Draw a timeline of your life from birth to now. Mark your biggest moments: the good, the bad, and the ones that changed everything. Then share them side by side.

☐ **Silent Dinner.** Have dinner together without speaking, just eye contact, smiles, and presence. You'll realize how much is said without words.

☐ **Read Childhood Journals or Yearbooks.** If you're brave enough, share your awkward middle school poems or yearbook messages. It's endearing, funny, and grounding.

☐ **The Values Test.** Each write down your five core values (honesty, growth, freedom, etc.) and compare lists. Talk about what they really mean to you.

☐ **Meditation Date.** Try a 10-minute guided meditation for couples. Hold hands. Breathe. It's weirdly bonding to do nothing together on purpose. I personally love guided meditations. My favorites are Jason Stephenson, The Honest Guys and Dauchsy.

☐ **The "Tell Me When" Game.** Take turns saying "Tell me when you felt..." happy, scared, proud, small, alive. It opens doors people usually keep shut. Don't worry...I got you with some questions to start.

50 Prompts

1. Tell me when you first realized love could hurt.
2. Tell me when you last felt completely safe.
3. Tell me when you laughed so hard you couldn't breathe.
4. Tell me when you knew you'd outgrown someone.
5. Tell me when you felt truly seen.
6. Tell me when you thought you'd ruined everything, but hadn't.
7. Tell me when you last cried in front of someone.
8. Tell me when you realized you were stronger than you thought.
9. Tell me when you were the most lost and how you found your way back.
10. Tell me when you last felt proud of yourself without needing validation.
11. Tell me when you first felt like an adult.
12. Tell me when you knew you were healing.
13. Tell me when you felt like you couldn't be loved and what changed.
14. Tell me when you realized someone didn't love you the way you needed.
15. Tell me when you've been the happiest version of yourself.
16. Tell me when you learned how to forgive.
17. Tell me when you knew you had to walk away.
18. Tell me when you've pretended to be okay but weren't.
19. Tell me when you've felt the most peace.
20. Tell me when you made someone proud.
21. Tell me when you felt jealous and why.
22. Tell me when you've said "I'm fine" and meant the opposite.
23. Tell me when someone surprised you in a good way.
24. Tell me when you stopped chasing something or someone.
25. Tell me when you've felt the most beautiful.
26. Tell me when you've been the most afraid to lose something.
27. Tell me when you were the bravest you've ever been.
28. Tell me when you knew you were in love.
29. Tell me when you first felt heartbreak, the real kind.
30. Tell me when you realized you were becoming like your parents.
31. Tell me when you felt misunderstood.
32. Tell me when you knew you'd hurt someone and couldn't undo it.

33. Tell me when you've had to start over.
34. Tell me when someone believed in you more than you did.
35. Tell me when you've had a moment of pure calm.
36. Tell me when you last took a risk that changed you.
37. Tell me when you realized what you actually want out of love.
38. Tell me when you let someone in who deserved it.
39. Tell me when you last surprised yourself.
40. Tell me when you stopped needing to be chosen.
41. Tell me when you realized you were the problem and fixed it.
42. Tell me when someone broke your trust and what that taught you.
43. Tell me when you've been proud of how far you've come.
44. Tell me when you laughed during the worst moment because it was all too much.
45. Tell me when you've had to be your own comfort.
46. Tell me when you've felt grateful to be alive.
47. Tell me when you've loved someone you couldn't have.
48. Tell me when you knew you'd never be the same again and it was a good thing.
49. Tell me when you've been completely honest, even when it cost you something.
50. Tell me when you last felt infinite, even if just for a second.

☐ **Recreate Your First Date.** Even if it's been years, same outfit, same meal, same jokes. It's nostalgia, but warmer the second time around.

☐ **The Compliment Challenge.** Each person has to give 10 specific compliments, not just "you're cute," but "you make me calmer when I overthink." Watch how the energy shifts.

☐ **Future You Letters.** Write a letter to your partner "from" your future self — one year, five years, or a lifetime from now. What do you hope you've built together?

☐ **Take a Personality Test Together.** Do Myers-Briggs, Enneagram, or love languages. Compare results, but go deeper, talk about where you *don't* match and why. Here are some example tests, if you can't find the real ones.

Myers-Briggs (MBTI) — 20-Item Mini Test
How to take it: For each item, pick **A** or **B**.

Scoring map: 1–5 = **E–I**, 6–10 = **S–N**, 11–15 = **T–F**, 16–20 = **J–P**. Count how many A vs B in each 5-item block. More A or B tells you your letter for that pair.

More A = E, More B = I
More A = S. More B = N
More A = T. More B = F
More A = J. More B = P

1–5 (E–I)

1. A Prefer group energy to think; B Prefer solitude to think
2. A Talk to clarify ideas; B Think to clarify, then talk
3. A Many acquaintances; B Few deep relationships
4. A Act first, reflect later; B Reflect first, act later
5. A External stimulation fuels me; B Quiet time refuels me

6–10 (S–N)

1. A Trust facts/what is; B Trust patterns/what could be
2. A Concrete, step-by-step; B Conceptual, big-picture
3. A Details before themes; B Themes before details
4. A Proven methods; B Novel approaches
5. A Present realities; B Future possibilities

11–15 (T–F)

1. A Logical consistency first; B Human impact first
2. A Critique to improve; B Encourage to inspire
3. A Fair = equal rules; B Fair = needs/context
4. A Comfortable with debate; B Prefer harmony
5. A Decide with head; B Decide with heart

16–20 (J–P)

1. A Plan it, then do it; B Explore, then decide
2. A Love checklists; B Love options
3. A Closure feels good; B Keeping it open feels good
4. A Structure → freedom; B Freedom → structure
5. A Arrive early, prepared; B Arrive flexible, adaptable

Result: Combine your four winners (e.g., ENFP, ISTJ).

Go deeper together: Share not just letters, but **where you differ** and how you can cover each other's blind spots.

Enneagram — 27-Statement Quick Sort

How to take it: Rate each statement 1–5 (1 = not me, 5 = very me). Group the items by type below, sum each type's three items, and your highest total is your likely core type. The second-highest is a likely wing.

Type 1 – The Reformer (principled, improvement)

1. I notice what's wrong and want to fix it.
2. I feel responsible for doing things the "right" way.
3. I'm hard on myself when I fall short.

Type 2 – The Giver (helpful, relational)
    4. I sense what people need and like being needed.
    5. I often put others first and forget my own needs.
    6. Appreciation matters a lot to me.

Type 3 – The Achiever (driven, image-aware)
    7. I set goals and move fast to hit them.
    8. I adapt my image to fit the room.
    9. Being seen as successful motivates me.

Type 4 – The Individualist (deep, expressive)
    10. I want a life that feels authentic and meaningful.
    11. I feel different from others, in good and hard ways.
    12. Strong feelings come in waves and color my days.

Type 5 – The Investigator (observant, private)
    13. I conserve energy and prefer lots of solo time.
    14. I like mastering topics before engaging.
    15. Too many demands feel draining.

Type 6 – The Loyalist (prepared, vigilant)
    16. I scan for risks and make backup plans.
    17. I'm loyal to people and systems I trust.
    18. Anxiety eases when I have guidance or proof.

Type 7 – The Enthusiast (optimistic, variety-seeking)
    19. I chase possibilities and reframe negatives quickly.
    20. I dislike feeling limited or stuck in pain.
    21. Plans are fun especially spontaneous ones.

Type 8 – The Challenger (direct, protective)
    22. I speak plainly and respect strength.
    23. I protect the people and spaces I care about.
    24. I'd rather take charge than be controlled.

Type 9 – The Peacemaker (steady, harmonizing)
    25. I avoid conflict and merge with others' agendas.
    26. I can minimize my own priorities to keep peace.
    27. Routine and comfort help me feel okay.

Result tips (to discuss together):
- **Triads:** 2-3-4 relate to image/heart, 5-6-7 to thinking/future, 8-9-1 to gut/instinct.
- **Stress/Growth:** Note where your type goes under stress vs security and how your partner can **support the healthy direction**.

Love Languages — 20-Item Mini Quiz

How to take it: Rate each item **1–5**. Sum per category. Highest one or two are your primary languages.

Words of Affirmation (A): 1, 6, 11, 16
1. Hearing specific praise makes me feel loved.
2. Texts that say what you appreciate about me matter.
3. Encouragement helps me try hard things.
4. I replay compliments in my head for days.

Quality Time (Q): 2, 7, 12, 17
1. Undistracted time together feels like love.
2. Shared routines/rituals mean a lot to me.
3. I'd rather have a deep talk than a fancy gift.
4. Being fully present beats multitasking.

Acts of Service (S): 3, 8, 13, 18
1. Helping with tasks relieves my stress.
2. Doing what you said you'd do is romance to me.
3. Thoughtful prep (coffee, car gassed up) melts me.
4. Support during busy weeks feels intimate.

Gifts (G): 4, 9, 14, 19
1. Tangible symbols of love feel meaningful.
2. Small surprises make ordinary days special.
3. I remember who gave me things that matter.
4. I notice thoughtfulness more than price.

Physical Touch (T): 5, 10, 15, 20
1. Hugs/handholds change my mood fast.
2. Sitting close calms me.
3. Affectionate touch helps me feel secure.
4. I miss touch quickly when it's absent.

Result: Highest total(s) = your primary love language(s).

Compare & go deeper: Share concrete **do/don't** lists for each other (e.g., "Do: leave me a voice note," "Don't: cancel our 1:1 time last-minute").

Get the Love Language Bingo Game:

https://www.etsy.com/listing/4406594158/love-languages-bingo-relationship-card

☐ **Share Your Scars.** Literal or emotional. The story behind that tiny mark on your knee or the heartbreak that changed how you love. This one's quiet magic.

☐ **Digital Detox Day.** No phones, no screens, no photos. Just each other. Rediscover how to be bored together, it's more intimate than it sounds.

☐ **Trade Core Memories.** Each of you tells a story that shaped who you are, but not a highlight reel moment. The one that still lives under your skin. The one that made you a little braver, or a little harder.

☐ **Take the Emotional Baggage Tour.** Pack metaphorical "luggage" for your past relationships, the things you're done carrying. Write each one on a slip of paper, throw them in a suitcase, and toss it in the closet. Closure can be a team sport.

☐ **Ask Each Other's Families About Them.** With permission, call or text one of their relatives or friends and ask for a story from before you met. You'll get gold you'd never hear firsthand.

☐ **The 'How I Was Raised' Dinner.** Cook each other's favorite childhood comfort food. Tell the story behind it: who made it, when, and why it still matters.

☐ **Watch Home Videos Together.** Nothing humbles a person like hearing their own toddler voice. It's tender, embarrassing, and adorable in equal measure.

☐ **Interview Each Other Like a Documentary.** Set up your phone like a film crew and ask hard questions as if you're filming *The Story of Us*. The trick: stay serious, like you're narrating your own character study.

50 Questions for *The Story of Us*

1. How would you describe yourself in one sentence?
2. What's the first memory that really shaped who you are?
3. What were you like as a kid?
4. Who taught you the most about love?
5. When did you first realize you were growing up?
6. What's a moment you wish you could relive?
7. What's something you've never told anyone?
8. What scares you the most about getting older?

9. What's your definition of home?
10. What's the hardest truth you've had to accept?
11. What chapter of your life are you in right now?
12. When was the last time you felt truly seen?
13. Who would play you in the movie of your life?
14. How would your friends describe you versus how you'd describe yourself?
15. What's something you thought you'd have figured out by now?
16. What's your love language in real life, not the quiz?
17. What do people misunderstand about you?
18. When did you feel most confident in your life?
19. What's a memory that still makes you laugh uncontrollably?
20. What do you wish your younger self knew about love?
21. What's a habit you've picked up from me?
22. What do you think I've learned from you?
23. When did you first know this connection was different?
24. What's your favorite version of us?
25. What's the hardest thing we've gone through together?
26. What surprised you most about me?
27. What would our highlight reel look like?
28. What would our blooper reel look like?
29. What's the most cinematic moment we've ever had?
30. If our love had a soundtrack, what song plays first?
31. What's your favorite quiet moment between us?
32. What's the scene you replay in your mind the most?
33. How do you handle conflict when the cameras aren't rolling?
34. What's your biggest strength in this relationship?
35. What's something you're still working on?
36. How has love changed you?
37. What's your proudest moment so far?
38. What's your biggest "character flaw" in this story?
39. How do you want this story to end?
40. What's the lesson love keeps trying to teach you?
41. When did you feel most vulnerable with me?
42. What's a risk you took that changed everything?
43. What's the one word that describes our relationship?
44. What's a dream we haven't said out loud yet?
45. How do you want to be remembered in my story?
46. If this was a documentary, what would it be called?
47. What's the question you hope I'll ask you next?
48. What part of me do you think the audience would fall in love with first?
49. What part of you do you wish people understood better?
50. When the credits roll, what do you hope people feel watching *us*?

- ☐ **"Before You Knew Me" Night.** Each of you picks one song, one photo, and one memory from before you met. Lay them out on the table like evidence and tell the story behind them.

- ☐ **Recreate a Moment You Regret.** If there's ever been tension or a fight you'd redo, reenact it, but with empathy this time. The rewrite might be more healing than the apology.

- ☐ **The Love Language Experiment.** Spend an evening giving your partner their top love language *to the extreme*: gifts, words, acts, touch, or time, even if it's not yours. See what happens.

- ☐ **Write Each Other's Obituaries.** It sounds morbid, but it's actually revealing. What do you hope your life adds up to? What do you want to be remembered for? Then, talk about how you can help each other get there.

- ☐ **Take a Walk Without Talking.** Go for a 30-minute walk in silence, no music, no phones. Just notice each other's pace, breath, and energy. Then talk about what you noticed.

- ☐ **Build Your Shared Code.** Come up with secret phrases, hand signals, or inside jokes only you two understand. It becomes a language no one else speaks. Instant intimacy.

- ☐ **Trade Vulnerabilities.** Each person writes down something they've never told a partner before, something they hide out of fear or shame. You don't have to fix it; just hold space for it.

- ☐ **Make a "When We…" Jar.** Write down moments you want to create together "when we buy our first couch," "when we see the Northern Lights." Each time one happens, read the note aloud.

- ☐ **The Mirror Exercise.** Sit facing each other and describe what you see. Not appearance, but energy. How they hold themselves, what you think they're feeling. It's unnerving, beautiful, and unforgettable.

- ☐ **Exchange "Love in Translation" Notes.** Describe how you *show* love versus how you *receive* it. Then swap papers and see if you've been speaking different languages this whole time.

☐ **Make a Photo Timeline Together.** Print out 10 photos each, from childhood to now, and lay them chronologically. The patterns you notice say more than you expect.

☐ **Take a 'First Time' Walk.** Visit a place meaningful to your partner and let them narrate it. First heartbreak, first apartment, first big risk. Be the listener who sees the full picture.

☐ **Share Your Favorite Smell.** Bring an item or scent that reminds you of home: a candle, cologne, old T-shirt, shampoo. Smell is the fastest way into memory; this one hits deeper than expected.

☐ **Describe Each Other in Metaphors.** Skip adjectives. Use images. "You're the sound of a record skipping but never stopping." "You're sunlight on hangover mornings." Poetry sneaks up on people.

☐ **Do a "Truth Walk."** Every block, you each have to say one true thing you've never said aloud. Start small. Let it build. The rhythm of walking makes honesty easier.

☐ **Share Your 'Almosts'.** Tell each other about something you almost did: a job, a person, a dream you almost chased. Regret often says more than success ever could.

☐ **Record a Time Capsule Message.** Film a video together meant for your future selves. Tell the camera who you are right now and what you hope stays the same.

☐ **Take Turns Being the Listener.** Set a timer for ten minutes each. One talks. One listens. No interruptions, no advice. Then switch. It's harder (and more healing) than it sounds.

☐ **Build a Couples "If I Die First" List.** Morbid but practical. Each partner writes the songs, items, or people they'd want honored. It's love disguised as logistics.

☐ **Learn Each Other's Attachment Style.** Take the quiz online and talk through it. Not to label, to understand why you react how you do when things feel off. Free quizzes are available at The Attachment Project, Trauma Solutions and Personal Development School by Thais Gibson.

☐ **Tell Your Origin Stories.** Not "how we met," but how you became *you*. The long messy version. The one no one's ever fully heard.

☐ **Do a Fear Swap.** Each of you writes down a real fear and trades it. Over the next week, design a tiny "obstacle course" to gently defuse your partner's fear. A task where messing up is part of the fun, a small ask to face rejection, or a surprise plan to ease control issues. At the end, sit together and talk about what actually happened: the fear, the feeling, and the truth underneath. Most fears shrink once you bring them into the light.

Fear Swap Challenge Ideas

1. **Fear:** Failure
   Obstacle: Try something you are both bad at, such as pottery, karaoke, or cooking a new recipe, and allow it to be messy.
2. **Fear:** Rejection
   Obstacle: Ask a stranger for something simple, like directions or a photo, and notice how kind people usually are.
3. **Fear:** Losing Control
   Obstacle: Let your partner plan an entire mystery day and agree to follow without any input.
4. **Fear:** Vulnerability
   Obstacle: Record a one-minute video confessing something real and then watch each other's.
5. **Fear:** Being Judged
   Obstacle: Wear something silly or bold in public together for one hour and own it completely.
6. **Fear:** Abandonment
   Obstacle: Spend a solo day doing everything you love and then meet again that night to talk about what actually felt good.
7. **Fear:** Not Being Enough
   Obstacle: Write a letter listing what you admire in your partner and read them aloud to each other.
8. **Fear:** Public Speaking
   Obstacle: Tell a story at an open mic or make a toast at dinner, even if your voice shakes.
9. **Fear:** Intimacy
   Obstacle: Hold eye contact for two minutes in silence and notice what comes up.
10. **Fear:** Change
    Obstacle: Do one small thing differently for a day, such as driving a new route or rearranging a room.
11. **Fear:** Confrontation
    Obstacle: Role-play a past argument, but this time swap roles and talk about what you learned.

12. **Fear:** Uncertainty
    Obstacle: Write a list of random activities, pick one from a jar, and go do it without overthinking.
13. **Fear:** Losing Independence
    Obstacle: Allow your partner to take over one task you usually control and practice letting go.
14. **Fear:** Being Seen
    Obstacle: Share something creative, such as a short post, drawing, or photo, publicly with your name on it.
15. **Fear:** Disappointment
    Obstacle: Plan a simple and imperfect date night. No expectations, just connection.
16. **Fear:** Repeating the Past
    Obstacle: Visit a place that once carried pain and rewrite the memory together.
17. **Fear:** Commitment
    Obstacle: Create a small shared goal for the week, such as cooking or walking daily, and keep each other accountable.
18. **Fear:** Success
    Obstacle: Describe your dream life out loud as if it already exists and observe your emotions as you do.
19. **Fear:** Being Alone
    Obstacle: Spend one day completely solo with no phone or partner, then share what you discovered about yourself.
20. **Fear:** Losing Someone You Love
    Obstacle: Begin a gratitude ritual for seven days where you each name one thing you would miss about the other.

Get the Fear Roulette Game:

https://www.etsy.com/listing/4406675469/fear-roulette-couples-game-intimacy-and

☐ **Make a Ritual Together.** It can be anything: morning coffee, Sunday night cards, a three-second forehead kiss before work. Small rituals become emotional glue.

Sexy & Flirty

☐ **Blindfolded Taste Test.** Feed each other mystery bites: sweet, salty, spicy, or suspiciously familiar. No talking while tasting; just reactions. At the end, guess what you've been fed and who had the better poker face. Bonus points for feeding each other something that requires a little clean-up.

☐ **Two Truths and a Lie: After Dark Edition.** The classic icebreaker gets a glow-up. This time, the lies can be flirtier, the truths can be riskier, and each reveal gets you one inch closer on the couch.

☐ **Reenact a Romantic Movie Scene.** Choose a famous movie kiss or confession, and recreate it as seriously or dramatically as possible. Whether it's *The Notebook* in the rain or *When Harry Met Sally* on your kitchen counter, it's an instant chemistry test.

☐ **Paint Each Other.** Grab a couple of canvases or use your bodies as the canvas. It can be artsy, abstract, or accidentally scandalous. Either way, it's a mix of creativity, laughter, and lowkey tension.

☐ **Stay-at-Home Spa Night.** Light candles, grab massage oil, and turn your living room into a spa suite. Alternate being "the client" and "the professional." Just know, this spa does not offer refunds or clothing.

☐ **Truth or Tease.** A twist on Truth or Dare. Every truth gets you one step closer to the dares you both secretly want to pick. It's basically foreplay disguised as a game night.

Possible Dares

1. Kiss your partner somewhere *unexpected* (not the lips) and make them guess where you'll go next.
2. Take off one item of clothing slowly while maintaining eye contact.
3. Whisper exactly what you'd do *if you weren't being watched right now.*
4. Glide an ice cube along your partner's wrist or neck and trace the path with your finger.
5. Blindfold your partner for one minute and make them guess what you're doing. Touch optional, anticipation mandatory.
6. Whisper one fantasy you've had about them. No explanations allowed.
7. You have thirty seconds to make your partner's heartbeat speed up. No kissing allowed.
8. Spray your favorite perfume or cologne on their neck and tell them not to forget how it smells.

9. Say something that sounds innocent but isn't, while biting your lip.
10. Lean close and say something so softly they have to close their eyes to hear it.
11. Use only one fingertip to trace a word on their arm. They have to guess it or you write another.
12. Stand together in front of a mirror and compliment what you see. Both reflections count.
13. Hug for one full minute without saying anything. If either person laughs or breaks eye contact, they owe a kiss.
14. Unbutton one button, theirs or yours. No reason needed.
15. Take a photo of your partner looking at you like they shouldn't be. Keep it for "private viewing."
16. Record a one-line message they'll want to replay later.
17. Run your hand through their hair and tell them what it makes you think of.
18. Lightly bite something they're holding: straw, sleeve, pen while looking at them.
19. Pretend you just met. Say exactly what you'd say if you were trying to take each other home.
20. Trade items of clothing for five minutes, no matter what they are.
21. Tell your partner one thing you love about their body, but you can't name it directly.
22. Get within inches of their ear and say something that would make them blush in public.
23. You have ten seconds to make them want to kiss you.
24. While touching, stay completely still for thirty seconds. Whoever moves first owes a favor.
25. Say something that will keep them thinking about you long after the date ends.

☐ **Five-Minute Flirt Challenge.** Set a timer and flirt like it's your very first date. Eye contact, witty banter, all of it. Whoever breaks character owes the other a drink or something better.

☐ **The Kiss Lottery.** Write five body parts on slips of paper (keep it classy). Each person draws one and gets to kiss that spot. Repeat until someone folds.

☐ **Late-Night Dance Break.** Dim the lights, put on a slow song, and dance like the room is watching. Then change the song to something upbeat and see who gets more competitive.

☐ **Role-Swap Date.** Dress and act like each other for an evening. Mimic their walk, phrases, and habits. It's hilarious, slightly humiliating, and shockingly revealing.

☐ **Dessert First.** Skip dinner entirely and start with something sweet. Eat it straight from the box in bed or while streaming your favorite show. Sticky fingers optional.

☐ **Flirtation Station.** Go somewhere public but pretend you're strangers meeting for the first time. The mission: make each other laugh or blush without breaking character.

☐ **Photo Shoot Date.** One person is the photographer, the other is the muse. Use your phone, natural light, and confidence. You'll end up with new photos *and* new appreciation.

☐ **Scent Memory Game.** Blindfold your partner and have them smell perfumes, candles, or skin. Guess each scent. Whoever wins gets to pick where the next scent goes.

☐ **The Whisper Date.** Speak only in whispers the entire night. It's oddly intimate and requires sitting way too close for comfort.

☐ **The Ice Game.** One ice cube, two people, zero rules. Start at the wrist. See how long you can keep it interesting.

☐ **The Hot Seat.** Set a timer for 60 seconds and ask each other anything. No skipping. Then switch roles. It's equal parts thrilling and dangerous.

☐ **The "If You Dare" Jar.** Write down spicy dares on slips of paper. Some mild, some wild. Keep the jar for rainy nights, birthdays, or courage tests.

☐ **Serendipity Jar.** Fill a jar with spontaneous ideas and draw one each weekend.

Get all 16 Jars:

https://www.etsy.com/listing/4405604819/complete-couples-jar-collection-16-date

☐ **The Towel Negotiation.** After showers, only one towel is allowed. Solve it however you want: diplomacy, strategy, or surrender.

☐ **The Elevator Game.** Imagine you're strangers stuck in an elevator for five minutes. You can say anything you want to pass the time. Anything. Or, again, pretend you're two strangers who just met in an elevator and only have three floors to make an impression. No names. Just instinct. The possibilities are endless.

☐ **The Strip Trivia Game.** Choose a trivia topic: movies, music, or random facts. Each wrong answer costs a layer. Knowledge is power... literally.

☐ **The Secret Confession Exchange.** Each person writes one secret they've never told anyone. Fold and swap. Read in silence. It's vulnerability meets tension.

☐ **Flirty Scavenger Hunt.** Hide notes or little gifts around the house with flirty messages. Each clue gets more personal until the final one leads to you.

☐ **The "What Happens After Midnight" Pact.** Go out late, like, after the world goes quiet. Walk, get milkshakes, or drive nowhere in particular. Anything said or done after midnight doesn't count.

☐ **The Strip Card Game.** Choose any card game you know: Go Fish, Uno, or poker and add a twist. Every loss costs a layer, a truth, or a dare. Just make sure the stakes feel worth it.

☐ **Moonlit Walk and Make-Out.** Go for a nighttime walk somewhere quiet. Talk until words stop being enough. Bonus points if it starts to drizzle and you don't run for cover.

☐ **Candle Countdown.** Light five candles and blow one out every fifteen minutes. When the last one goes dark, the game ends or something else begins.

☐ **Massage Roulette.** Write different body parts on folded slips. Draw one and give a two-minute massage there. Keep drawing until someone can't keep track of time.

☐ **The "Don't Kiss Me" Challenge.** Spend an entire date trying *not* to kiss. Flirt, tease, lean in close, but hold back. Whoever breaks first loses, but honestly... everyone wins.

☐ **Lipstick Test.** Kiss a sheet of paper or their skin with different lipstick shades and let them pick their favorite. Leave evidence everywhere.

☐ **Truth or Shot.** Ask the kind of questions that make people gulp. If they won't answer, they drink. If they do answer, you drink for surviving the honesty.

☐ **Private Chef Night.** Cook together wearing aprons and minimal common sense. Feed each other bites like it's a Michelin-star competition with zero decorum.

☐ **The Hotel-at-Home Trick.** Turn your bedroom into a "hotel." Fresh sheets, robe, room-service menu, maybe a fake accent at check-in. You'll forget you never left.

☐ **The Hand Game.** Sit facing each other and let your hands explore arms, wrists, and shoulders. No words, no rush. It's somehow more electric than anything else.

☐ **Slow Burn Movie Night.** Watch a film that simmers instead of sizzles (*Before Sunrise*, *The Age of Adaline*). Then talk about what scenes felt the most magnetic and why.

☐ **The Secret Note Drop.** Throughout the evening, slip folded notes into their pocket or bag: one sweet, one bold, one impossible request. They'll find them later and text you accordingly.

☐ **Blindfold Karaoke.** One sings, the other can't see. Guess the song, then trade places. Confidence counts more than talent.

☐ **The "I Dare You Not to Laugh" Game.** Each of you tells a ridiculously flirty pickup line while keeping a straight face. Whoever cracks up first has to admit one desire.

☐ **The Ice Cream Taste-Off.** Buy three pints of outrageous flavors and feed each other spoonfuls while blindfolded. Loser has to buy breakfast.

☐ **The Compliment Echo.** Every time your partner compliments you, you must respond with one thing you love about them, but it can't be physical. Watch how fast it gets emotional.

☐ **The "Kiss Where It Hurts" Game.** Ask each other where you feel tense: neck, back, shoulders and kiss it better. It's therapeutic, technically.

☐ **Couple's Truth Board.** Write spicy truths or fantasies on sticky notes and put them on a board. Take turns pulling one at random and talking it through or acting it out.

☐ **Late-Night Drive with Rules.** Windows down, playlist on, and one rule: no talking about real life. Only hypotheticals, dreams, or what you'd do if you weren't afraid.

☐ **Write Each Other's Dating Profiles.** Create honest but flirty versions of each other's bios. Then read them aloud dramatically. Prepare for ego boosts and confessions.

☐ **Private Dance Lesson.** Take an online salsa, tango, or slow-dance class. The learning curve is just foreplay with better posture.

☐ **The Surprise Text.** Send a short, mischievous message while you're in the same room. Don't say a word, just watch their reaction.

☐ **The Memory Re-Creation.** Revisit a moment that used to make you nervous around each other. Same outfits, same place, new confidence.

☐ **Flirty Crossword.** Make a personalized crossword using inside jokes, secret nicknames and favorite things. Every correct answer earns a reward.

☐ **The "Stay or Go" Game.** Ask each other, "If I did this on a first date, would you stay or go?" The answers are revealing *and* hilarious.

Sample Questions

1. Showed up ten minutes late but brought you coffee.
2. Talked about their ex... twice.
3. Ordered for you without asking what you wanted.
4. Said, "You look better in person" like it was a compliment.
5. Brought their dog and expected it to sit at the table.
6. Asked to split the bill *before* ordering.
7. Spent the first ten minutes talking about crypto.
8. Said they don't really like movies.
9. Pulled out a coupon at dinner.
10. Took a phone call mid-date and said, "Sorry, it's my mom."
11. Told you they Googled you before meeting.
12. Mentioned they "don't believe in therapy."
13. Corrected your grammar mid-sentence.
14. Said, "You remind me of my ex."
15. Called the waiter "boss."
16. Didn't ask a single question about you.
17. Talked about marriage before dessert.
18. Asked, "So what do you bring to the table?"
19. Tried to feed you from their plate without asking.
20. Brought a friend "just to tag along."
21. Said they don't really have friends "people just don't get me."

22. Complained about their job for the whole meal.
23. Checked their reflection in every shiny surface.
24. Wore sunglasses inside.
25. Asked how many people you've dated.
26. Snapped at the server.
27. Talked about their astrology sign like it was a medical diagnosis.
28. Used the phrase "alpha male" unironically.
29. Didn't tip.
30. Said, "I'm just brutally honest," then insulted you.
31. Tried to impress you by quoting Andrew Tate.
32. Asked you to "guess their age."
33. Said they "don't like labels."
34. Pulled out their phone to show pictures of their ex's dog.
35. Wore a Bluetooth headset the entire time.
36. Said they're "not really into emotions."
37. Asked if you'd ever been arrested — before asking your middle name.
38. Talked about how "crazy" their ex was (for ten minutes straight).
39. Brought up their divorce within five minutes.
40. Ordered milk with dinner.
41. Said, "You'd look prettier if you smiled more."
42. Asked for a bite of your food before you even took one.
43. Tried to hold your hand while crossing the parking lot after Date #1.
44. Asked, "Are you a good cook?" in a tone that felt like an audition.
45. Told you their biggest goal is "to be famous."
46. Said they don't believe in Wi-Fi.
47. Tried to play a song they wrote about an ex.
48. Admitted they "forgot your name" halfway through.
49. Wore flip-flops to a nice restaurant.
50. Said, "You seem like high maintenance" and smiled like it was flattery.

☐ **The Bubble Bath Interview.** Get in the tub and take turns asking "deep-light" questions, enough vulnerability to match the bubbles.

☐ **Couple's Bucket List.** Write down ten outrageous or intimate things you want to do together. Fold, mix, and draw one whenever you're bored.

If you have no idea where to start on your bucket list, get my book *Bucket List*. It has over 10,000 entries ☺
https://amzn.to/4nSNtfM

☐ **The Blindfolded Artist.** One person draws the other without looking. The result is terrible art and uncontrollable laughter.

☐ **The Private Fashion Show.** Pick each other's outfits. Model them like it's Fashion Week, minus the cameras. Make sure you have the sultry eyes.

☐ **The Timer Game.** Set a five-minute timer for anything you want to do: kissing, dancing, staring contest. When it rings, stop. Unless you both agree to reset it.

☐ **The Secret Menu.** Write down three "menu items" you'd like to try together: cute, adventurous, or decadent. Pick one without reading the others.

☐ **The Elevator Rule.** Every time you ride an elevator together, anywhere, you have to kiss before the doors open. Permanently enforceable law.

☐ **The Candle Color Code.** Assign each candle color a theme: red = passion, white = calm, black = mystery. Light the one you're craving that night.

☐ **The "One Bed" Scenario.** Classic rom-com setup: there's only one bed, and neither of you can sleep on the floor. Role-play accordingly.

☐ **The Polaroid Collection.** Capture ten snapshots from one night: funny, messy, real. Don't filter them; that's the point.

☐ **The "Read My Mind" Game.** One person thinks of something flirty; the other asks yes/no questions until they guess it. Wrong guesses earn forfeits.

☐ **The Private Performance.** Sing, dance, or recite something ridiculous just for them. Confidence is the real aphrodisiac.

☐ **The Sunday Morning Rule.** Stay in bed. No phones, no chores, no plans. Just slow coffee, messy hair, and eye contact that lasts a beat too long.

☐ **The Goodbye That Lingers.** When the date ends, don't rush the goodbye. Stretch it out with eye contact, breath, stillness. Make them think about it all night.

Roleplay & Fantasy

☐ **Strangers at a Bar.** Meet like you've never met before. New names, new backstories, new chemistry.

☐ **Murder-Mystery Dinner.** Host a themed whodunit and commit fully to your character — alibi and accent included.

☐ **Movie-Character Night.** Dress as your favorite film duo and live the dialogue for one evening.

☐ **Travel-Vlogger Adventure.** Pretend you're influencers discovering your own city. Over-narrate everything for comedic effect.

☐ **Fake Dating App Challenge.** Build each other's fake profiles and see who "wins" the most matches in an hour.

☐ **Secret Agent Mission.** Assign code names and secret tasks to complete during the night. Debrief over martinis.

☐ **Celebrity & Paparazzi.** One of you is famous; the other is their handler dodging fans and flashbulbs.

☐ **Art-Heist Duo.** Visit a museum and plan a (purely imaginary) heist of your favorite piece.

☐ **Royal Couple in Exile.** Spend a day speaking in regal tones and demanding the finest local coffee "the realm" offers.

☐ **Time-Travel Tourists.** Pick a decade and dress, talk, and act accordingly. Try ordering like it's 1924 or 1987.

☐ **Runaway Elopement.** Pretend you just met, fell madly in love, and decided to "elope." Create your spontaneous wedding story.

☐ **Detective & Suspect.** Interrogate each other playfully until one "confesses" to stealing your heart.

☐ **Boss & Intern.** Swap power dynamics for an evening of mock meetings, feedback sessions, and creative "reviews."

☐ **Faux Reality-Show Contestants.** You're on a dating show — compete for each other's rose, confessionals required.

☐ **Therapist & Client.** Role-play a life-coaching session and see what truths slip out between laughs.

☐ **Travel Agents.** Design each other's dream vacation on the spot — complete with imaginary brochures and absurd add-ons.

☐ **Fictional Bandmates.** Make up a band name, genre, and first hit song. Bonus: perform your "single" at karaoke.

☐ **Undercover Critics.** Visit a restaurant or event pretending you're elite critics. Review everything in exaggerated seriousness.

☐ **Neighbors with a Secret.** You just moved in next door — and there's definitely a subplot.

☐ **Spy vs. Spy.** Each of you hides a secret word or object the other must uncover by observation alone.

☐ **Matchmaker & Client.** One person plays the professional matchmaker, the other the hopeless romantic in need of guidance.

☐ **Movie Audition.** Pretend you're auditioning for a film together. Make up the genre, improvise the scene, and overact shamelessly.

☐ **Haunted Hotel Guests.** Pick a spooky inn or Airbnb and pretend it's haunted. Leave dramatic voice-notes documenting "paranormal activity."

☐ **Fortune-Teller & Seeker.** One reads tarot, palms, or tea leaves; the other seeks answers only the stars can give.

☐ **Runaway Criminals.** On the lam — but for something ridiculous like stealing the world's best donut.

☐ **Reporters on Assignment.** Interview locals, take notes, and "file your story" about the night's discoveries.

☐ **Wedding Crashers.** Dress up, attend a random event (even virtually), and invent your outrageous backstory as guests.

☐ **Personal Stylists.** Each of you becomes the other's fashion consultant for the day. Run a "red-carpet reveal."

☐ **Detectives in Love.** You're partners on a cold case who can't stop flirting between clues.

☐ **Host & Guest on a Talk Show.** One interviews the other about their "latest scandal." Applause break required.

☐ **Coffee-Shop Novelists.** Pretend you're famous writers researching characters, which suspiciously resemble each other.

☐ **Space Explorers.** You've just landed on a new planet (your neighborhood). Document your findings and report back to "mission control."

☐ **Lost Royalty.** Pretend you're descendants of rival kingdoms forced to share one throne — or one dessert.

☐ **Startup Founders.** Pitch your fake billion-dollar idea to each other Shark Tank-style, complete with buzzwords.

☐ **Runaway Detectives.** You're hiding out under new identities after solving one last case together.

☐ **Fashion Week Designers.** Host a mini runway show at home with outfits from your closets and absurd brand names.

☐ **Museum Curators.** Assign each other one household item and create its dramatic "historical significance."

☐ **Lost Tourists.** Speak in fake accents and ask locals for directions to nonexistent landmarks.

☐ **Hollywood Agents.** Negotiate each other's "contracts" for life, love, and movie rights over dinner.

☐ **Pirates on Shore Leave.** Talk like seafarers, invent your treasure map, and end the night "dividing the loot."

☐ **Superheroes on a Day Off.** You saved the city, now decide what normal people do for fun.

☐ **Detective Noir.** Dress in trench coats, dim the lights, and narrate your evening in hard-boiled 1940s slang.

☐ **Game-Show Contestants.** Create absurd challenges and trivia rounds about each other's quirks.

☐ **Hotel Strangers.** Meet in a hotel lobby like two travelers whose flights got canceled.

☐ **Dream Architects.** Pretend you design dreams for a living. Interview each other about tonight's client: each other.

☐ **Villain & Hero.** Pick your sides and debate morality over cocktails.

☐ **Royal Court Intrigue.** One's a monarch, the other a scheming advisor — plot, flatter, and outwit.

☐ **Retro Diner Date.** 1950s outfits, milkshakes, jukebox songs, and over-the-top accents.

☐ **Alien Anthropologists.** You've just arrived on Earth to study human dating rituals. Observe yourselves accordingly.

☐ **CEO & PR Crisis Manager.** You've got a brand disaster — fix it before "the board" calls.

☐ **Movie Director & Star.** One directs, the other performs; make your own absurd commercial or scene.

☐ **Magician & Assistant.** Learn a simple magic trick and dramatize it like a Vegas act gone rogue.

☐ **Time-Capsule Builders.** Pretend you're archiving your love story for a future civilization to find.

A Little Sexier...

☐ **The Gardener.** One tends to the plants; the other can't stop "checking on progress." Dirt under the nails, slow afternoon, charged glances.

☐ **The Pizza Delivery.** Knock at the door, wrong address, irresistible aroma, you decide whether to tip or invite them in for a slice.

☐ **The Housekeeper & The Homeowner.** Cleaning turns into conversation that's a little too personal. How dirty are you going to get your hands.

☐ **The Personal Trainer.** One pushes form and focus; the other keeps breaking concentration. Endorphins are the plot.

☐ **The Photographer & The Muse.** Lighting, poses, compliments that sound dangerously honest. Every click gets bolder.

- [ ] **The Masseuse.** A late appointment, quiet room, and the power dynamic of who relaxes first.

- [ ] **The Celebrity & The Bodyguard.** Fame, danger, and one moment of privacy no one's supposed to see.

- [ ] **The Chef & The Food Critic.** High-pressure kitchen, sizzling pans, and a review that gets personal.

- [ ] **The Tattoo Artist.** One sketches designs while the other debates placement. Art meets anticipation.

- [ ] **The Teacher & The Guest Speaker.** An after-hours faculty event turns into unexpected chemistry and witty debate.

- [ ] **The Pilot & The Passenger.** Turbulence, tiny cabin, "fasten your seatbelt" delivered like a secret.

- [ ] **The Bartender.** You're the regular; they know your order and that you never stay long.

- [ ] **The Fashion Designer & The Model.** Last-minute fitting before the big show, measurements, compliments, and chaos backstage.

- [ ] **The Journalist & The Source.** An interview in a quiet café, too many follow-up questions, and the story keeps changing.

- [ ] **The Art Thief & The Detective.** Cat-and-mouse energy, stolen glances, mutual confession that neither intends to keep.

- [ ] **The Royal & The Body Double.** One lives the crown; the other wears it for a day. Mistaken identity never felt so intriguing.

- [ ] **The Neighbor Who Helps Out.** Borrowed tools, weekend projects, and a running joke that's not quite innocent.

- [ ] **The Hotel Guest & The Concierge.** Requests get progressively more personal, service with curiosity.

- [ ] **The Rockstar & The Fan.** Backstage pass, autograph session, moment that lasts too long.

- [ ] **The Movie Director & The Lead Actor.** Rehearsing the same scene again and again until it feels a little *too* real.

☐ **The Coffee-Shop Stranger.** You've been watching each other for weeks; today one finally orders "the usual" for both.

☐ **The Mechanic.** One's stranded, the other's covered in grease and calm competence. Sparks, literally.

☐ **The Librarian & The Researcher.** Late night stacks, whispers, and books no one else has checked out.

☐ **The Traveler & The Local Guide.** New city, hidden spots, and directions that keep leading somewhere unexpected.

☐ **The Casino High-Roller.** Luck, risk, and someone who keeps winning hands they shouldn't.

☐ **The Billionaire.** Because I read enough smut, to know that's what sells. *50 Shades of Grey* didn't gross a billion, because we want cookie-cutter.

Fun/Holiday/Games/ Miscellaneous

☐ **Go to a Virtual Reality (VR) café / arcade.** These are becoming more and more popular. Check on Google maps to see if one has popped up in your area. If there is one in your area, check it out together. You can have an action-packed, creative, or relaxing date at the VR arcade. This is especially memorable if neither of you has tried a full VR set up.

☐ **Have a water gun/balloon fight.** This one is definitely a summertime date idea. Running around spraying each other with water and lobbing water balloons can be a great way to have fun and beat the heat. Just make sure to have something lined up for when you finish as this is kind of a short date idea.

☐ **Go to a local nonprofessional sports game.** Like a high school football game or a little league game. Choose a side to cheer for or cheer for opposing teams. Lots of fun and usually quieter than professional sports games. Plus, a lot cheaper. It'll give you a lot of chances to talk, and you'll be able to support a local team!

☐ **Rent a skateboard or longboard and give it a go.** So, this one. This one is a bit risky. It can be a lot of fun no matter what your or their skill level is. But if one of you gets seriously injured, well that's not fun at all. A trip to the hospital does not make for a good date. So, choose this date idea with an ounce of caution.

☐ **Rent and beat a game together.** This is a great date idea if you are both gamers. You can rent a game and try to beat it together in one marathon session. Just make sure it is either two-player or you both can pass the controller at regular intervals.

☐ **Do a themed 5k or fun run type of race.** You can take these as seriously or as laid back as you want. A lot of people just walk them. So they are perfect for any fitness level. And there a lot of fun themed races, some have bubbles, some you eat during them, some involve getting messy in some way or another. Always good for a date day.

You know like the color blast ones or the tough mudders. I am sure there so many that you want to try.

☐ **If you both play an MMORPG, an online multiplayer shooter, or some other online game you could have a date in game.** Entirely depends on both of you being into gaming, but if you both are, it can be a great date idea and a great way to do something you both love.

☐ **Jump around at a trampoline park or obstacle course.** If your city or town has one of these, they are a blast. A lot of laughs, a decent workout, and a whole lot of fun. Just make sure not to get injured.

☐ **Go Fly a Kite.** Check the wind map, grab a couple of kites or ribbons, and head to a breezy park or hill. It's pure rom-com energy: laughter, tangled strings, and that perfect mix of play and nostalgia.

☐ **Search "challenge" on YouTube and do whatever buck-wild challenges you want.** It kind of goes without saying that you should definitely film yourself doing the challenges. Just don't go overboard and end up in the hospital, while it may make for a good story / video, it would be a lousy date. Have fun with it and see how crazy your date can be.

☐ **Set up an obstacle course in the back yard or at a park.** This is a really fun one for double dates. Each couple is a team and it often leads to some hilarious antics. Just remember, as with all the competitive date ideas, try not to take it too seriously. Oh, and try not to injure yourself.

☐ **Buy a cheap drone and take turns flying it around and probably crashing it.** You can get a drone for the price of a couple of drinks these days, and they are a ton of fun to play around with. I would recommend outdoors away from people, but some drones work okay indoors too. Just make sure not to fly it around breakable stuff. Relax and chat while it charges up after you burn through the battery.

☐ **Try your hands at movie / Halloween makeup and watch horror movies.** Go to the local party store, buy some fake blood or Halloween makeup. Spend some time putting it on together then curl up on the couch and have a scary movie marathon.

☐ **Plan a Game Night.** This is the perfect free group date activity. Split up into teams and let the dice (and the good times) roll.

☐ **Play a Messy Game of Twister.** Take it to the backyard and play game of messy Twister. The same rules as regular Twister apply, but put coordinated paint colors on the Twister circles and let the games begin! Pro Tip: Wear something you don't mind getting covered in paint.

☐ **Play Old-School Video Games.** Dust off the old controllers and turn on that Nintendo 64! Be Mario, Princess Peach or Toad for the night and have an old school face-off playing Mario Kart, Mario Party and all of the classics.

☐ **Go to an escape room.** These are popping up in more and more places. You go into a room and see if you can solve a mystery using the clues provided. A lot of fun, and can be a great way to spend an hour or two.

☐ **Rage Room Date.** Suit up, grab a bat, and take turns smashing old TVs, plates, or printers. It's weirdly therapeutic and way more fun than couple's therapy.

Destruction Therapy & Chaos Dates

☐ **Car Smash Experience.** Some places let you go full action-movie: helmets, sledgehammers, and one junk car begging for a final scene.

☐ **Break Plate Art.** Write something you're ready to release on ceramic plates, smash them, then turn the shards into mosaic art. Symbolic, satisfying, and surprisingly deep.

☐ **Demolition Derby Night.** Watch cars collide in glorious chaos while you cheer and snack on something fried.

☐ **Junkyard Therapy.** Visit a salvage yard, find an object you both hate (old printer, anyone?), and ceremoniously destroy it.

☐ **Guitar Smash.** Buy a cheap, broken instrument, paint it together, then channel your inner rockstars with one dramatic finale swing.

☐ **Exploding Paint Balloons.** Fill balloons with paint, toss them at a canvas, and call the mess "abstract couple's therapy."

☐ **Destruction & Rebuild.** Build a cardboard tower, knock it down, and rebuild it better. A metaphor for love if there ever was one.

☐ **Paper Shredder Confessionals.** Write down old grudges or bad habits, feed them to the shredder, and toast to a clean slate.

☐ **Rage Yoga.** Take a yoga class that swaps "om" for screaming. Stretch, yell, and breathe out everything that doesn't serve you.

☐ **Glass Blowing Workshop.** Shape molten glass into art or chaos together. It's heat, danger, and beauty, all at once.

☐ **Smash Cake Date.** Order a gorgeous cake just to destroy it. Smear frosting on each other like toddlers or models, your choice.

☐ **Destruction Art Gallery.** Visit or make your own chaos-inspired art exhibit. Rip, burn, or deconstruct something and display it proudly.

☐ **Sledgehammer Symbolism.** Find a demolition experience or art space that lets you literally break down walls. Name the wall after something you're done with.

☐ **Go get henna tattoos together.** It's like getting regular tattoos together but a much lower level of commitment. Just be sure that it isn't in a place that will interfere with your job, they last 1 to 4 weeks.

☐ **Have an impromptu 4th of July celebration.** Or any holiday really. Make a Thanksgiving dinner for the two of you or wear green and go out and have a bunch of beers and bring green food coloring for the beer.

☐ **Do a seasonally themed date.** Do some stereotypical seasonal activities together like building a snowman if it's winter or going to the beach or pool if it's summer. For fall or spring, you could carve a pumpkin or paint Easter eggs. Have seasonal food and drinks after the activity.

☐ **Build sandcastles together (no beach necessary).** No beach nearby? Not to worry. The hardware store sells play sand. Get some of that, a flat surface, some water, a place you don't mind getting wet and sandy, and you are good to go. You could do a full-on beach day away from the beach.

☐ **Both of you download an app/game in which you have to walk or travel around the real world to achieve goals in the game.** There are a lot of these games for both Android and iOS. If you search augmented reality games, you'll probably find quite a few.

☐ **Do a photo booth crawl and make silly photos at every booth you can find.** This one is a spinoff of the "crawl" idea I mentioned earlier and can be a great way to have a lot of fun on a date. It's a perfect excuse to act silly. On the way to the next booth, you can plan out what theme you are going to do for your next set. Bonus points if you pick up props for the photos at a dollar store.

☐ **Meet each in a bar, assume new identities, and try to pick each other up.** This depends a lot on whether you are into role-playing or not. And is definitely more for couples who have been together for a while. That being said, it can be a great way to spice things up.

☐ **Create your own couple holiday including traditional food and activities and then celebrate it every year.** Make your own holiday that is customized to you and your SO. This works better for established couples and can be a lot of fun setting up a new tradition. You can even break it up into two dates. The first date for planning and the second one for celebrating the holiday.

☐ **Change the World.** Find the superhero in your significant other. Talk about what matters most to both of you and explore local groups or causes that align with your shared values. Whether it's animal rescue, community gardens, or neighborhood clean-ups, join people who are building something better and use your power for good together.

☐ **Find a world record and try to break it.** There are some crazy world records out there. Find a few that look like it would be fun to try, and all of you give it a shot. You probably won't beat the record, but I'm sure you'll all have fun trying. And if you do beat it, how cool would that be?!

☐ **Play laser tag together.** Not as much fun as paintball, but also less expensive and less painful. Just make sure your date is up for it. Laser tag, even though it's pretty awesome, is not everyone's idea of a fun date.

☐ **Chuckle at a comedy show.** If a typical two-drink-minimum comedy club isn't your thing, look up comedy podcast tapings. They're just as fun, and you can listen to your episode later on.

☐ **Date like a kid.** Whether it's arcade games or laser tag, find a spot that lets you indulge your younger self. Laughter is basically guaranteed.

☐ **Pop by a cat café.** Both fans of felines? Get cozy with some cats while you sip some beverages. Your date gets bonus points if they wind up adopting one, of course.

☐ **Visit a Sunflower Field.** Wander through golden rows, take photos, and get lost together in the color of summer.

☐ **Pick Wildflowers.** Find a local field or trail, build your own bouquet, and press the prettiest ones in a book later.

☐ **Explore a Pumpkin Patch.** Hunt for the perfect pumpkin, carve your initials into it, and roast the seeds together.

☐ **Apple Orchard Afternoon.** Pick apples, sip cider, and take that rom-com photo of you two sharing one caramel apple.

☐ **Corn Maze Challenge.** Team up or compete to see who escapes first, loser buys hot cocoa.

☐ **Vineyard Harvest Day.** Go grape-picking or attend a tasting event. Toast to the season's sweetness.

☐ **Hayride Under the Stars.** Bundle up with blankets and thermoses, and ride through crisp fall air under twinkle lights.

☐ **Farmers Market Scavenger Hunt.** Pick five random ingredients and figure out what to cook together.

☐ **Leaf-Peeping Drive.** Take a road trip just to chase color, the redder the better.

☐ **Bonfire Night.** Bring flannel, marshmallows, and a playlist. Stay until the fire dies out.

☐ **Strawberry or Cherry-Picking Day.** Fill your baskets, then go home to bake something together, messy is part of the fun.

☐ **Butterfly Garden Visit.** Walk through a greenhouse alive with color and quiet magic.

☐ **Baby Animal Farm.** Go see lambs, goats, or chicks. Nothing sparks serotonin like baby animals.

☐ **Lavender Field Getaway.** Wander through purple rows and take home a bundle to dry for your room.

☐ **County Fair Night.** Ferris wheels, fried food, and that one ride that makes you cling to each other.

☐ **Firefly Watching.** Find a quiet field, bring a blanket, and let the glow remind you how simple magic can be.

☐ **Christmas Tree Farm.** Hunt for the perfect tree, even if you don't need one. It's about the smell, not the size.

☐ **Winter Market Walk.** Sip mulled wine or hot chocolate and browse handmade gifts like you're in a snow-globe.

☐ **Snow Day Escape.** Build a fort, make cocoa, and act like kids again until your cheeks turn pink.

☐ **Holiday Lights Tour.** Walk or drive through the brightest neighborhood and rank each house's display.

☐ **Cozy Cabin Weekend.** Trade phones for firelight and let the world stay outside for a while.

☐ **Cider Mill Visit.** Taste fresh cider and warm donuts, and see who ends up with the most cinnamon sugar on their face.

☐ **Scarecrow or Pumpkin Carving Contest.** Go full creative chaos and see who can make the funniest or creepiest creation.

☐ **Hot Cocoa Crawl.** Visit every café in town, sample their cocoa, and rate them like professional tasters.

☐ **DIY Ornament-Painting Night.** Paint ornaments together, add inside jokes, and hang them every year as proof of your shared chaos.

Other Ideas That Really Need No Explanation:

☐ Get lost in a hedge maze
☐ Give each other haircuts
☐ Get a tattoo or piercing together
☐ Record a podcast together with what you are passionate about.
☐ Play your favorite video game
☐ Cheer on your local team
☐ Play with some puppies
☐ Play some squash
☐ Play some pool
☐ Go on a ghost tour.
☐ Take over an empty playground

Pop Culture & Media- Inspired Dates

☐ **Binge a Nostalgic Series.** Pick a TV show you loved as kids and marathon it with themed snacks and inside jokes.

☐ **Oscars Night In.** Dress up, roll out a towel as red carpet. Give each other awards like "Best Line Delivery" or "Best Supporting Partner."

☐ **TikTok Challenge Marathon.** Try every couple trend you've ever said you'd never do, film the chaos.

☐ **Book-to-Film Debate.** Watch a film adaptation after reading the book, then passionately argue who did it better.

☐ **Director's Cut Night.** Watch the extended or alternate version of a classic and decide if the edits were genius or indulgent.

☐ **Album Listening Party.** Pick an iconic album and listen from start to finish, phones off. Discuss which tracks aged like wine or milk.

☐ **Podcast Date.** Pick a random episode of a thought-provoking or absurd podcast and react together in real time.

☐ **Cult Classic Cinema.** Find a weird, beloved movie you've both never seen and embrace the fandom for one night only.

☐ **Rock Documentary Double Feature.** Watch two music docs back-to-back: one inspiring, one tragic and talk about fame's price.

☐ **Band Biopic Night.** Similar, but different. Watch two musician biopics and create a fake pitch for your own. (*Working title: "Your Love Is My Chart Topper."*) What type of band would you be in? How did you meet your demise? Who broke up the band? Were you the base player, the drummer or the lead singer?

☐ **Celebrity Chef Night.** Follow a recipe from a famous TV chef, critique it like you're judges on *Top Chef*, and film the results.

☐ **Spoiler-Free Movie Swap.** Each person picks a film for the other without revealing *anything*. No trailers. No clues.

☐ **YouTube Rabbit Hole Night.** Go down a random theme spiral: conspiracy theories, 90s commercials, or celebrity interviews, etc.

- **Concert Movie Party.** Watch a recorded live concert and turn your living room into a front-row experience.

- **Fictional World Feast.** Create a meal inspired by a fantasy world: *Hogwarts*, *Westeros*, *Middle-earth*, or *Panem*.

- **Book Blind Date.** Wrap a book, write three teasing hints on the cover, and swap to read for the week.

- **TV Theme Song Karaoke.** Sing along to old show themes like it's your national anthem. Bonus points for choreography.

- **True Crime & Tacos.** Watch a true-crime docuseries and make tacos, because nothing says romance like mystery and salsa.

- **Character Cosplay Dinner.** Dress as your favorite TV or book character and stay in character through dinner.

- **Late-Night Talk Show.** One's the host, the other's the celebrity guest. Interview each other like you're promoting a new hit.

- **Director's Commentary.** Watch a film you know by heart but add your own "commentary" as if you made it.

- **Fan Fiction Read-Aloud.** Find the most dramatic fanfic online and take turns performing it like Shakespeare.

- **Documentary & Debate.** Choose a random doc and see which side you each take. Healthy disagreement, popcorn optional.

- **Vintage Commercial Marathon.** Watch retro ads from the 80s–90s on YouTube and rate them on weirdness, nostalgia, and accidental genius.

- **Fictional Awards Night.** Give awards to characters from your shared favorite series "Most Likely to Text Back," "Best Villain Redemption Arc."

- **Movie Trailer Recreation.** Film your own dramatic trailer about your relationship using only your phones and household props. "In a world, where Dan & Gina met…"

- **Celebrity News Roast.** Read the most ridiculous entertainment headlines to each other and assign fake PR damage control roles.

- **Pop Culture Trivia Showdown.** Compete to see who knows the most random celebrity facts or award-show flubs.

☐ **TV Pilot Experiment.** Watch the first episode of five new shows and vote on which one to commit to for a full binge.

☐ **Cameo Night.** Order a personalized celebrity video message for each other or just watch Cameo videos until you cry-laugh. From heartfelt birthday shoutouts to absolute chaos from washed-up reality stars, it's equal parts hilarious and weirdly touching. (Obviously, use some AI software for this one.)

☐ **Album Art Museum.** Print your favorite record covers, hang them like gallery pieces, and rate them over drinks.

☐ **Pop Icon Style Swap.** Pick a celebrity and dress in their signature aesthetic, paparazzi photo shoot optional.

☐ **Cult TV Watch Party.** Choose a show with a rabid fanbase (*Twin Peaks*, *Firefly*, *The Office*) and dive in together.

☐ **Audiobook Drive.** Choose a dramatic audiobook for your next road trip and perform commentary like co-hosts.

☐ **Music Video Re-creation.** Recreate an iconic video scene: props, lighting, and all. Low-budget brilliance encouraged.

☐ **Celebrity Chef Crawl.** Visit restaurants owned or endorsed by famous chefs and rank them like food critics.

☐ **Oscar Predictions Game.** Watch the nominees and predict winners. Loser buys champagne for the afterparty.

☐ **Movie Genre Swap.** Watch a rom-com like it's a thriller or a horror film like it's a comedy and narrate it that way.

☐ **Favorite Childhood Movie Night.** Revisit a film from your early years and rate how it holds up as adults.

☐ **Celebrity Couple Debate.** Each of you defends a famous couple you think will last.

☐ **The Temptation Playlist.** Each of you adds five songs you think are secretly sexy. Play them on shuffle.

The Soundtrack Series

☐ **Shuffle Playlist Drive.** Put both your playlists on shuffle and let the music set the mood.

☐ **Soundtrack Swap.** Each person makes a playlist inspired by a favorite movie and explains why it fits their "life's soundtrack."

- [ ] **The Playlist War.** Create playlists that capture your chemistry and battle it out. Whoever's list gets more skips has to make breakfast.
- [ ] **Make a "What I've Never Said" Playlist.** Each of you adds songs with lyrics that say what you can't. Play it, no explanations until it's over.
- [ ] **The Playlist Exchange.** Create a playlist called "Us, if we were a movie." Swap and talk about why you chose each song.
- [ ] **Lost Highway Playlist.** Make a joint playlist called *Lost Highway* and drive until the last song ends.
- [ ] **The Decade Swap.** Each of you picks a decade and builds a playlist of its best hits. Debate which era had the superior vibe.
- [ ] **The Firsts Playlist.** Fill a playlist with songs tied to your "firsts" — first date, first road trip, first dance in the kitchen.
- [ ] **The Cover Story.** Build a playlist of cover songs better (or worse) than the originals. Rank your favorites.
- [ ] **The Lyrical Confession.** Each choose three songs with lyrics that describe how you really feel right now. Listen together and let the words do the talking.
- [ ] **The 3 a.m. Playlist.** Songs for late-night drives, insomnia talks, and quiet, half-dreaming moments.
- [ ] **The Reverse Playlist.** Build a playlist that plays backward through your relationship — from now to the beginning.
- [ ] **The "You" Playlist.** Create a list of songs that remind you of the other person, from obvious to oddly specific.
- [ ] **The Alternate Universe Playlist.** Songs that would play if your story had gone differently — fun, bittersweet, cinematic.
- [ ] **The Future Soundtrack.** Choose songs that match where you want to be a year from now, and listen while you make plans.
- [ ] **The Genre Challenge.** Pick a genre neither of you usually listens to and find its hidden gems. You might discover a new favorite together.

Get the Mix-Tape Madness Game:

https://www.etsy.com/listing/4406759222/mix-tape-madness-couples-game-101

Late Night Dates

- ☐ **Two a.m. Diner Run.** Find the nearest all-night spot and order breakfast like you're the only people left in the world.

- ☐ **Night Swim.** Pool, lake, or ocean. The rule is to keep it quiet enough to feel like a secret.

- ☐ **Neon Bowling.** Late-night lanes, bad lighting, good competition. Winner chooses dessert.

- ☐ **City-Light Drive.** Cruise through town after midnight with no destination, windows down, playlist up.

- ☐ **Glow-Stick Hike.** Wrap yourselves in glow sticks and walk a short trail. It feels like another planet.

- ☐ **Night-Market Crawl.** Visit local markets or food trucks open past ten and try one thing from every stall.

- ☐ **Late-Night Movie Marathon.** Pick a trilogy or theme and stay up until you finish it. Pajamas optional.

- ☐ **Rooftop Stargazing.** Find a parking deck or rooftop, bring snacks, and count satellites.

- ☐ **Moonlight Walk.** Choose a quiet neighborhood and stroll in near silence. No phones allowed.

- ☐ **Laundromat Hangout.** Bring snacks, fold clothes, and talk about life while the machines hum.

- ☐ **Flashlight Hide-and-Seek.** Play in your yard or a park after dark. Silly but unforgettable.

- ☐ **Night Photography Walk.** Capture long exposures of empty streets and glowing windows.

- ☐ **Late-Night Dessert Hop.** Visit three dessert spots before midnight. Share every plate.

- ☐ **Candlelight Dinner at Home.** Turn off the lights, light every candle you own, and slow down.

☐ **Midnight Bike Ride.** Quiet streets, empty parks, and that feeling of flying.

☐ **24-Hour Store Challenge.** Go to a big box store late at night and see who can build the funniest outfit from what's inside.

☐ **Watch Planes Take Off.** Park near an airport runway and guess where each flight is going.

☐ **Moon Bathing.** Lie outside under the moonlight, listen to soft music, and do nothing at all.

☐ **Board Game Café.** Stay until closing time and order one last round of caffeine you don't need.

☐ **Night Fair or Carnival.** Ride the Ferris wheel, eat cotton candy, and make it cinematic.

☐ **Late-Night Workout.** Go to a 24-hour gym or stretch in the living room to reset your energy.

☐ **Lightning-Storm Watch.** If it's safe, sit under shelter and count seconds between flashes.

☐ **Parking-Lot Picnic.** Fast food, tailgate, good playlist. Simple and weirdly romantic.

☐ **Nighttime Art Museum Event.** Find a gallery with evening hours or special exhibits.

☐ **Shadow Puppets Movie.** Turn off the lights and create stories using a flashlight and your hands.

☐ **Glow-in-the-Dark Mini Golf.** Compete quietly like you're in a spy movie.

☐ **Neighborhood Lights Tour.** During holidays, drive around rating decorations on originality.

☐ **The Three a.m. Question Game.** Stay up late and ask each other questions you'd never ask in daylight.

☐ **Midnight Market Challenge.** Grocery shop after midnight and make breakfast right then.

☐ **Night Zoo or Aquarium.** Visit if open late or watch animal-cam livestreams together.

☐ **City Skyline Hunt.** Find the best nighttime view in town. Bonus if it's from somewhere you shouldn't technically be.

☐ **Late-Night Road Trip.** Pick a town within two hours and watch the sunrise there.

☐ **Night-Themed Photoshoot.** Bring fairy lights or sparklers and capture that cinematic glow.

☐ **24-Hour Donut Shop.** Sit at the counter, split a pastry, and talk about everything that matters and nothing that does.

☐ **Watch the Sunrise.** Stay up to see morning light, then get breakfast together.

The Unexpected

Industrial Tourism & Back-of-House

☐ **Tour the Water Plant.** Follow your city's drinking water from source to tap and toast to what keeps you alive every day.

☐ **Visit a Recycling Facility.** Watch bottles and cans get sorted into second chances. It's oddly hypnotic and surprisingly romantic.

☐ **Explore a Freight Yard.** Find a public overlook and count the colors of the cargo cars rolling past.

☐ **Watch a Newspaper Press Run.** Smell the ink, hear the thunder of printing, and grab a fresh copy with your names in it.

☐ **Peek into a Commercial Kitchen.** Ask a local bakery or restaurant for a five-minute back-of-house tour and watch the rhythm of the line.

☐ **Visit a Quarry Overlook.** Marvel at the geometry of human excavation and talk about what you've both been digging for emotionally.

☐ **Walk the Airport Perimeter.** Find a legal observation area and watch the choreography of takeoffs and landings.

☐ **Tour a Power Plant Visitor Center.** Learn how the lights stay on and talk about the sparks that do the same for you.

☐ **See a Bridge Open.** Find a drawbridge and time your arrival for its lift, the mechanical poetry of motion.

☐ **Visit a Wind Farm.** Stand beneath a turbine, listen to the low hum, and feel the scale of modern wind.

☐ **Explore a Postal Hub.** Watch the belts and bins sorting mail and imagine the stories behind each envelope.

☐ **Port Observation Deck.** Watch cranes move containers like toy blocks and talk about destinations you still want to see.

☐ **Visit a Theme-Park Workshop.** Take a sanctioned back-lot tour and learn how illusions are built to look effortless.

Civic Curiosity & Public Rooms

☐ **Attend a City Council Meeting.** Watch democracy in action and predict how each vote will go.

☐ **Sit in a Courtroom Gallery.** Observe real-life drama unfold, then discuss the shades of justice over coffee.

☐ **Visit a Zoning Office.** Look at maps of your neighborhood's future and plan your own imaginary development.

☐ **Dig into Public Records.** Find an old deed, photo, or family mention and trace it to the present.

☐ **Join a Neighborhood Meeting.** Show up, listen, and leave inspired to fix something tiny together.

☐ **Budget Hearing Bingo.** Print the agenda and quietly play bingo with phrases like "fiscal responsibility."

☐ **Attend a School Board Night.** Cheer for student awards, then talk about your own favorite teachers.

☐ **Explore a Polling Place.** Volunteer for a shift or visit during setup and see what participation really looks like.

☐ **Go to an Art Commission Review.** Watch artists pitch public sculptures and choose your winner.

☐ **Adopt a Storm Drain.** Decorate a sign, name it, and check it after storms as your civic pet.

☐ **Visit the City Archives.** Handle old maps, faded letters, or newspapers and imagine the lives behind them.

☐ **Write a Two-Minute Public Comment.** Practice giving a calm, persuasive speech together about anything.

☐ **Walk a Redevelopment Zone.** Explore a neighborhood mid-change and talk about what progress really means.

☐ **Ride Public Transit End-to-End.** See your city through the eyes of everyone who keeps it moving.

☐ **Explore a Courthouse Hallway Exhibit.** Many have art or history tucked behind security. Quietly take it in.

Analog Time Machine Days

- [ ] **Live Like It's 1995.** No phones, no GPS, just cash, paper maps, and conversation.

- [ ] **Film-Only Photography.** Use one roll of film and wait to see how memory looks when it can't be edited.

- [ ] **Paper Map Adventure.** Choose a random point on a physical map and go there.

- [ ] **Radio Roulette.** Spin the dial until you land on a station. Listen for an hour no matter what it is.

- [ ] **Recipe Card Dinner.** Cook from an old family recipe card and pass it down in your own handwriting.

- [ ] **Library Research Date.** Find a random subject and learn everything you can about it without using the internet.

- [ ] **Typewriter Messages.** Borrow a typewriter and write notes like telegrams.

- [ ] **Polaroid Prompts.** Snap instant photos during the night and label each one with a single word.

- [ ] **Postcard Chain.** Buy postcards, write micro-diary entries, and mail them to yourselves as an ongoing story.

- [ ] **Cash-Only Challenge.** Withdraw a small bill limit and see what kind of date it buys.

- [ ] **Walk Without Tech.** Leave phones home, follow your senses, and talk about what you notice differently.

Cartography & Boundary Quests

- [ ] **Trace the City Edge.** Walk or drive the outer boundary of your city and see how the landscape changes.

- [ ] **Old Map Overlay.** Compare a century-old map to today's streets and look for what survived.

- [ ] **Contour Line Picnic.** Choose a single elevation on a topo map and picnic where the line passes through.

☐ **Longitude Challenge.** Stay within one line of longitude for the whole day just for fun.

☐ **Street-Name Scavenger Hunt.** Collect photos of every street that shares your initials.

☐ **Follow a River from Source to City.** Even a small creek tells a story worth walking.

☐ **Coordinate Roulette.** Use random coordinates within fifty miles and navigate there exactly.

☐ **Boundary Walk.** Walk the line between two zip codes or school districts. Half of you on each side.

☐ **Historic Route Recreation.** Recreate a section of an old trade route or wagon road with modern snacks.

☐ **Map Store Date.** Pick a map and plan your dream road trip on paper.

☐ **Elevation Coin Flip.** Flip for up or down, hills or valleys only.

☐ **Time Zone Marker.** If one's nearby, stand in two times at once and count down together.

☐ **Urban Grid Puzzle.** Try to draw your city entirely from memory, then test your accuracy on a real map.

☐ **Compass Challenge.** Navigate a park using only a compass and instinct.

Borrowed Professions

☐ **Bakery Apprentice.** Ask to watch shaping for a few minutes and learn a folding trick.

☐ **Florist's Assistant.** Help trim stems and build your own small bouquet.

☐ **Bike Mechanic Lesson.** Learn to fix a flat at a community shop and ride home with pride.

☐ **Radio Station Visit.** Observe a live broadcast, then record a playful faux commercial together.

☐ **Art Gallery Sit.** Volunteer as docents for a day and invent secret backstories for the paintings.

- ☐ **Farmhand for a Morning.** Pick fruit, feed animals, or help water crops. Trade sweat for simplicity.

- ☐ **Coffee Barista Swap.** Ask your favorite café if you can shadow a barista during slow hours.

- ☐ **Museum Volunteer Shift.** Offer to help at a family event. It's chaos, laughter, and free education.

- ☐ **Hotel Concierge Roleplay.** Take turns playing concierge and designing dream itineraries.

- ☐ **Bookstore Shift.** Ask to help shelve or recommend titles. You'll leave smelling like pages.

- ☐ **Pet Shelter Assistant.** Walk dogs or clean cages while cheering each other on.

- ☐ **Stage Crew for a Night.** Help at a local theater and see a show from behind the curtain.

- ☐ **Brewery Bottling Line.** Join a volunteer bottling day if offered. Instant community, instant story.

- ☐ **Cooking Class Guest Chef.** Offer to teach one signature dish at a community center.

- ☐ **Florence Night-In.** Learn basic first aid and make a care kit for each other.

Micro-Documentary Fieldwork

- ☐ **One-Minute Portraits.** Film each other answering one meaningful question.

- ☐ **Neighborhood Interviews.** Ask three shop owners how they got started and cut it into a tiny film.

- ☐ **Sound Collage Walk.** Record ambient noises from a day together and play them back that night.

- ☐ **Photo Essay Challenge.** Tell a full story using ten photos only.

- ☐ **Mini Nature Documentary.** Narrate a bug, bird, or puddle like you're David Attenborough.

☐ **Object History.** Pick a thrift-store item and research its origin before bedtime.

☐ **Five-Question Street Series.** Ask strangers the same question and edit the responses.

☐ **Time-Lapse Morning.** Set up your phone at sunrise and capture your coffee ritual.

☐ **Food Origin Story.** Trace an ingredient from farm to plate and film the journey.

☐ **Memory Reconstruction.** Revisit a childhood place and document how it's changed.

☐ **Local Legend Hunt.** Track down the story behind a rumored haunted spot.

☐ **Archive Voiceover.** Use old family footage or photos and record your own narration.

☐ **Pet Documentary.** Follow a pet (or friend's) for a day as if they're a celebrity.

☐ **Cultural Festival Capture.** Attend a festival and make a micro-vlog of the colors and sounds.

☐ **Audio Diary Swap.** Record your inner monologue for one day and listen to each other's later.

Weather, Light & Sound Phenomena

☐ **Inversion Morning.** Drive above the fog line and watch the clouds sit below you.

☐ **Tide Walk.** Explore tidal pools at the lowest tide of the month.

☐ **Echo Experiment.** Find a tunnel and record echoes of your laughter.

☐ **Golden Hour Race.** Leave ten minutes before sunset and reach your chosen lookout in time.

☐ **Puddle Reflections.** Photograph reflections after rain and pick your favorite.

☐ **Window Rain Concert.** Sit by a window during a storm and rank the rhythms.

☐ **Streetlight Safari.** Catalog the colors and sounds of different lamps around town.

☐ **Thermal Vision Walk.** Use a thermal app to watch buildings breathe heat.

☐ **Shadow Theater.** Create stories with a single lamp and your hands.

☐ **Star Halo Chase.** Find a night with ice crystals and look for halos around the moon.

☐ **Lightning Countdown.** Safely watch a storm and count seconds between flash and thunder.

☐ **Snowflake Microscope.** Catch flakes on black paper and study their symmetry.

☐ **Fog Photography.** Walk during morning fog and capture ghostly frames.

☐ **Soundless Snow Walk.** Experience silence deeper than any conversation.

Psychology & Perception Experiments

☐ **Mirror Gazing.** Sit across from each other and hold eye contact for two minutes. Discuss what changed.

☐ **Synesthesia Game.** Describe music as colors or emotions and compare.

☐ **Dream Decode Night.** Write down a dream and interpret each other's symbols.

☐ **Memory Swap.** Each tell a story the other must retell later from memory.

☐ **Yes-And Conversation.** Do ten minutes where you can only respond with "yes, and…" to whatever the other says.

☐ **Word Association Duel.** Trade words until someone repeats or hesitates.

☐ **Future Visualization.** Close eyes and describe your ideal life in five years while the other listens quietly.

☐ **Body Language Challenge.** Try to communicate a sentence using gestures only.

☐ **Time Perception Test.** Sit in silence and guess when one minute has passed.

☐ **Emotional Charades.** Act out feelings instead of movie titles.

☐ **Mindfulness Mirror.** Copy each other's movements slowly for one minute.

☐ **Personality Prediction.** Take turns guessing the other's reaction to hypothetical scenarios.

☐ **Noise Sensitivity Walk.** See who notices more sounds on a city block.

☐ **First Impression Replay.** Recreate the first time you met and see what details differ.

☐ **Color Memory Test.** Look at a scene, close your eyes, and describe every color you remember.

☐ **Micro-Expression Challenge.** Try to spot each other's smallest smiles or sighs.

Luck, Fate & Probability

☐ **Lottery Date.** Each buy one scratch ticket and promise to do something fun no matter the result.

☐ **Random Restaurant Generator.** Use a map app and eat wherever your finger lands.

☐ **Dice Adventure.** Assign numbers to six activities and roll for your fate.

☐ **Deck of Cards Date.** Assign categories to suits and pull one card to pick the theme.

☐ **Weather Roulette.** Plan the date type based on that day's forecast no matter what it is.

☐ **Horoscope Night.** Read both your horoscopes and act them out ironically.

- ☐ **Fortune Cookie Futures.** Keep your fortunes and see which comes true first.

- ☐ **Museum Randomizer.** Visit the first exhibit number you draw from a hat.

- ☐ **Predictive Text Poetry.** Use your phone's predictive text to write spontaneous poems.

- ☐ **Bus Stop Game.** Wait at a stop and take whichever bus arrives first.

- ☐ **Guess the Number.** Simple, silly, and still somehow competitive.

- ☐ **Lucky Penny Hunt.** Whoever finds one first gets to make the next wish.

Art of the Absurd

- ☐ **Museum of You.** Curate objects from your home and give each one a dramatic label.

- ☐ **One-Word Date.** Each of you picks one word and must use it in every sentence.

- ☐ **Invisible Art Show.** Pretend you're in a gallery full of invisible art and critique what you "see."

- ☐ **Slow Motion Hour.** Move and speak slowly for fifteen minutes. Time feels elastic.

- ☐ **Compliment Auction.** Bid fake money on compliments you most want to hear.

- ☐ **Ridiculous Walk Parade.** Create your own absurd stroll down the block.

- ☐ **Monologue Night.** Each write and perform a one-minute dramatic piece about your day.

- ☐ **Reenact a Commercial.** Choose an old TV ad and recreate it seriously.

- ☐ **Word Ban Game.** Ban three common words for the evening and invent replacements.

- ☐ **Fake Interview.** Pretend one of you is a celebrity and the other a late-night host.

☐ **Opposite Day Outing.** Do everything backward, from dessert first to walking the opposite route.

☐ **Improvised Theme Song.** Create a jingle for your relationship on the spot.

☐ **Invisible Audience Game.** Narrate your actions like you're in a documentary for exactly five minutes.

☐ **Prop Night.** Each choose one household object to use in every interaction, no explanation allowed.

☐ **Tiny Awards Show.** Give each other absurd trophies for "Best Shoe Choice" or "Most Dramatic Bite."

Other Books by Sarah Melland

Red Flag Translator

The savage, laugh-out-loud guide that exposes what men *really* mean when they say things like "no drama" or "I'm just focusing on myself." It's not about fixing them; it's about seeing them clearly and walking away faster. Once you learn the language of red flags, you'll never fall for "I'm not ready for a relationship" again, and that's exactly the point.

https://amzn.to/3LCzbm3

A Single Girl's Guide to Hilarious Facts You Never Knew About Sex

From Cleopatra's bee-powered dildo to the surprising anti-aging perks of sperm (yep, you read that right), this book is packed with the wildest, weirdest, and most entertaining sex facts you never knew you needed. Think history, science, and hilarity rolled into one unapologetically fun read. Complete with playlists, orgasm trivia, and enough conversation starters to keep you laughing for days. Just… maybe save a few of them for date number two.

https://amzn.to/446Djkq

If you loved some of the dating games like the Triathlon Challenge or the *Amazing Race*, or the ones that made you laugh so hard you forgot it was technically a date, you're going to lose your mind over what's next. Explore *hundreds more hilarious, connection-building, and slightly chaotic dating games* on my Etsy store!

https://www.etsy.com/shop/YourDatingUnExpert

About

Sarah Melland is the unapologetic voice behind *Your Dating UnExpert*, a brutally honest and hilariously relatable brand that turns the chaos of modern dating into comedy, clarity, and catharsis. Drawing from years of real-life experience, sharp observation, and a knack for translating emotional nonsense into savage truth, she's built a loyal following of women who are done settling for mediocrity. Equal parts storyteller, researcher, and professional pattern-spotter, Sarah writes about dating with the precision of a therapist and the humor of your funniest friend because she's lived it, decoded it, and survived to tell the story.

Follow on all social platforms: @yourdatingunexpert